PQ 7797 .B635 .Z5
SHA

QMW Library

23 105

KW-089-811

WITHDRAWN
FROM STOCK
QMUL LIBRARY

DATE DUE FOR RETURN

NEW ACCESSION

CANCELLED

- 8 DEC 1994

20 JAN 1995.

13 FEB 1995

0 1 MAR 1995
16 MAR 1995

- 5 MAY 1995

2 0 MAY 1996

0 4 MAR 1997
- 9 MAY 2000

BORGES' NARRATIVE STRATEGY

LIVERPOOL MONOGRAPHS IN HISPANIC STUDIES
11

BORGES' NARRATIVE STRATEGY

DONALD L. SHAW

X
FRANCIS CAIRNS

Published by Francis Cairns (Publications) Ltd
c/o The University, Leeds, LS2 9JT, Great Britain

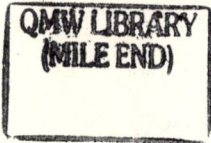

QMW LIBRARY
(MILE END)

First published 1992

Copyright © Donald L. Shaw 1992

All rights reserved. No part of this publication may be reproduced, stored in a retrieval system, or transmitted, in any form or
by any means, electronic, mechanical, photocopying, recording,
or otherwise, without the prior permission of the Publisher.

British Library Cataloguing-in-Publication Data
A catalogue record for this book is available from the British Library

ISBN 0-905205-84-7

Printed in Great Britain by
Redwood Press Ltd, Melksham, Wiltshire

CONTENTS

This book is respectfully dedicated to the
Brown-Forman Corporation of Louisville, Kentucky,
in grateful appreciation of its generous endowment
of the Chair of Spanish American Literature
in the University of Virginia.

CHAPTER 1

UNDERSTANDING A BORGES STORY

Most serious writing about the stories in Borges' main collections —
Historia universal de la infamia (1935), *Ficciones* (1944, augmented
1956), *El Aleph* (1949, augmented 1952), *El informe de Brodie* (1970),
El libro de arena (1975) and *Veinticinco agosto 1983 y otros cuentos*
(1983) — has been primarily concerned with elucidating and
interpreting their meaning.[1] Despite some half-hearted protests by
Borges himself and by a few critics, this is quite as it should be. There
is no autonomy of form in literature. We cannot discuss form in
terms of its functionality or otherwise without having arrived at some
notion of what it is that the author is seeking to achieve by using the
particular formal arrangement and devices which he has selected or
created. So that to understand the patterning of a Borges story, as
distinct from merely recognizing it, we have necessarily to start from
some conclusion about the meaning, or the various layers of the
meaning, which we think the story contains.[2] The task then is to try to
relate the formal pattern which we have recognized to what we think
the story is about.

Understanding a Borges story involves at least four interconnected

---

[1] The texts used in this study are Jorge Luis Borges, *Prosa completa*, 2 vols.
(Barcelona: Bruguera, 1980), and *Veinticinco agosto 1983 y otros cuentos* (Madrid:
Siruela, 1983). All quotations are accompanied by the appropriate page reference, the
latter book being indicated by the abbreviation *VA*. The English translations
accompanying the quotations are my own.

[2] For a cogent discussion of some of the issues involved here, see Eric D. Hirsch,
Validity in Interpretation (New Haven: Yale Univ. Press, 1967) and *The Aims of
Interpretation* (Chicago: Chicago Univ. Press, 1976).

processes. The first of these is concerned with focusing our minds consciously on the story in its own right, and not (in the first instance) as an enigmatic statement about, say, the human condition, reality or literature. In the unrelenting search for meaning we all too often overlook the intrinsic interest of the stories themselves, their intriguing novelty, their economy of means, their immediate engagement of our attention, their cunning build-up of suspense, their unexpected climaxes, in brief, their success in producing pure reader-enjoyment of a traditional kind. Without this instant appeal — and not only to a minority intellectual audience — Borges' stories could never have attained the world-wide level of sales they have achieved. First and foremost, then, we must recognize Borges' mastery of the art of story-telling itself.

But, once we have read the stories for pleasure and pause to reflect on them, we easily perceive that they are often like parables or fables which illustrate aspects of the general collapse of rational or religious certainties in our modern world, and the bewildering possibilities which thus emerge. Like his great predecessor in literature in Spanish, Unamuno, Borges is concerned to shake our comfortable and rather complacent confidence in our ability to understand either ourselves or the reality in which we live. Many who have been present at his public-speaking engagements have heard him ask, for instance, "How do we know that we are not the first immortal generation?" All we really know, that is, is that everyone has always died eventually *up to now*. But this does not necessarily guarantee that it is still the case or that it will always be so in the future. Suppose we, in this generation, were immortal without knowing it? This is a somewhat crude example, which Borges relegated to his platform or drawing-room appearances. But it reminds us that many of his stories contain an implicit "What if ...?" or "Suppose that ...". What if the world were as the idealist philosophers suggest that it is? Suppose that it became possible for someone never to forget anything whatsoever, even the most fleeting visual impressions. What would follow? Here are the basic models, clearly, for "Tlön, Uqbar, Orbis Tertius" and "Funes el memorioso". The possibilities which are explored as the stories develop are enjoyably fantastic and unexpected. But they usually lead to implicit conclusions which call into question one or other of our accepted ideas and beliefs. So that the second stage in understanding a Borges story is concerned with separating the story itself from its deeper implications. These, it should be emphasized, are rarely simple. Attempts to suggest that

Borges stories often have only one level of meaning and that when we have found it we have "cracked" the story in question are to be resisted as simplistic and reductive, except in the case of a few stories which are relatively unambiguous. Many of Borges' stories are modelled on, or contain, puzzles or riddles; but they are puzzles or riddles to which there are no simple answers. One of the consequences is that major critics of Borges frequently disagree about the meaning of given stories.

But interpretation is one thing and analysis of technique is another. Close and detailed examination of his narrative strategy is the neglected aspect of Borges' fiction. Attention to it is the third process involved in understanding a Borges story. As we shall try to illustrate in a moment, what Borges may be saying and the particular method he adopts in order to say it can sometimes be closely related. Indeed, a close examination of the patterning of a given story may allow us to attach more weight to one interpretation of it than to another. But, independently of its possible relation to meaning, the *dispositio* of a Borges story is always worth a long, hard look.

Finally, we must notice that many Borges stories contain what he has called "inlaid details", small indications or clues, held out to the alert reader, which suggest something about how to understand the tale. To identify those details which are significant in this sense, among others which are not, calls for careful critical discrimination. But a Borges story has not been fully understood until all the important details fit.

A fair amount of Borges criticism is flawed by failure to keep these four stages adequately in view. Too much effort has been expended on the second stage, meaning, and not enough on technique. It is time to recognize that we now probably possess enough familiarity with Borges' outlook to be able to proceed to consider his craftsmanship more closely in the light of that familiarity. One of the best ways forward in Borges criticism is to examine his individual stories much in the way that individual poems of Neruda or Vallejo have been analysed, with great benefit to studies of their work.

An example: "La casa de Asterión"

"La casa de Asterión" (II, 52-54) is told in the first person by a mysterious being who turns out to be the Minotaur of Greek legend, the offspring of Queen Pasiphae and a bull. The strange creature describes his life in the labyrinth which he inhabits, his loneliness and his wish for some sort of "redemption". At the end an anonymous narrative voice informs us that he was killed by Theseus without a struggle. The story has been interpreted in various ways. Wheelock, for instance, asserts that "the narrator, Asterion, is the idealist consciousness" and that "the labyrinth he lives in is the conceptual universe", that is, "his own mind".[3] Paoli, for his part, suggests that Asterion represents the Unconscious, the repressed, the socially unacceptable part of ourselves or of our fellow men, while the labyrinth stands for the form of repression or segregation.[4] Probably more authoritative is Alazraki, who argues that Asterion represents man in general and his labyrinth the construct which he inhabits and regards as reality.[5] The labyrinth, that is, represents man's imposition of a bearable form of order on the chaotic flux of experience. McMurray follows this interpretation, writing that "Asterion conceivably represents modern man who, finding himself alone and insecure in the chaotic, labyrinthine universe, builds his own, more comprehensible, labyrinth. Thus Asterion's house becomes a metaphor of culture, that is, of man's concept of reality".[6] Borges himself, characteristically, is not very helpful. To Irby he remarked that Asterion is essentially a freak, a monster, though he could stand for the essential loneliness and unhappiness of man in general.[7] Similarly, in *Review*, in 1973, he said of the story and presumably of its protagonist, "It stands for feeling lonesome, for feeling useless."[8]

While there is an element of consensus here, differences of emphasis seem strongly pronounced. Above all, a number of questions are left unanswered. Why, for instance, are the doors of Asterion's labyrinth open, and what is outside? Who are the people he encountered when he occasionally left it? Why would he like the company of another creature like himself in the labyrinth? If Asterion is man, who is Theseus? Plainly, not all the details fit. Is the text itself any more help?

Surely it is. The clue, which is too explicit to be an inlaid detail, is

---

[3] Carter Wheelock, *The Mythmaker. A Study of Motif and Symbol in the Short Stories of Jorge Luis Borges* (Austin: Univ. of Texas Press, 1969), p. 27.

[4] Roberto Paoli, *Borges, percorsi di significato* (Messina-Firenze: D'Anna, 1977), p. 131.

[5] Jaime Alazraki, "Tlön y Asterión: metáforas epistemológicas", in his *Jorge Luis Borges, el escritor y la crítica* (Madrid: Taurus, 1976), pp. 183-200, esp. p. 196.

[6] George R. McMurray, *Jorge Luis Borges* (New York: Ungar, 1980), p. 24.

[7] James E. Irby, *Encuentro con Borges* (Buenos Aires: Galerna, 1968), pp. 28-29.

[8] Quoted in Emir Rodríguez Monegal, *Jorge Luis Borges. A Literary Biography* (New York: Dutton, 1978), p. 45.

the sentence: "La casa es del tamaño del mundo; mejor dicho, es el mundo" (II, 53) (The house is the size of the world, or rather, it is the world). At first sight the conclusion is obvious: if the labyrinth is the world, its inhabitant, Asterion, must represent man. So far, there is no problem. But we must now ask: what kind of man? Clearly he does not stand for the whole of mankind, for the people outside, variously referred to in the first paragraph as "la plebe" (the mob), "la gente" (the people) and "el vulgo" (the rabble), are quite obviously men and women also. The difference appears to be that they are normal, while he is a monster; and, furthermore, that they are potential victims, since at intervals nine men from somewhere outside are put into the labyrinth and killed by Asterion. It would seem from this that insofar as Asterion represents man, he represents man the monster. Significant perhaps in this connection is the fact that Borges suggested to Burgin that there might be a connection between Asterion and Hitler. Equally significant, in my view, is the fact that "La casa de Asterión" was published quite near in time to "Deutsches Requiem", in which the central character, Zur Linde, a Nazi war criminal, might be regarded as symbolizing much the same as Asterion. Lonely, stupid and illiterate, Asterion is a freak with delusions of grandeur; perhaps not fully aware of his partly bestial nature, he suffers from a certain persecution mania and is characterized by cold, murderous cruelty.

These characteristics suggest that "La casa de Asterión" is really a moral fable. It is about evil: specifically about man possessed by evil. In "Deutsches Requiem" Borges shows us that men tend to need a construct of reality, a means of imputing order to life's chaos, and that certain men can experience a "conversion" to evil, as others can to good. In each case they have found a habitat, a way of structuring their experiences and of coming to terms with existence. Those converted to evil have taken refuge in an arbitrary, cruel order in preference to having no order in their lives. Asterion, the monster, inhabits a "world", his world, of evil. That world, however, is empty, monotonous, futile and not fully comprehensible. As early as "El asesino desinteresado Bill Harrigan" in *Historia universal de la infamia*, Borges had suggested that the world of the psychotic killer was lonely and destructive of the personality: "Mientras el dedo del gatillo no le falló, [Billy the Kid] fue el hombre más temido (y quizá más nadie y más solo) de esa frontera" (I, 274) (While his trigger-finger did not fail him, he was the man who was most feared [and perhaps most without human personality and most alone] on that frontier). The parallel with Asterion is plain. The latter claims to prefer his own world to the alternative world of normality outside. But in fact he is uneasily aware of his differences and of the emnity and fear which he and his world inspire in those who do not share it with him. He longs to try to explain it, to achieve communication with others who might be willing to join him in it. When he shows himself to the "normal" inhabitants of the wider world outside, he elicits the classic response to the archetypically evil historical figures: fear, hostility or worship. But all the time that part of him which is human and not bestial prompts him to long for relief from the monotony and futility of evil and the pretence that it is satisfying or the source of a sense of superiority. He has accepted his "order", but not without a nagging desire to be released from it.

Who is to be his redeemer? The word itself may well provide the clue. Wheelock sees Theseus as standing for whatever "can deliver man from the confusing complexity of consciousness";[9] McMurray sees him as the representative of Death, which provides a welcome deliverance from the absurdity of existence.[10] McGrady, on the other hand, identifies an inlaid detail: the reference to the *Book of Job*, 19. 25 — "... sé que mi redentor vive, y al fin se levantará sobre el polvo" (II, 54) (I know that my redeemer lives and at last he will stand upon the earth) — and identifies the redeemer as God or Christ, releasing Asterion from his weariness with life.[11] Where I differ from McGrady is in seeing the reference to Christ as ironic, as an inversion of the traditional myth or doctrine, in line with many similar inversions of Christian myths to be found in modern Spanish American fiction. McGrady's own acceptance of Borges' "conocida antipatía hacia el judaísmo y el cristianismo" (well-known antipathy towards Judaism and Christianity) seems to lend support to this view.[12] Christ as Redeemer *died himself* in order to save man, who is essentially *good* but accidentally evil because of Original Sin. Theseus as Redeemer *kills* man the monster, who is radically *evil*, in order to save other, normal men.

The various interpretations of this story have been alluded to in some detail, not only to show the way they can — and usually do — differ, but also in order to illustrate with a specific example what was

[9] Wheelock, *The Mythmaker*, p. 28.
[10] McMurray, p. 24.
[11] Donald McGrady, "El Redentor del Asterión de Borges", *Revista Iberoamericana*, 135/136 (1986), 531-35.
[12] ibid., p. 531.

said earlier about the need to work towards an interpretation in which the significant details fit. This must always be the acid test. It provides the main incentive for taking a particularly close look at the text itself when dealing with a Borges tale. The other incentive is to familiarize oneself with his skills, as distinct from his thought, and here, too, "La casa de Asterión" provides us with an excellent illustration.

Every good Borges story is a mechanism: each part of it is functional. A useful exercise with his shorter tales is to number the paragraphs and then attempt to analyse precisely the contribution that each of them makes to the overall pattern. The opening paragraph is, of course, critically important. An appropriately selected group of such initial paragraphs, looked at comparatively, provides a rich field of study because of the variety of gambits which Borges deploys to get his stories started and the purposes — usually more than one — which he makes them serve. Always, of course, their primary function is to create interest. Here, as in "La lotería en Babilonia", the method used is that of the hidden item of information: the story begins in the first person but we do not know who is speaking. In this case our attention is riveted by the fact that an unknown voice is overheard making quite extraordinary statements in a tone of querulous indignation. From the opening phrases Borges is manipulating us effectively, luring us into feeling intrigued and curious. At the same time he is fitting together the elements of Asterion's self-presentation on the one hand, and his description of his home on the other. The difficulty, from Borges' point of view, is that each of the elements must be, at one and the same time, both part of the fascinating oddity of the story's opening and part of the symbolism which we will subsequently recognize in it.

If we pause at the end of the first paragraph and ask what it is that predominates, we see that it is the identity of the speaker, rather than his personality or the weird details of his surroundings. The story, that is, works basically on the model of a puzzle, with the solution at the end. It involves a technique of systematic postponement, followed by fulfilment. The reader who is more or less familiar with classical legends will suspect the answer quite early in the tale, but will read on to see if his suspicion is confirmed. Other readers will grasp the point only at the end, or when they understand the reference to Theseus, Ariadne and the Minotaur. But this reference is preceded by four clues (if we ignore the epigraph, which, taken by itself, would alert only classical scholars). These are designed for the

intelligent and informed reader to congratulate himself on picking
them up. The first clue is the mention in paragraph one of the pale flat
faces of those outside the labyrinth, in implicit contrast to Asterion's
muzzle. The second is the double reference to the Queen (Pasiphae)
in the epigraph and the first paragraph. The third clue, apart from the
growing realization that the creature's home is a labyrinth, is the
refence to his victims, at the beginning of the fourth paragraph. The
fourth is the juxtaposition of "toro" (bull) and "hombre" (man) just
before the word "minotauro" (Minotaur) is mentioned in the last
sentence, along with the appearance of Theseus and Ariadne.

The very fact that this tale is modelled on a puzzle is significant,
since reality itself is a puzzle for Borges. The technique, that is,
already reflects and even symbolizes a fundamental part of the
author's outlook. We shall see presently how this is developed much
further. In addition, however, we must notice the effect both of its use
and of the supply of the answer at the end. If we analyse our
reactions, we can perceive that the use of the puzzle model is a
distancing technique. That is, it is the complete opposite of what
predominates in the bulk of nineteenth-century realist fiction. There
the aim was to draw the reader into close self-identification with the
characters and the situations. The pleasure derived from problem-
solving is a quite different kind of pleasure from that derived from
imaginative and emotional self-involvement with personages or
plots. This is an important point, not only for the way we read some
of Borges' fiction, but also for the way we read some of the Spanish
American "new novels" on which he has exerted so much influence.
The fact that we are eventually given the solution is important in
another way. Borges writes especially for the alert reader and his tales
are full of traps for the less alert. We may conjecture that a
considerable sector of readers of this story will rest content, like
McGrady initially, with the realization that it is about the Minotaur
("... el cuento era sencillamente un rompecabezas cuyo objeto era
descifrar quién era el narrador" [the story was simply a puzzle the
object of which was to make out who the narrator was]).[13] At this
stage the postponement technique has performed its function of
sustaining the reader's interest and curiosity, which is now rewarded
with the answer. We now know for certain who the "speaker" is. The
puzzle has been solved.

Or has it? The more alert reader, going back over the story, will

[13] ibid., p. 532.

notice that the crucial opening paragraph does more than capture our interest and present the chief characteristics of Asterion. From the third sentence the story bifurcates. On the one hand we have the speaker; on the other his mysterious dwelling. Interestingly, in the title itself, we read, not "Asterión y su casa" (Asterion and his House), but "La casa de Asterión" (The House of Asterion). If the "I" of the story denotes the Minotaur, what does his house denote? Having recognized the solution to the first puzzle, we are immediately presented with another. Why is Asterion's house a labyrinth? Why is it (said to be) infinite? If it is infinite, how can he go outside it? Why is he alone in it? One, relatively easy to solve puzzle has led to another, more difficult one.

This is a common Borges technique. We see it in another guise in "La muerte y la brújula", which belongs to an archetypal class of puzzle-stories, the detective story. In this case the detective, Lönnrot, is lured to his death by the mobster Scharlach. Once more we have a hidden item of information: the identity of the criminal. Once more we have a series of clues: the tetragrammaton, the lozenges, the mysterious letter which Lönnrot receives. Once more the method of first creating suspense and curiosity and then postponing the solution works very efficiently, perhaps better than in "La casa de Asterión", since in this case we cannot perceive the solution to the puzzle before reaching the end. But when we do reach the end, and realize that the whole scenario has been stage-managed by Scharlach, we are again forced back to the beginning of the tale to ask ourselves more searching questions about it. Why is Treviranus, the unimaginative Inspector, right about Yarmolinsky and Lönnrot led into error and death by his impatience with the obvious? Why are Lönnrot and Scharlach's names so closely connected? What is the story really about? Clearly, what we have in both "La casa de Asterión" and "La muerte y la brújula" is a puzzle within a puzzle.

In "La casa de Asterión" the clues to the first puzzle — the identity of the speaker, Asterion — are unambiguous, like the solution. If we do not discern the answer from one or more of them, it is given to us. At this level it is in a sense as if we were reading a comforting nineteenth-century narrative in which events are presented in chronological order and the motivation of the characters is omnisciently expounded. The inference is that we can understand them, ourselves and the outside world. But the clues to the second puzzle, the meaning of Asterion's abode, are highly ambiguous, not to say contradictory. Having reinforced our confidence in our powers of understanding at one level, Borges deftly pulls the carpet from under our feet. What we can readily understand, the technique seems to be telling us, is only the surface level of reality, deceitful as even that level sometimes is. But what we come to underneath is more baffling. Even here Borges tempts the unwary ready to jump to a conclusion, when Asterion asserts that his house is the world. We are tempted to assume that Asterion is not just the Minotaur but a metaphor of mankind, and his labyrinth not only that of Crete but a metaphor of our surrounding reality. Yet all the details do not fit. For, as we have noted, Asterion's "world" has a somwhere else around it.

There is a possible key. It is Asterion's curious reference to "el intricado sol" (II, 53) (the intricate sun). Here we have, in my view, another inlaid detail. Once Asterion calls the sun, which he can see as a simple glowing disc, "intricate", we find our suspicions about his power to interpret reality and his reliability as a narrator (already aroused by his tone) confirmed. We no longer accept uncritically what he affirms. He may assert that his dwelling is "the world", but he precedes the assertion by describing how he left it for another world outside. Once we recognize that there is a monstrous "world" and a non-monstrous "world" enclosing it, we feel that we may be on the track of a solution to the second stage of the puzzle. But our confidence has been shaken, and part of Borges' object achieved.

Now, characteristically in the middle of a paragraph, the emphasis shifts again. The entire story consists of only six paragraphs all told. We can see that they divide into four plus two. The first four paragraphs form a unit of rather static description. At the beginning of paragraph five, however, we are conscious of a change: figures penetrate into Asterion's labyrinth. More especially, we perceive a new element: that of the redeemer. It is an element which does not fit at all with the classical myth on which the story rests. On the other hand, it does fit in to some extent with the idea of the labyrinth as a world and the Minotaur as man inhabiting it; but not in a conventionally Christian way. We have been betrayed again. We thought we understood the story when we realized who Asterion was. Then we thought we had understood it when we reached a conclusion about the meaning of his dwelling. But now we are faced with a new problem: why is Theseus, his killer, seen by the Minotaur as a redeemer? I have suggested a possible answer.

But this is less important perhaps than the strategy which we can now see Borges has employed. The story is made like a Chinese box: a riddle leads to another riddle and this in turn to a third, each more ambiguous than the last. Each phase of the story is a framing device for the next phase and we are dextrously led from one to another without at first reading being really aware of it. What we have here is a metaphor of Borges' outlook, figured forth in the actual technique of the story itself. Reality, too, is a puzzle within a puzzle within a puzzle. As we apparently solve one of life's easier mysteries, another, more complex enigma awaits us.

Arguably, "Deutsches Requiem" and "La casa de Asterión" carry the implication that there is an answer: the moral life. It is not necessarily Borges' preferred answer, for that is perhaps more often to be found in a display of physical courage. But despite the important role played by courage in some of Borges' most meaningful stories, we recognize that (as he himself has suggested) it reveals in some measure the presence of a compensatory fantasy for his not having been able to follow the example of his military forbears.[14] Moral courage, however, is a different matter. Whatever the range of his scepticism, there is reason to believe that Borges' attachment to it, and to moral behaviour in general, was rather strong.

---

[14] See the "Epílogo" to Jorge Luis Borges, *Obras completas 1923-1972* (Buenos Aires: Emecé, 1974), p. 1144. In the same paragraph he reproached himself for having given way, because of his cult of courage, to "la veneración atolondrada de los hombres de la hampa" (thoughtless veneration for slum-dwellers).

CHAPTER 2

EARLY STRATEGIES

Unlike Horacio Quiroga before him in the well-known "Decálogo del perfecto cuentista"[1] or Julio Cortázar after him in "Algunos aspectos del cuento",[2] Borges never seems to have felt the need to gather together his ideas on the writing of short stories. His comments remain scattered in prologues, epilogues and interviews, and in any case chiefly refer to individual stories. For this and other reasons, including the fact that most writing about the Spanish American short story takes the form of simple historical surveys, it is not easy to perceive clearly what made *Ficciones* such a turning-point in the 1940s. But certainly one of the major factors was the greater sophistication of Borges' narrative technique compared to that of his predecessors, with sporadic exceptions.

This is an easy assertion to make, but a more difficult one to prove. Even with regard to the traditional novel, belonging to the period before what we now call the Boom, useful studies of narrative strategies are not easy to come by, much less anything approximating to a survey of their evolution in the nineteenth and early twentieth century. Brushwood, whose *Genteel Barbarism* covers a number of representative nineteenth-century novels with this issue in mind, is extremely (and justifiably) cautious in reaching any conclusion. He goes no further than the relatively safe postulate that investigation would "probably show a growing awareness of technique in the

[1] Reproduced in Pedro G. Orgambide, *Horacio Quiroga, el hombre y su obra* (Buenos Aires: Stilcograf, 1954), pp. 130-31.
[2] *Casa de las Américas*, 2, nos. 15/16 (1962-63), 3-14.

course of the century".[3]

In the case of the short story, Pupo-Walker has suggested that the major defect of the genre in the last century was its "tradición descriptiva" (descriptive tradition) and excessive interest in the "registro minucioso del mundo físico" (meticulous recording of the physical world).[4] He quotes Luis Leal as affirming that subsequently, in the shift from *Costumbrismo* (a pre-realist mode of writing which often privileged the merely picturesque) to Naturalism, Spanish American short-story writers began to achieve "una estructura precisa" (a precise structure), but argues that, on the whole, the short-story writers of the Mexican Revolution represented a regression to mere descriptive sketches and reportage. Meanwhile, Antonio Muñoz affirms, in the short stories of writers belonging to the *modernista* movement at the end of the century and beyond, the "organización poética del discurso narrativo a menudo se hace a expensas de la fábula" (poetic organization of the narrative discourse often comes into being at the expense of story-telling).[5] He goes on to quote an illuminating statement by Amado Nervo in *Almas que pasan* (1906): "Es cierto que para escribir un cuento suele no necesitarse la imaginación; se ve correr la vida, se sorprende una escena, un rasgo, se toman de aquí y ahí los elementos reales y palpitantes que ofrecen los seres y las cosas que pasan, y se tiene lo esencial. Lo demás es cosa de poquísimo asunto: coordinar aquellos datos y ensamblear con ellos una historia" (It is certainly true that to write a short story one normally does not need imagination; one watches life pass by, one happens on a scene, a trait, one picks up from here and there the real, palpitating elements offered by the human beings and things going by, and one already has all that is essential. The rest is a minor matter: to co-ordinate the data and assemble a story out of it).[6] The striking elements here are the emphasis — by a poet — on photographic realism and the utterly casual attitude to artistic structure implied by the verbs "co-ordinate" and "assemble". In fact, it is broadly true to say that what really took on importance in the *modernista* short story was style. Careful interior organization of the narrative remained a subordinate consideration.

[3] John S. Brushwood, *Genteel Barbarism* (Lincoln: Nebraska Univ. Press, 1981), p. 204.

[4] Enrique Pupo-Walker, "Prólogo" to his *El cuento hispanoamericano ante la crítica* (Madrid: Castalia, 1973), p. 11.

[5] Antonio Muñoz, "Notas sobre los rasgos formales del cuento modernista", ibid., pp. 50-63.

[6] ibid., p. 59.

Oddly enough, this is exactly what we also find missing in Quiroga's famous "Decálogo ...". We find mention of the importance of the opening and closing paragraphs of short stories, and of the need to proceed directly from one to the other without digressions or redundancies. As we might expect in the aftermath of *Modernismo*, there is also reference to style. But the "Decálogo ..." completely ignores narrative organization. In fact, as we see from other remarks by Quiroga, this was typical of his approach. In "El eterno traidor", for example, he writes: "La idea es naturalmente lo esencial en el arte. Al acto de sentirlas suele llamársele 'Tener algo que decir'. De aquí que el tener ideas primero, y la suerte luego de hallar las palabras que las expresen definitivamente, son las dos facultades maestras del escritor" (Ideas are naturally essential to art. We call feeling their presence "Having something to say". It follows that first of all having ideas and then having the good luck to find the words which give them hard and fast expression are the two master faculties of the writer).[7] We notice the leap from thematics to stylistic expression, bypassing any question of narrative structure. There seems, as in Nervo, to be no sense of technique. Why is this? Examination of Borges' mature stories (and a side-glance at Cortázar's earlier mentioned essay) suggests a possible answer. If in general, as we see from Nervo and Quiroga, short-story writers before the 1940s tended to take matters of narrative organization somewhat for granted, it was because they did not usually question the view that comprehension and, therefore, description of reality was achieved by perceiving it in linear chronological sequence based on the notion of cause and effect. Hence they tended to organize their stories straightforwardly on the assumption that reality, too, was generally straightforward. The keyword for the pre-Borges short story in Spanish America is sequentiality: one event following, and following from, another. The basic technique is simple juxtaposition. At best we are offered flashbacks, used explanatorily, which interfere with, but do not call into question, our normal sense of time as monolinear and ongoing, and some variation in narrative viewpoint. But rarely (even in writers like Rafael Arévalo Martínez, whose fantastic short stories are often thought of as prefiguring the importance of fantasy in, for example, Borges and Cortázar) do we break away from linear juxtaposition and sequentiality.

---

[7] Horacio Quiroga, "El eterno traidor", in his *Sobre literatura* (Montevideo: Arca, 1970), p. 76.

In Borges, and subsequently in Cortázar, whose essay — disappointing in other respects — is categoric on this point, the idea that comprehension of reality can be founded on rationalistic recognition of straight lines of cause and effect no longer holds good. Linear juxtaposition and authorial omniscience, the staple techniques of writers who, like Nervo, saw their task more or less in terms of reproducing an observable, intelligible reality, were no longer able to convey a vision of reality in which those presuppositions no longer consistently apply. The old comforting metaphor which such techniques had figured forth had been gradually replaced by one which was much less reassuring. Not only new themes, but also new techniques were needed to express it. At the beginning of his career as a writer of fiction Borges was not as fully aware of this as he was subsequently to become. Apart from professional inexperience, this was one of the reasons why his first collection of tales is not fully satisfying.

In the early stories of *Historia universal de la infamia* (1935) Borges has not as yet developed the complex strategies which we shall be attempting to identify in some of the technically more interesting later ones. Describing the tales in the prologue to the first edition (I, 241), he reduces their significant techniques to three: "enumeraciones dispares" (disparate enumerations), "la brusca solución de continuidad" (sudden breaks in continuity) and "la reducción de la vida entera de un hombre a dos o tres escenas" (the reduction of an entire life to two or three scenes). At first sight the first of these, which is certainly a stylistic feature of some of the stories and was to reappear at significant moments in later ones — the description of the visions granted to Tzinacán in "La escritura del Dios" or to the narrator in "El Aleph", for instance —, does not seem relevant to narrative technique in the wider sense. But in the case of "El asesino desinteresado Bill Harrigan" it is. In general the opening strategy of these early tales is quite conventional. Borges opts, not for a framing device or an enigmatic statement, but simply for a context. In "El atroz redentor Lazarus Morell", since the story has to do with slavery, Borges begins with the origin of Negro slavery in the New World in 1517 and gradually narrows the focus to the lower Mississippi valley region and then to one inhabitant, Morell. In "La viuda Ching, pirata" he introduces two European women pirates by way of preparing us for the Asian one. The story of Monk Eastman is preceded by a brief dissertation on early twentieth-century New York street gangs. Writing in part to provide copy for the Saturday supplement of the newspaper *Crítica*, which he was then editing, Borges at this stage was adapting rather than creating and seems to have been ready to settle for such straightforward openings. He is content to catch the reader's attention with an unexpected adjective (*"Atrocious* Redeemer", *"Disinterested* Killer", *"Uncivil* Master of Ceremonies") in the title and to hold it by relying on the exotic subject-matter which follows.

"El asesino desinteresado Bill Harrigan" is the exception, for here Borges employs a quite different opening ploy (I, 271): "La imagen de las tierras de Arizona, antes que ninguna otra imagen: la imagen de las tierras de Arizona y de Nuevo México, tierras [...], tierras vertiginosas y aéreas, tierras [...], tierras [...] En esas tierras, otra imagen ..." (The image of these lands in Arizona, before any other image: the image of the lands in Arizona and New Mexico, lands [...], dizzying, airy lands, lands [...], lands [...] In these lands, another image ...). The technique is to combine enumeration with the "visual intention" which Borges in the prologue declares that he aimed at. The retina of the mind's eye becomes a screen onto which are projected, first the background — "... tierras vertiginosas [...] de los delicados colores [...] con blanco resplendor de esqueleto pelado" (dizzying lands [...] with their delicate colours [...] with the white magnificence of a clean skeleton) —, then Billy the Kid himself — "... el jinete clavado sobre el caballo" (the rider firmly seated on his horse). The incantatory repetition and the absence of verbs create an effect of dramatic superimposition of one image on the other, with the solitary horseman, frozen into immobility, starkly outlined against the vast, metallically glittering desert. Borges never again begins a story with that kind of static visual effect. But it shows that he had become aware of the need for an opening impact different in both kind and degree from those he was satisfied to achieve in the other stories of *Historia universal de la infamia*. What that realization led to we recognize in the superb opening of "Hombre de la esquina rosada" and in the carefully crafted beginnings of other stories to be examined shortly.

The other two techniques which Borges mentions in the prologue — the use of sudden shifts in the story-line and the reduction of a biographical account to two or three scenes from the individual's life — have to do essentially with narrative economy achieved by the elimination of unnecessary detail. The author dispenses with causal sequences, with intrusive commentary, with any illusion of completeness, and merely privileges a small group of significant incidents.

In "El incivil maestro de ceremonias Kotsuké no Suké" he praises his source, Mitford, for ignoring "local colour" and sticking closely to the "*movimiento* del glorioso episodio" (I, 277) (*movement* of the glorious episode). This seems to imply that the *disposition* of the episodes in a rapid, active sequence is as important as the *selection* of them. Not long afterwards, in "El acercamiento a Almotásim" (1935), he slightly amplified his remarks, affirming that the proper way to write a story involves the avoidance of obvious allegory, although a certain element of symbolism is permissible. Clearly, in the 1930s Borges had doubts (or insecurities) about "deep theme" or inner meaning in fiction. At intervals during the rest of his career he affected to have retained those doubts. But it was clearly an affectation. What we should rather conclude is that, in the period before *Ficciones* began to take shape, Borges had not evolved the kind of narrative strategies which later allowed him to half-conceal in a tale a deep theme or several levels of possible meaning in such a way that even critics would frequently be misled or overlook important areas of signification. One cannot agree with Lyon that the content of the stories lacks originality "but the literary devices are certainly esthetically mature".[8] In proportion as he developed the techniques alluded to in our earlier commentary on "La casa de Asterión" (which is in fact highly allegorical, albeit not in the way which Borges had rejected twelve years before), he was able to incorporate into his tales the often plural implications which we are still in process of identifying.

An example of the rather simple construction of these early stories, which places them in illuminating contrast both to the complexity of canonical stories like "El inmortal" or "El Aleph" and to the deceitful simplicity of some of the late stories, is "El atroz redentor Lazarus Morell" (I, 245-52). It can be seen to consist of three main sections. The first employs the focusing technique already alluded to, re-emphasized by the succession of subheadings: "La causa remota" > "El lugar" > "Los hombres" > "El hombre" (The Remote Cause > The Place > The Men > The Man). It is, in miniature, the same technique of moving from milieu, through moment, to man which Domingo Faustino Sarmiento had used to brilliant, if misleading, effect in *Facundo*, the story of one of the most infamous Argentine historical figures in the nineteenth century. The end of this section is

[8] Thomas E. Lyon, "Borges and the (Somewhat) Personal Narrator", *Modern Fiction Studies*, 19, no. 3 (1973), p. 364.

the first "scene": Morell preaching, while his gang steals the horses of the fascinated congregation. The second section describes Morell's method of enriching himself by exploiting the hopes and credulity of slaves. The third covers his grand design to promote a slave rebellion and its collapse after his sudden illness and death. The shift to vivid direct speech which marks the climax of the introduction, together with the symmetrical arrangement of the second and third parts of the tale, a rising and then a falling movement, are already marks of an accomplished narrator. In particular, the ending, in which the second "scene", Morell's own description of an especially cold-blooded murder, is followed by a semi-ironic anticlimax when Morell dies in his hospital bed, is highly effective. But what strikes us is the lack of interaction among the three parts of the tale, which are simply juxtaposed in a linear chronological way.

The story has no metaphorical meaning, though there is a moment in it when that potentiality is clearly present. It comes when Borges describes Morell's method of deceiving his victims as unique, because of "la abyección que requiere, por un fatal manejo de la esperanza y por el desarrollo gradual, semejante a la atroz evolución de una pesadilla" (I, 248) (the abjection which it requires, using a fatal manipulation of hope and a gradual development like the atrocious evolution of a nightmare). Here, surely, is the germ of such later stories as "La muerte y la brújula" or "El muerto", where the element of abjection, though present, is somewhat attenuated, but the exploitation of hope and credulity and the slow nightmarish development are prominent features. Also they are in some sense related metaphorically to a view of the human condition. Whereas here their function is simply to accentuate Morell's unambiguous cruelty and evil. The story flickers for a moment and seems about to light up, but then fails to do so. The reason is clear. These stories, being about or connected with evil, are essentially "declaratory" stories. However playfully they exemplify it through the characters and the events, they do not question or deepen our understanding of the phenomenon of evil (as, for instance, "Deutsches Requiem" will do). Although in "El proveedor de iniquidades Monk Eastman" Borges ironically compares a dispute over territory between rival New York gangs to international border disputes, and the subsequent shoot-out to battles at Troy or Junín (a major battle in the Spanish American Wars of Independence), and even a street-affray to World War I, it would be far-fetched to postulate an interpretation of the story with these not entirely serious ploys as a basis. In the same way the cat which, "Desconocedor feliz de la muerte" (I, 270) (Happily unaware of death), contemplates Eastman's corpse prefigures the far more symbolically important cat in "El Sur", which Dahlmann strokes before leaving for his own death, real or imaginary. But it is there in "El proveedor de iniquidades ...", like the hospital bed in "El atroz redentor ...", only to provide an unexpected note of anticlimax at the end.

This is, in fact, one of Borges' most noteworthy strategies in *Historia universal de la infamia.* Since a number of these stories are biographical (Lazarus Morell, Monk Eastman, Billy the Kid), Borges is faced with the problem of the predictable ending. We have just seen in two instances how he resolves it. In the Billy the Kid story the last four sentences provide an even more striking example of unexpectedness which balances the story's unique opening (I, 275). Billy has been shot down. A lesser writer would perhaps have been content at this point with the contrast between "Billy the Kid el Héroe" (Billy the Kid the Hero) and the corpse with "ese aire de cachivache que tienen los difuntos" (that air of useless rubbish which dead people have), and left it at that. But Borges startles us with the next words: "Lo afeitaron" (They gave him a shave). The story, just as it is apparently over, bursts into life again. Billy's corpse, shaved and dressed up in new off-the-peg clothes, is exhibited in a shop-window for days, even touched up with cosmetics for a while, and then — crushingly — buried "con júbilo" (with rejoicing). But Billy is presented in the story as a psychotic killer. The charade after his death which ends the tale has no ironic features or deeper significance. It questions no received value, any more than did the public exhibition of the corpse of Mussolini after his shooting by a partisan. Only momentarily does "El asesino desinteresado ..." flicker, like "El atroz redentor ...". It is when Billy, at the peak of his fame is described as "quizá más nadie y más solo" (I, 274) (perhaps more lacking in human personality and more alone) than any other man on the frontier. For an instant we think of the Negro in "El fin", who, after killing Fierro, "ahora era nadie" (I, 524) (was now nobody), of Rufo/Homer/Cartaphilus/Borges in "El inmortal", who finds that immortality is a weary synonym for "no soy" (II, 19) (I am nonexistent"), and of Zaid in "Abenjacán el Bojarí, muerto en su laberinto", who will become "nadie" (II, 99) (nobody) in death. Here, however, Borges seems to be implying, not the non-existence of the individual personality, which would undermine our sense of being ourselves, but merely that evil is a form of solitude and non-existence: a moral, not an ontological, threat. Once more, what we see in "El asesino desinteresado ..." is a story in which Borges uses unusual and effective opening and closing strategies together with extreme selectivity in the choice of details and scenes to illustrate Billy's life. But there are none of the disturbing or thought-provoking implications with respect to evil that we find in the later work.

A possibly transitional figure is Bogle in "El impostor inverosímil Tom Castro" (I, 253-58). In appearance this story is no more than a sketch of the circumstances of the famous case of the Titchborne Claimant which aroused popular curiosity in Great Britain in the mid-nineteenth century. Like "El atroz redentor ...", it falls logically into three sections. The first describes Orton/Castro's early life and his meeting with Bogle. The second outlines the plot hatched by Bogle for Orton/Castro to impersonate Titchborne. The third deals with the failure of the plot after Bogle's death. But now, for the first time, Borges takes a hesitant step towards the technique of many of his later stories. Bogle stands apart from Morell, Eastman and Billy the Kid. He is not just a murderous ruffian, a flat cardboard figure, nor is his plot motivated by greed or mere gratuitous violence. On the one hand, he is a confidence trickster of genius and audacity; on the other, he is a parody of the man of faith who communes with the Almighty before each important occasion for action and assumes that his behaviour is dictated from on high. At the same time an ironic destiny brings his plans to nought. This is, in other words, the first of several stories, culminating eventually in "El Evangelio según Marcos", in which Borges touches on religion with a certain gentle mockery. There is more than just a flicker of the later Borges in this tale. The references to Psalm 107, to "las visitas del dios" (I, 254) (the god's visits) and to the motto of the Jesuits, *"Ad majorem dei gloriam"* (I, 256), are not casual. Like the clues to the identity of the Minotaur in "La casa de Asterión", though more crudely, they suggest to the reader alert enough to notice them that there is more to this story than was the case in "El atroz redentor ..." or "El proveedor de iniquidades ...". The god who visits Bogle is an early version of the "tosca divinidad" (II, 126) (coarse divinity) who stands behind Bandeira in "El muerto", leading his victim on towards an illusory goal, only to destroy him. From another point of view Bogle, for whom Orton/Castro is merely a phantom animated by his genius, prefigures the wizard in "Las ruinas circulares".

The point at issue here, however, is not whether Borges is moving towards the thematic complexity of some memorable later stories, but that in doing so, he is not as yet fully able to make the structure of his tale significant in relation to its content. The ambiguous figure of Bogle, who alludes ironically, like Asterion or Otálora later, to certain aspects of man and the human condition as Borges sees them, as well as the clues to this allusion, are simply inserted into an otherwise conventional linear précis of a series of events which actually happened more or less as described. Once more there is no interaction. The events in question do not contain that element of unreality which confirms, as Borges suggested in *Discusión*, "el carácter alucinatorio del mundo" (I, 204) (the hallucinatory nature of the world). "El impostor inverosímil ..." simply does not work like a mature Borges story, because Borges is still writing to some extent within the postulate of a pre-existing reality (in this case an actual set of historical events) which is somehow more "real" than imagined reality. He can rather timidly propose an interpretation of that reality, in which Bogle believes himself to be manipulating Orton/ Castro at the behest of a god, while in fact being pursued by a relentless destiny. But the reality itself remains fixed by the subtext, which is constituted by the reports of the Titchborne Claimant's trial and their various re-elaborations. This is a trap which Borges will later avoid by postulating imaginary subtexts which are rather more tractable.

Of all the stories in *Historia universal de la infamia* perhaps the one which most concretely illustrates the contrast with the mature tales is "El incivil maestro de ceremonias Kotsuké no Suké" (I, 277-81). It is a story of subtle revenge and, as such, can be thought of as foreshadowing "La muerte y la brújula" and more especially "Emma Zunz". The latter is the more relevant of the two because, as in "El incivil maestro ...", we proceed directly from the offence to the revenge, whereas in "La muerte y la brújula" the revenge element is part and parcel of the surprise ending. In other words, the formula of "El incivil maestro ..." and "Emma Zunz" is basically the same. There is an opening scenario which motivates the vengeance. There is a carefully thought out deception in preparation for this last. Then follows the vengeance itself and its consequences. But here the similarity between the two tales ends. "El incivil maestro ..." begins even more conventionally than the other stories in *Historia universal de la infamia* which we have so far mentioned, with an unambiguous announcement of the theme: the triumph of loyalty over dishonour. The rest of the first paragraph merely suggests, with only the faintest hints of rhetorical over-emphasis — "la gratitud de todos los hombres" (the gratitude of all men), "una empresa inmortal" (an immortal enterprise), "la minuciosa gloria" (meticulous glory) —, the theme's universal significance. After acknowledging his source, Borges proceeds to recount the events in a compact, linear way, ending with an infelicitous final sentence implying that the undertaking was in fact immortal since we go on telling the tale. The reader familiar with the technique of Borges' later stories, who has been waiting for the rhetoric of the opening to be revealed as gently ironic, is brought up short. He recognizes that, unless we are intended to see the sacrifice of their lives by Takimi no Kami's forty-eight admirers as disproportionate to the offence — a possible, but not likely reading of the story, given that the macrotheme of the collection is infamy and self-degradation —, his expectations have been disappointed. Instead of an anticlimax we have something almost approximating to a moral.

This is, in other words, a story which metaphorically affirms precisely what "Emma Zunz" will later deny: that it is possible by guile to impose a willed pattern on reality, which in turn submits passively to human designs. It presents us with a reassuring metaphor of the way things are rather than a disturbing one. To be sure, Borges offers something similar in "Biografía de Tadeo Isidoro Cruz", but there Cruz's suddenly-discovered loyalty is to an outlaw, not to the victim of an ignoble scoundrel. The conventionality of the narrative lay-out of "El incivil maestro ..." reflects a conventional vision of a hierarchy of moral values. Good triumphs over evil by means of a combination of cunning and heroism. We are not called upon to interpret the story, but merely to accept it. Quite the reverse is the case with "Emma Zunz", where, as we shall see, the offence is presented ambiguously, the strategem backfires on Emma and the vengeance changes its meaning. Instead of confirming our accepted moral values, "Emma Zunz" questions their applicability to a reality which cannot be assumed to be passive and predictable, but which may instead have unforeseen revelations in store for us. Instead of being a conventional working-out of the vengeance-plot, as in "El incivil maestro ...", Borges' strategy in "Emma Zunz" is to make the later segment of the story comment ironically on the earlier one. Therein we see the difference between the later stories and the earlier ones brought into sharp focus.

Perhaps what is most striking about the tales of *Historia universal de la infamia* is that none of them is a puzzle-story except "Hombre de la esquina rosada" (I, 289-96). This story passes, correctly, for the first of those in which Borges alludes to the value of personal courage and honour for their own sake, a theme which was to re-emerge in some of his best-known later stories, most notably "El Sur". To perceive what a huge technical advance the tale represented, we need to compare it not only with the others in the volume but also with the original version, published first in *Martín Fierro*, 38, 26th February 1927 and reproduced in Borges's *El idioma de los argentinos* (1928).[9] Originally entitled "Leyenda policial" and later, in *El idioma ...*, "Hombres pelearon", it consists of a first-person introduction and eight brief paragraphs of third-person narrative without dialogue. It tells how "El chileno" from the southern section of the Buenos Aires slums set out to challenge "El mentao", the hero of the northern section, only to meet his death in the encounter. As a story it is even more primitive than those of *Historia universal de la infamia*. It is also different from them in that it does not deal with infamous or criminal behaviour. On the contrary, it exalts the incident as one of pure courage and manliness in the case of both men, who are uncontaminated by any base motive. The victim "Murió de pura patria" (Died like a true patriot) and will be remembered, the tale concludes, on the Day of Judgement.

Scarcely anything of this brief sketch survives in "Hombre de la esquina rosada", except the idea of the challenge and the presentation of the tale as an oral account of the incident. The following are the main differences:

1 In "Hombre de la esquina rosada" the narrator both witnesses and participates in the action, while in "Leyenda policial"/ "Hombres pelearon" we do not even know whether the narrator was present or is relating an incident which is part of the mythology of the slum neighbourhood in question.

2 In "Hombre de la esquina rosada" the challenge is refused and the challenger is killed in mysterious circumstances, not by his famous rival but by the narrator, a bystander. Thus the whole thrust of the tale is altered.

3 The language of "Hombre de la esquina rosada" gives a much more convincing impression of the speech of an *orillero* (a Buenos Aires slum-dweller) of the period than the utterly artificial pseudo-oral style of the earlier version, overloaded as it is by self-conscious imagery and unlikely vocabulary (e.g. "Las estrellas

---

[9] Jorge Luis Borges, *El idioma de los argentinos* (Buenos Aires: Gleizer, 1928), pp. 151-54.

iban por derroteros eternos y una luna pobre y rendida tironeaba
del cielo" [The stars followed their eternal courses and a poor
worn-out moon tugged from the sky]).

The first point is the basic one. By comparing the two versions of
the tale we can see that between the first and the second Borges
almost certainly changed his mind about its implications and
developed a completely different narrative strategy in order to
suggest them. "Leyenda policial"/"Hombres pelearon" is a declaratory story told in a would-be poetic but straightforward linear
way, leading directly to the narrator's final approving comments. By
contrast, "Hombre de la esquina rosada", while retaining death as
the outcome, reserves implicit approval for Rosendo's refusal to
become involved in what the earlier version, at its climax, had
exalted: a duel for its own sake as a test of courage. The subsequent
killing is presented as the result of shame and jealousy based on local
pride and rivalry. Once the fighter who receives the challenge, now
called Rosendo Juárez, refuses it, a new figure is required to contrast
both with him and with his rival. For this purpose the role of the
narrator is developed into that of an active participant.

But, more important still, in the new version Borges begins to
develop the techniques of ambiguous narration, aimed at the alert
reader, which we saw exemplified in "La casa de Asterión". A feature
which instantly differentiates "Hombre de la esquina rosada" from
the other tales in *Historia universal de la infamia* is the creation of
suspense at the opening. The essential characteristic of the beginnings
of the other tales is that they are simply expository. The reader's
interest is aroused by the novelty of what the stories promise to be
about rather than by how the promise is made. Here what awakens
our curiosity is the thrice-repeated reference to one specific night (I,
289): "Arriba de tres veces no lo traté, y ésas en una misma noche" (I
didn't have to do with him more than three times, and they were all
on the same night); "... una noche nos ilustró la verdadera condición
de Rosendo" (one night revealed to us Rosendo's real character); and
the alluring "... la historia de esa noche rarísima empezó ..." (the
story of that very strange night began). As in "La casa de Asterión",
a mysterious voice is speaking, we do not know to whom. We read
on, intrigued by the implicit promise that the events of the night in
question will, in fact, justify the adjective "rarísima" and to
investigate the identity of the speaker. We have no means of knowing
that Borges is already playing with us, leading us toward the
assumption on which the whole success of the tale's trick ending

depends, i.e. that the speaker was simply an onlooker at the events which he describes. As in future stories, the curiosity interest, gradually converted into suspense as the tale develops, functions both as a lure and as a distraction. The more the narration grips us, the less we notice that we are being manipulated. Meanwhile, having begun the story with one of the adversaries, Borges now deflects our attention to the other, Rosendo Juárez. We are deftly led to make a second assumption: that the point of the story will be the revelation of the latter's true character. What we are intended to overlook is the crucially important detail that on the night in question "vino la Lujanera, porque sí, a dormir en mi rancho" (I, 289) (La Lujanera came to sleep at my place, just like that), the significance of which (as so often in future stories) only becomes apparent when, having finished the tale, we go back to the beginning and reread it to see how it all fits. As an opening this is not, perhaps, quite in a class with those of "La casa de Asterión", "La lotería en Babilonia" or "Tlön, Uqbar, Orbis Tertius". But it leaves far behind the exposition, for instance, of "El atroz redentor ..." or the merely visual effect of the first paragraph of "El asesino desinteresado ...". With it a watershed has been crossed.

The originality of Borges' strategy in the rest of the story is seen when we contrast it with those mentioned below in Chapter 5. Since a major feature of his short-story technique will continue to be that of suggesting assumptions to the reader and then betraying them, pivotal episodes assume a particular importance. For it is the primary function of such episodes (e.g. the receipt by Lönnrot of the map and the compass or the devirgination of Emma Zunz) to initiate the process by which the stories curl back on themselves, ironically changing their implications. There is, in other words, as Alazraki has pointed out, a characteristic symmetry or two-part arrangement in a number of Borges' best stories.[10] The first part invites us to perceive the story in a certain way, which the second part then modifies, often without our having noticed it on first reading. What Borges does in "Hombre de la esquina rosada" is to elide the pivotal episode, leaving it as a hidden element, so that the reader has to work out for himself what happened between the moment Real, the challenger, and La Lujanera left the dance-hall and their return with the former mortally wounded. The shift which takes place between "A lo mejor

---

[10] Jaime Alazraki, *Versiones, inversiones, reversiones: el espejo como modelo estructural en los cuentos de Borges* (Madrid: Gredos, 1977), pp. 36 & 41.

ya se estaban empleando los dos en cualesquier cuneta" (They were probably having it off in some ditch or other) and "Cuando alcancé a volver" (When I managed to get back) (I, 293) is a shift in the very theme of the story itself. From being, as promised at the beginning, the story of Rosendo's true character, it becomes that of the character of the narrator.

It is arguable that some critics, including Alonso and Alazraki, have missed the point of the story by misinterpreting the hidden detail.[11] It should not be forgotten that, like the others in the collection, this is a story connected with infamy. Far from being one in which "el compadrito hace del coraje su religión y su ley" (the hoodlum makes courage his religion and his law),[12] this is a story of treachery, a parody of *pundonor*, the Hispanic code of honour, not an example of it. Carlos Santander is clear on this point: "Es decir, en vez de un héroe, tenemos aquí un traidor" (That is to say, instead of a hero, we have here a traitor).[13] Similarly, Costa writes of the narrator: "Thus he is depicted ultimately, and ironically, not as the hero of the tale, but as the villain."[14] Borges himself has declared that "el más leído de sus cuentos fue 'Hombre de la esquina rosada', cuyo narrador es un asesino" (the short story of his which was most frequently read was "Streetcorner Man", whose narrator is a murderer).[15] Borges appears to have realized that even critics have been misled. For much later he makes Rosendo explain in "Historia de Rosendo Juárez" that "lo mataron [i.e. Real, his adversary] a *traición* esa misma noche" (II, 387) (he was killed *treacherously* the same night). Jealousy and resentment, not honour, motivate the narrator. The whole point of the missing episode is that it converts a potentially virile, if barbarous, challenge, resisted with a moral courage which transcends physical courage, into a petty act of vengeance.

Borges' problem in the second part of the story is to present the second episode, the death of the challenger, Real, in such a way as to

[11] See Amado Alonso, "Borges narrador", in his *Materia y forma en poesía*, 2nd ed. (Madrid: Gredos, 1960), pp. 341-54, esp. pp. 346 ff.; Jaime Alazraki, *La prosa narrativa de Jorge Luis Borges* (Madrid: Gredos, 1968), p. 104.

[12] Alazraki, *La prosa narrativa ...*, p. 104.

[13] Carlos Santander, "Estructura narrativa en 'Hombre de la esquina rosada'", *Revista Chilena de Literatura*, 1 (1970), p. 29.

[14] René de Costa, "A Note on Narrative Voice in Borges's Early Fiction", *Modern Philology*, 76 (1978-79), p.195.

[15] Jorge Luis Borges, *Obras completas 1923-1972* (Buenos Aires: Emecé, 1972), p. 1144.

balance the opening one, the challenge and Rosendo's response, while at the same time eluding an explanation of it until the trick ending. There is a certain symmetry about the two episodes, created by the descriptions of Real's two entries into the dance-hall. In the first (I,290), "llamaron a la puerta con autoridá, un golpe y una voz. En seguida un silencio general, una pechada poderosa a la puerta y el hombre estaba dentro" (someone knocked on the door authoritatively, one knock and a shout. Then right away a general silence, a heavy charge at the door and the fellow was inside). In the second (I, 294), we do not hear of a knock at the door, though the later notation "Cuando golpeó" (When he knocked) indicates that there was one. But now the voice has changed to a terrible tone of serenity "como si ya no juera de alguien" (as if now it didn't belong to anyone). Real's original dramatic entry is repeated, but this time preceded by La Lujanera, the reference to whose audible weeping prepares us, like Real's voice, for what is to come. The true parallel between the first and the second episodes of "Hombre de la esquina rosada", however, is implicit. Both episodes illustrate courage: the first, Rosendo's moral courage in the face of insult and ridicule; the second, Real's physical courage in the face of death. His passing, like that of the victim in the earlier version, is described with solemnity and admiration, in terms of manly pride and quiet stoicism, the narrator pronouncing a simple obsequy: "... era de los hombres de más coraje que hubo en aquel entonces, dende la Batería hasta el Sur" (I, 294-95) (he was one of the bravest guys around at that time, from the Battery to the Southside).

We now reach the crucial point in the story: the ending. Throughout his work Borges seems willing to postulate only two absolute values: attachment to the ethical principle and courage. Religious and aesthetic values, social and philosophical doctrines, all other presumptions about goodness and truth tend to be called into question. But ethical behaviour and bravery survive untarnished by Borges' scepticism and gentle but pointed satire. Here all the emphasis has been on bravery. As far as the two episodes go, the story is quite unambiguous. But they are not the whole story. Rosendo and Real are not the only protagonists now, as the two rivals were in "Leyenda policial"/"Hombres pelearon". In the reflective interlude which separates the first episode from the second, and at the end, the narrator comes into his own. The critical question is whether he, too, belongs to the human category of Rosendo and Real or whether his role in the story is to exalt their behaviour by

contrast. Borges provides us with very few clues. Even the reference
to a treacherous attack on Real in "Historia de Rosendo Juárez",
since it is not part of the internal data of the story, does not constitute
a clinching argument. We are forced back on to other evidence. The
key phrases are: "Debí ponerme colorao de vergüenza" (I, 292) (I
must have flushed with shame) and "... en cuanto lo supe muerto y
sin habla, le perdí el odio" (I, 295) (as soon as I knew he was dead and
speechless, I lost my hatred of him). Shame and hatred are the
motivating emotions behind the intervention of the narrator in the
events described, together with the desire to avenge the humiliation
inflicted on the neighbourhood by the apparently successful challenge
to its leading fighter. These are not noble motives. The tone of the
narrator's reflections as he steps out from the hall into the night is of
smouldering resentment and inferiority, compounded by anger and
envy that the newcomer may be at that very moment triumphantly
enjoying the favours of La Lujanera as his reward.

While no definite conclusion can be advanced, since La Lujanera's
brief account of what happened omits any description of an actual
fight, it seems likely that Borges intended to imply more at the end of
"Hombre de la esquina rosada" than simply that the narrator had
avenged the honour of the neighbourhood. The last sentence, in
which the narrator's knife is described rather curiously as "como
inocente" (as if innocent) seems to imply a doubt, not about the
narrator's responsibility for the death of Rosendo, which is made
clear, but about the acceptability of his conduct. The mystery of
Real's death is explained, but the ambiguity of the narrator's action
remains to qualify the emphasis on the courage of the two other
protagonists.

The cunningly fashioned opening, the use of the hidden item of
information to preserve curiosity and suspense, the trick ending, the
hint of moral ambiguity alongside the theme of courage, all combine
to make "Hombre de la esquina rosada" Borges' most carefully
crafted early story, whose narrative strategy, now almost fully
developed, portends the technical brilliance exhibited by the stories
of the decade of the forties now soon to follow.

CHAPTER 3

OPENING STRATEGIES

A novel normally has an exposition; a short story only has an opening. One of the tests of a short-story writer is how quickly he can grasp the reader's interest and focus it on the tale without pausing to insert more than the minimum of background material or character presentation. Economy is all. But equally, if the short story is to combine subtlety with its brevity, the opening must work for its living and often perform more than one function. We saw in "La casa de Asterión" how in the first paragraph Borges not only intrigues the reader by using an unnamed narrator, but also how, by the third sentence, he insinuates the question of Asterion's house, the second object of mystery. At the same time he contrives to hold a balance between straight narrative and symbolic elements. The critical question, then, when we focus our attention on the opening of a Borges story, is whether we can perceive it functioning simultaneously in different ways.

A ploy which Borges has used several times is the one seen in the opening of "Tlön, Uqbar, Orbis Tertius": "El hecho se produjo hará unos cinco años" (I, 409) (The event took place some five years ago). We find it again in "El encuentro": "El hecho aconteció, por lo demás, hacia 1910" (II, 389) (The event happened, moreover, around 1910); "El Evangelio según Marcos": "El hecho sucedió en la estancia Los Alamos, en el partido de Junín, hacia el sur, en los últimos días del mes de marzo de 1928" (II, 424) (The event happened on Los Alamos ranch, in the southern part of the district of Junín, in the last days of the month of March, 1928); in "El otro": "El hecho ocurrió en el mes de febrero de 1969" (II, 457) (The event occurred in the month of February, 1969); and in "Avelino Arredondo": "El hecho aconteció en Montevideo, en 1897" (II, 523) (The event happened in Montevideo, in 1897).

Why is it such a favourite with Borges? The difference in type among the five stories offers a clue. The first four are, to a greater or lesser extent, fantastic stories or at least stories containing an element of fantasy. "Avelino Arredondo", on the other hand, is a fictional evocation of a historical event, with overtones of moral courage. In the former stories the concrete time or time and place reference forms part of Borges' confessed method of placing a certain emphasis on "realistic" details in order to lull the reader before drawing him into the realm of the "unreal". The opening of "Tlön, Uqbar, Orbis Tertius" itself, with its accumulated references to real places — "una quinta de la calle Gaona, en Ramos Mejía" (I, 409) (a villa on Gaona Street in Ramos Mejía) — and to real people (Bioy Casares, Mastronardi, Ibarra, Martínez Estrada, Drieu la Rochelle, Reyes, Xul Solar, Amorim), is a prime example of this technique. In a much later story, "Ulrica", Borges telescopes it into the pseudo-ingenuous "Mi relato será fiel a la realidad" (II, 465) (Mi story will be faithful to reality), before producing the familiar ploy "Los hechos ocurrieron hace muy poco" (The events happened not very long ago) and providing a series of concrete references to the city of York and its famous Minster. Only when we have been softened up by this evocation of a familiar world does the story suddenly slip into fantasy. But the reappearance of the specific time notation in "Avelino Arredondo", which is not a fantastic tale, indicates that creation of a sense of reality is not the only reason for its use. If we turn to the end of this last story, we read: "Así habrán ocurrido los hechos" (II, 527) (That is how the events must have happened). The opening formula, that is, grasped our attention with the alluring reference to "El hecho" (The event), but the actual assassination with which the tale is concerned is then put off until the climax of the story. The pattern is one of announcement followed by postpone-ment, a classic short-story strategy.

In "Tlön, Uqbar, Orbis Tertius", the story of the discovery of materials relating to a fantastic imaginary land, which then begins to affect our world, the "hecho" in question is not the climax of the story, but only the first event: the finding of the (falsified) encyclo-paedia. Since the fantastic elements of the story are much more prominent than in "Ulrica", the manipulation of the reader has to be more sophisticated. In the opening section, therefore, the extra pages at the end of volume XLVI of the encyclopaedia are presented as an intriguing, but spurious, interpolation into the comforting, reliable reprint of the *Encyclopaedia Britannica*. Any threat the contents of these added pages may imply to our sense of knowing our own world is defused when we learn at the end of the section that the interpolation is an isolated case, not even present in other copies of the volume. We relax, only to be caught off guard by the sudden appearance, not of part of an encyclopaedia of Uqbar (which, since we are consciously reading a story and therefore expect something to happen, we could regard as an expansion of the earlier practical joke), but of part of an encyclopaedia of Tlön, a region as imaginary to the inhabitants of Uqbar as Uqbar is to us! Suddenly we are a long way from Ramos Mejía.

What has happened? As in so many of Borges' stories, we have passed from the comforting security of the real to the disconcerting novelty of the fantastic. And not just at one remove away from provincial Argentina (i.e. to Uqbar), but at two (i.e. to Tlön). The original "hecho", the finding of the partially-falsified volume of the first encyclopaedia, with its predominant references to this world, turns out to have been merely a prelude to a second "hecho", the appearance of a wholly-falsified volume of another encyclopaedia referring to a world so imaginary that even those who imagined it — the inhabitants of Uqbar — are assumed to be unreal. The reason why the explanation of the first "hecho" was not long postponed was that there was this second "hecho", Ashe's volume, still to come, more important and — in the end — more threatening. Ramos Mejía produced Uqbar; Uqbar (and Adrogué) produce Tlön, but then Tlön unexpectedly invades Argentina and our familiar, reassuring world. The story broadens out to embrace a description of an unreal world, but then curls back on itself to bring this astonishing place into disturbing contact with the world we know and trust to be real.

We can now return to the opening and notice that the phrase "El hecho se produjo hará unos cinco años" does not come at the beginning of the story as do similar phrases in, for instance, "El otro". It is preceded by references to a mirror and to an encylopaedia. We know why the encyclopaedia is there. It is, of course, a symbol of our power to catalogue, and hence — hopefully — to understand, reality; a symbol which becomes ironic as soon as Uqbar is included in its contents. But, more practically, without its intercalated pages, there would be no Uqbar and, therefore, no Tlön. But why the mirror? Everyone familiar with Borges is aware that mirrors for him

are threatening presences. The appearance of the mirror in the
opening sentence of the story implies already a sinister sequel. But
this is not the only significance of "espejo" (mirror) as the seventh
word in the story. The main point is surely that Tlön, with its radical
idealism, forms a kind of mirror-image of our materialist world: it is
what our world would be like if philosophical idealism were a
description of reality. This initial symbol is only clarified by the
ending of the story, the significance of which it, in turn, clarifies on
second and subsequent readings.

At this point we begin to appreciate the complexity of the opening
of "Tlön, Uqbar, Orbis Tertius". Beginning from what it has in
common with other Borges openings — the use of the ploy "El hecho
se produjo" dangled in front of us to arouse our curiosity —, we
move to a recognition of Borges' skill in creating an air of plausibility
by deftly mixing together the real and the imaginary so that the
former can be used as a springboard to the latter. But behind both
strategies lies another which is symbolic: the mirror reflecting the
corridor in Ramos Mejía portends the reflection of our world in
Tlön. More broadly still, the intervention of the imaginary in the
"real" world, as Borges and Bioy Casares find the spurious pages in
the rogue volume of *The Anglo-American Cyclopaedia*, portends the
way in which the products of the imaginary world of Tlön will
eventually intervene in our world. The whole opening of "Tlön,
Uqbar, Orbis Tertius" is not just designed to catch our interest or
draw us almost imperceptibly away from the embrace of the real. It is
also an extended and complex foreshadowing device preparing us for
the end of the story.

Foreshadowing is equally a feature of other story openings.
"Deutsches Requiem" and "El Sur" both employ it in a very similar
way. The beginning of "Deutsches Requiem" (II, 62) grasps the
reader's attention by presenting the story as the last statement of a
condemned criminal. The alluring sentence "En cuanto a mí, seré
fusilado por torturador y asesino" (As for me, I shall be shot as a
torturer and murderer) pulls us up short as we are absorbing the
banal factual details contained in the first three sentences. But what is
really important is not the sudden shock-effect of this laconic
statement, effective as it is. The real point is that it is not the opening
line of the story. It and the references to the trial and the plea of guilty
are sandwiched in between other references to Zur Linde's military
forbears. These in turn are situated between an epigraph from the
Bible and a footnote referring not just to some other ancestor of Zur

Linde, but to his "most illustrious" one, the theologian and possibly Jewish Hebrew scholar, Johannes Forkel, whom he has failed (significantly, we are forewarned) to mention. As so frequently in Borges' best tales, the point of the initial patterning is not really visible to the reader until the story is read through and we return to the beginning again for a closer look, to try to resolve some of our residual puzzlement. The ending, that is, sends us back to the beginning in order to work out what the story may be about, as distinct from what, at first sight, it seems to be about.

What "Deutsches Requiem" seems to be about is suggested by Borges' comment to Burgin that Zur Linde represents the archetypal Nazi, "The platonic idea of a Nazi [...] who feels that a violent world is better than a peaceful world and who doesn't care for victory".[1] Certainly the story can be read at this level, as a vignette of a totally evil mentality. As such, it reminds us once more that Borges' assumption of a stance of sceptical detachment is, at the ethical level, a thin façade, behind which we perceive a deep commitment to certain moral values. But if the story is only about the evil and violence inherent in the Nazi mentality, really only Zur Linde's military ancestors, those connected with the expansive force of German aggression in the past, are fully relevant. What are we to make of the epigraph and the footnote?

On a second reading of the story, they warn us that it is more than an exploration of a paradigmatic Nazi mentality. A major clue to the story's further meaning is almost certainly to be found in the well-known phrase from "Tlön, Uqbar, Orbis Tertius": "... bastaba cualquier simetría con apariencia de orden — el materialismo dialéctico, el antisemitismo, el nazismo — para embelesar a los hombres" (I, 423) (any symmetry with some semblance of order — dialectical materialism, antisemitism, Nazism — was enough to entrance mankind). The key word is "order". Men, Borges is suggesting, will gladly embrace any system of ideas which seems to offer the possibility of conferring order, and hence some kind of meaning and finality, on their lives. In other words, as Efron has put it, the story comes to be about "the unavoidable need to construct perspectives, and to believe in them".[2] That is, it is about man's need of a faith to make sense of his existence, and about how allegiance to

---

[1] Richard Burgin, *Conversations with Jorge Luis Borges* (New York: Avon, 1968), p. 30.

[2] Arthur Efron, "Perspectivism and the Nature of Fiction: Don Quixote and Borges", *Thought*, 50, no. 197 (1975), p. 160.

faith can survive and reinterpret every catastrophe which stands in the way of its triumph. Zur Linde's faith in Nazism is an ironic mirror-image of Christian faith. This is the point of the religious frame of reference hinted at in the beginning of the story. Zur Linde clings to his faith in Nazism as Job clung to his faith in God's goodness and mercy in the face of all contrary experience. His theological forbear, Johannes Forkel, is more illustrious than his military ancestors because it is faith in the mystique of Nazism, not its mere cruel and aggressive militarism, that Zur Linde embraces. It is this which allows him, on the Christian model, to work on behalf of the faith in an obscure and to him hateful way, sacrificing his own personality like a candidate for sainthood, rather than participating in Nazism's military triumphs.

Once we perceive that Zur Linde means what he says when he compares the dawn of Nazism to the early days of Islam or Christianity, we also perceive that Borges is alluding in the story to men's inherent tendency to accept any order that seems to involve an absolute, and to make any sacrifice for it, rather than recognize the absence of an absolute and accept the blind flux of life. A similar allusion is to be found in "La lotería en Babilonia", where the inhabitants of Babylon evidently prefer to believe in the existence of the Company and to view the lottery as "una interpolación del azar en el orden del mundo" (I, 444) (an interpolation of chance into the orderliness of the world) rather than to follow the heresiarchs (and Borges, probably) in accepting that Babylon — the world — "no es otra cosa que un infinito juego de azares" (I, 447) (is nothing but an infite interplay of chance). At this point it becomes clear that the arrangement of the opening of "Deutsches Requiem", from the epigraph on, includes an elaborate foreshadowing of the religious dimension of the story, and is deliberately designed to signal its presence to us.

Very much the same is true in the case of "El Sur", but in this later story the foreshadowing is — perhaps regrettably — much more explicit. On the other hand, there may be good reason for this. A noteworthy feature of Borges' tales is his tendency to lay traps for the unwary reader which either obscure from him a deeper level of meaning or allow Borges to overthrow his assumptions at a later stage in the story. In "El Sur" everything depends on the levels of meaning which we are prepared to identify. As Gertel has made clear, there are several.[3] An obvious one concerns Borges' notion, voiced in

³ Zunilda Gertel, "'El Sur' de Borges: búsqueda de la identidad en el laberinto",

Evaristo Carriego (I, 86), that "cualquier vida humana [...] consta en realidad de un momento: el momento en que el hombre sabe para siempre quién es" (any human life [...] in reality consists of one moment: the moment in which a man gets to know for ever who he is). We can perceive "El Sur" as being about a man who reaches, as it were, the centre of his own labyrinth, about self-discovery. Equally, since what Dahlmann discovers is his readiness to die in a traditional Argentine way, courageously in a knife-fight, we can interpret the story as connected with the discovery by Dahlmann of his visceral Argentineness. More than this even, we can see in the story something cognate with Zur Linde's attraction to the view, expressed by Schopenhauer in *Parerga und Paralipomena*, that in some sort we all, consciously or not, choose our own destinies. We know that Borges affects to hold this view himself. Thus the story contains implicitly the theme of choice and fate. But most of all, as nearly every critic has noticed, the story is about the ambiguity of reality. We do not know whether the events described in the later part of the tale are intended to be taken as "real" (in the fictional sense) or as a hallucination or dream of Dahlmann's while he is in the clinic (or even on the train).

To return to the opening paragraph (I, 529), it is plain that Borges is here deliberately foreshadowing the theme of Argentineness, using a method similar to the one he had employed in "Deutsches Requiem". We notice the gentle anticlimax suggested by the positioning of the notation of Dahlmann's ultra-pacific and insignificant post as librarian between the references to his two grandfathers, one a German evangelist, the other an Argentine frontier soldier. The contrast with Dahlmann's quiet heroism at the end is clearly intentional. But at the same time the emphasis falls on the "discordia de sus dos linajes" (discord between his two ancestries), one European and spiritual, the other Argentine and physical. Dahlmann opts for the latter, "choosing" the grandfather who had met death with physical courage. By so doing, he chooses his Argentine heritage. When we come to the final incident in the story we see what that choice has foreshadowed, and what Dahlmann's possession of a ranch-house to the south of Buenos Aires symbolized: that link with the heroic past which had been passive until February 1930 and then was suddenly activated.

The danger is that of being satisfied with the recognition that the

Nueva Narrativa Hispanoamericana, 1, no. 2 (1971), 35-55.

opening paragraph foreshadows the climax. For in a writer like Borges, who maliciously enjoys manipulating the reader's reactions, the very explicitness of the device in this case renders it suspect. When we take account of the fact that the core of the story may well have to do with something quite different from the choice of Argentineness — the realization (embodied in so much contemporary fiction) which Miguel Angel Asturias expressed when he remarked almost casually in Chapter 26 of *El Señor Presidente* (1946) that "Entre la realidad y el sueño la diferencia es puramente mecánica" (The difference between reality and dreams is purely mechanical)[4] —, we may see the functionality of the opening in a somewhat different light. It may be designed to "fix" an interpretation of the tale in our minds, so that Borges can first of all reinforce it and then, as so often, question it. For what seems to be a conscious decision on Dahlmann's part to accept the *compadrito*'s challenge may, in fact, simply be destiny operating through him deterministically, as Borges seems to believe it does through all our actions. In addition, at the end of the story, we do not know whether the choice (or the destiny) is not merely part of a dream. One technique of the story, visible at the beginning, points deliberately in one direction, which is later covertly contradicted by another. What was so explicit in the opening may have been there chiefly to give way later to the ambiguity of the ending. This is not quite the same use of the technique, then, as in "Deutsches Requiem".

Another kind of opening ploy can be seen in "El milagro secreto" (I, 507-13). The story of Hladík's arrest and condemnation to death is not only once more dramatic and suspense-creating in its own right, but could also be seen as a framing device, as discussed in the next chapter. This is true, however, only in the restricted sense that at the end of the tale Hladík is actually shot on the date fixed for his execution. It is not a genuine frame-story, like for instance those of Yu-Tsun, Teodelina Villar or the cousins Beatriz and Carlos Daneri, because it does not interact significantly with the main episode. Rather, what calls for attention, as in "Deutsches Requiem", is the fact that the suspense-creating notation — Hladík's condemnation to death by a firing squad — is not the first element of importance in the story. It is preceded by his strange dream of a chess-game.

As usual, Borges himself is not entirely helpful. To Irby he

---

[4] Miguel Angel Asturias, *Obras completas* (Paris: Klincksieck, and Mexico City: Fondo de Cultura Económica, 1978), III, 159.

declared: "... había incluido ese detalle para obtener un efecto de contraste. Al final del cuento, el protagonista escribe el tercer acto de su comedia en un instante. Queda bien, pues, que al principio haya un juego de ajedrez que se demora a través de generaciones y generaciones" (I had included that detail in order to create a contrasting effect. At the end of the tale the protagonist writes the third act of his comedy in an instant. So it's a good idea to have at the beginning a chess-game that lasts for generations and generations).[5] There is obviously more to it than that. But the meaning of the dream, and hence its wider functionality within the story's general narrative strategy, remains mysterious until we have read the whole tale and come back to the dream again to see where it fits. Like "Las ruinas circulares", "El milagro secreto" contains echoes of the Spanish thinker Unamuno's ideas. Its key sentence is the one which tells us that Hladík "procuraba afirmarse de algún modo en la sustancia fugitiva del tiempo" (I, 508) (tried to secure himself somehow in the fleeting substance of time). He sees the completion of his play *Los enemigos* (*The Enemies*) as a potential means of doing so. Both elements here — the triumph of the individual soul over time and death, together with survival by means of artistic creation — are profoundly Unamunesque. The difference is that Borges professes general indifference to, and disbelief in, either of them. Hence the story, instead of being "agonic" in Unamuno's sense of the word, is ironic. The possibilities which Unamuno desperately tried to believe in, Borges quietly rejects.

If this is accepted, it becomes apparent that Hladík's first dream is another foreshadowing device, but in this case an ironic one. The dream itself, the play which Hladík mentally completes and the story as a whole are all concerned with conflict. A game of chess is similarly a symbolic struggle. Both Unamuno — in *La novela de don Sandalio, jugador de ajedrez* and *La esfinge*, for example — and Borges — in the poem "Ajedrez II"[6] — use it as a symbol of life itself, seen as a conflict with a force which ultimately wears down all our resistance. A footnote to "Historia de los ecos de un nombre" clarifies the use of the symbolism here: "Buber (*Was ist der Mensch?*, 1938) escribe que vivir es penetrar en una extraña habitación del espíritu, cuyo piso es el tablero en el que jugamos un juego inevitable y desconocido contra un adversario cambiante y a veces espantoso" (II, 277) (Buber [*What*

[5] Irby, *Encuentro con Borges*, p. 26.
[6] Jorge Luis Borges, *Obra poética, 1923-1977*, 3rd ed. (Madrid: Alianza, 1983), p.125.

is Man?, 1938] writes that living means entering a strange room of the spirit, whose floor is the chess-board on which we play out an unknown and inescapable game against an ever-changing and sometimes fearsome adversary). The struggle in this case is the struggle against time, emphasized by the time-notations in the story, beginning with the first eight words. Paradoxically Hladík "knows" that within the lapse of time indicated (the 19th to the 29th of March) he is immortal, in the sense that a man who knows for certain the date of his death "cannot" die before it arrives. This is, in fact, pure illusion, like the illusion that a detail imagined beforehand cannot become reality. The dream in the opening paragraph can be seen in retrospect as foreshadowing the failure of Hladík's illusion: his inevitable failure to overcome time. The first part of the dream, with the mention of two hostile families ("Aryans" and Jews?) in a centuries-old conflict, links it to Hladík's actual situation as a man of Jewish origin in the power of the Gestapo. The second part, in which the dreamer races against time without knowing the rules of the contest, and wakes to his doom, links the dream to his situation in the condemned cell. Hladík can no more defeat time and death by means of artistic creativity than the dreamer can make a meaningful move in a game of whose rules he is ignorant. The dream, that is, is designed to undermine, from the outset of the story, Hladík's apparent success in his fight against time, and to emphasize the ultimate futility of that fight.

"El fin" (I, 521-24) is about the death of Martín Fierro, the hero of the Argentine poem of the same name, but the first word of the story refers to Recabarren, a spectator of the event. If we think of "El encuentro", which also deals with a fatal knife-fight, what strikes us is that Recabarren is an onlooker but, unlike the onlooker in the later tale, not the narrator. The first part of "El fin" is told from his viewpoint, but not by him. The second part, the conversation between Fierro and the Negro, is told impersonally. Still, since Recabarren reportedly could hear Fierro hiss through his teeth as he reined in his horse, dismounted and entered the store, we naturally assume that Recabarren overhears it from where he is lying, unable to move. However, the focus of the tale has suddenly moved away from him to the two speakers. The omniscient narrator does not report their dialogue using Recabarren as the reference-point, following the pattern of the earlier part of the tale, where, for instance, the sound of the Negro's guitar was linked to Recabarren's reaction: "Recabarren, patrón de la pulpería, no olvidaría ese contrapunto" (Recabarren, the owner of the store, would never forget that counterpoint). In the dialogue section the indications "con dulzura" (gently), "con voz áspera" (in a harsh voice), "sin apuro" (unhurriedly) etc. do not explicitly express Recabarren's impressions. Although his presence remains implicit and re-emerges for an instant at the end — "Desde su catre, Recabarren vio el fin" (From his cot Recabarren saw the end) —, it is clear that his role is essentially connected with the opening strategy of the tale. After that he is dispensed with until the brief notation associating him with the climax.

Why is Recabarren introduced at all, if he is not to be the narrator or even a minor participant in the action? What is his function? Since he does not tell the story and has no reported thoughts about the outcome, he does not comment on the event or the characters directly. Borges' opening strategy in "El fin" is not to go straight to the story of Fierro's death itself, but instead to begin by creating an individual and a set of circumstances apparently unconnected with it, except by physical proximity, and then leave the reader to establish the connection. Alazraki writes: "Es extraño que Borges haya recurrido en su cuento a un testigo, Recabarren, cuya función en el relato es dudosa" (It is strange that Borges should have had recourse in his story to a witness, Recabarren, whose function in the tale is doubtful) and concludes rather unconvincingly that the episode of Fierro's death may simply be a dream in the storekeeper's mind.[7] This suggestion may derive from Santí, who presents Recabarren as dying and delirious, a view for which I cannot find adequate evidence in the text.[8] What the text does tell us is that Recabarren is helplessly paralysed by a stroke, dumb, resigned and stoical. Twice Borges indicates his total absence of self-pity, his unmoved acceptance of his harsh destiny. Twice also he mentions that Recabarren's destiny is static: the storekeeper is confined within a reality que "ya no cambiaría nunca" (I, 521) (would now never change) and lives in a perpetual present. These circumstances and personal qualities have nothing to do with dreams or delirium. They suggest that Recabarren's primary function is to convey the fact that the theme of "El fin" is destiny and man's response to it.

Specifically, Recabarren exists in the tale as the standard against

---

[7] Alazraki, *Versiones ...*, p. 49.

[8] Enrico-Mario Santí, "Escritura y tradición: Martín Fierro en dos cuentos de Borges", *Revista Iberoamericana*, 87/88 (1974), p. 316.

which Borges suggests we should measure the two combatants. They
are differentiated by their respective levels of insight. Fierro has
already undergone the experience which the Negro is impatiently
awaiting. He knows what the Negro is about to discover: that neither
the causes nor the consequences of human actions should be viewed
simplistically. In his behaviour in front of his children he sets a non-
violent example — "... no quise mostrarme como un hombre que
anda a las puñaladas" (I, 522) (I did not want to show myself to be a
man who gets into knife-fights) — and specifically warns them to
avoid bloodshed: "Les dije, entre otras cosas, que el hombre no debe
derramar la sangre del hombre" (I, 523) (I told them, among other
things, that it is not for man to shed a man's blood). In this he appears
to accept some degree of moral responsibility. But at the same time
he views his situation as transcending his own possible guilt: "Mi
destino ha querido que yo matara" (My destiny willed that I should
kill). His stance seems to be equidistant from acceptance either of
free will or total determinism. Perhaps Borges is again hinting here at
Schopenhauer's idea that we will our own destinies or in some way
collaborate with fatality.

Fierro's words to the Negro are an implicit warning not to act, not
to bring on himself the level of insight that makes Fierro, like
Scharlach/Lönnrot at the end of "La muerte y la brújula", weary
and afflicted with a sense of abstract sadness. But destiny in Borges'
stories is almost always ironic. For Fierro to do more than hint to the
Negro that his vengeance will merely transfer guilt and remorse,
together with the sense of being reduced to a cipher by the
indifference of destiny, would indicate cowardice. The one man who
could explain to the Negro the futility of his vengeance is his intended
victim. Fierro is compelled to collaborate with a fatality the outcome
of which he knows only too well. The Negro, on the other hand,
represents illusion, the self-deceiving belief that his vengeance for his
brother's death will somehow be a solution, a fulfilment, a collaboration with justice. As we know from "Emma Zunz", Borges
detested vengefulness and always makes it turn on its representatives.
Emma's vengefulness subjects her to an experience which alters the
essential nature of the action she takes against Loewenthal; Scharlach, if we believe Borges' suggestion that the story is at one level
connected with the idea of suicide, kills at least a part of himself and
hence his "fatigada victoria" (I, 503) (weary victory) is accompanied
by a sadness no less great than his hatred. Fierro's last words to the
Negro suggest that the latter was too impatient to rush on to his

destiny, of which he could not weigh the consequences for himself, to have won the song-contest. But the implicit warning, that a second defeat awaits him even if he overcomes Fierro, goes unheeded. This, too, is associated with irony. For as Recabarren lay in his cot, he had heard the Negro strumming on his guitar music which is described as "una suerte de pobrísimo laberinto que se enredaba y se desataba infinitamente" (I, 521) (a kind of very poor labyrinth which twined and untwined itself infinitely). The combination of the ideas of the labyrinthine and the infinite, with all the resonance that they possess in Borges' work, places it beyond doubt that the music is a symbol. Its infinite entanglements and disentanglements symbolize life. Playing, as he waits to collaborate actively with his own ironically ambiguous destiny, the Negro is unconsciously commenting on the fact that the infinite complexity of life renders his vengeance futile and nugatory and will in the end only result in his changing places with his victim.

What, meanwhile, of Recabarren? He represents the third position. The Negro is impatient to act; his is rashness in the face of life's unpredictability. Fierro, reluctantly in view of his acquired insight, assents to action; his is the physical courage to risk his life (and lose it) for what he knows to be in vain. Recabarren endures stoically an affliction which makes it impossible for him either to act or to be drawn into action. His is the moral courage to accept his destiny without struggle or repining. He is "el sufrido Recabarren" (I, 522) (the long-suffering Recabarren). The phrase which Borges uses of Dahlmann in the clinic in "El Sur" — "condolido de su destino" (I, 530) (pitying himself because of his destiny) — comes to mind. Threatened by a petty, absurd death, caused by a banal, minor injury to his scalp, Dahlmann weeps with self-pity. But then, faced with the illusion or the fact of a death which will somehow fulfil a repressed, romantic Argentineness, like Fierro he learns to assent. But Recabarren, who can view his paralysed body "sin lástima" (I, 521) (without self-pity), and whose life, encapsulated in a perpetual present, is to that extent detached from causes and effects which link the past to the future, is the Schopenhaurian man of insight who has accepted detachment from action and freedom from involvement. He is thus liberated from life's squalid labyrinth in which Fierro and the Negro are trapped. Not only can he not act; he cannot even speak. In a sense he enjoys the awareness of the Immortals in "El inmortal" without their burden of everlasting life. Their awareness detaches them from pity, let alone self-pity. Like them, Recabarren contemplates passively a life in which action, whatever its motivation, good or bad, noble or ignoble, is pointless.

Wheelock extends this view of Recabarren by suggesting that he represents the human mind in general, paralysed and inarticulate in the face of life's ambiguities.[9] The problem with this interpretation is that it dissociates Recabarren too much from Fierro and the Negro. To be sure, they act, willingly or reluctantly, while he does not. But this does not mean that only he has universal reference. All three represent mankind in the sense that they all represent different options in the face of destiny.

The opening strategy of "El fin", then, is to foreground Recabarren first, in order to establish from the beginning a hierarchy of possible responses to individual destiny. Recabarren's situation and his responses to it are designed to comment implicitly on the respective situations and responses of Fierro and the Negro. By setting the former up at the beginning of the tale, Borges seems to be pointing to the ideal option: calm, stoical contemplation of the Self and the Other, which robs destiny of part of its power. Here, it is true, we see only a technique of juxtaposition. Recabarren cannot interact verbally or physically with Fierro and the Negro because he is paralysed and without speech. Yet a kind of interaction takes place in the reader's mind when we question Recabarren's role and come to recognize that without it the story would be incomplete.

One of the more interesting openings in Borges' later stories is that of "El duelo" (II, 406-10). Barrenechea writes teasingly: "El nivel de la supuesta realidad, la historia contada, es la emulación de dos mujeres de alta sociedad, amigas íntimas, diletantes de pintura" (The level of supposed reality, the story that is told, is that of mutual emulation on the part of two high-society ladies, close friends and amateur painters).[10] She goes on: "Los incidentes se encadenan y remiten a la existencia de otros niveles de comprensión, hecho hacia el cual el narrador se encarga de llamar la atención desde el comienzo" (The incidents link up and indicate other levels of understanding, a fact to which the narrator takes care to draw our attention from the beginning). But she does not clarify what these "other levels of understanding" might be. She contents herself with the remark that "Estas distintas capas de interpretación o lecturas no

[9] Wheelock, *The Mythmaker*, p. 376.
[10] Ana María Barrenechea, "Borges y los símbolos", *Revista Iberoamericana*, 100/101 (1977), p. 603.

son siempre claras y definidas" (These different levels of interpretation or readings are not always clearly defined). More recently
Agheana refers to the rivalry between Clara Glencairn and Marta
Pizarro as "an allegorical duel between figurative and non-figurative
painting", and asserts that in the tale it is painting which occupies the
centre of the stage, not the characters.[11] This possibly indicates one of
Barrenechea's "other levels of understanding", though there are
counter-arguments, as we shall see. But it hardly seems to do justice
to Borges' intentions if the story is as Barrenechea sees it.

What is it that Borges' narrator draws our attention to "from the
beginning"? It is: a) the link between Henry James and Clara, one of
the protagonists; b) the distinction between Henry James' approach,
which would have involved "más de cien páginas de ironía y ternura"
(II, 406) (more than a hundred pages full of irony and tenderness)
and the narrator's more laconic "resumen del caso" (précis of what
happened); and c) that there is something "esential" in the tale which
transcends national boundaries and that this element is connected
with the protagonists and their situation rather than with the
incidents which body it forth. It is perfectly possible to imagine "El
duelo" without its opening paragraph, which fulfils none of the
normal functions of an exposition, except that it indicates in passing
that "the events" took place in Buenos Aires. Unlike most of Borges'
openings, it seems quite separate from the story proper. At first sight
it constitutes simply a commentary on it, in the manner of the third
part of "El acercamiento a Almotásim", where Borges makes gentle
fun of James' practice of fiction under the guise of contrasting it with
his own. But in this case we are dealing with the ever-crucial *opening*
of the story. To see how unusual it is, one need only compare it with
any of the others in *El informe de Brodie* — notably that of
"Guayaquil", for instance — to see how different it is. This must give
us pause.

We can easily overlook, in the first place, the way this opening
functions as an authenticating device. Precisely by suggesting what
another author would have done with "the facts", as distinct from
what he is going to do with them (i.e. situate them where they actually
happened and present them without contrived dialogues or melo-
dramatic additions), the narrator implies that his is the more reliable
and accurate, more unadorned, hence more "true" account of them.

---

[11] Ion Agheana, *The Meaning of Experience in the Prose of Jorge Luis Borges* (New
York: Peter Lang, 1988), p. 203.

But the choice of James as the contrastive figure is not casual, as an "inlaid detail" later on in the tale confirms. The detractors of "abstract" painting accuse one of its practitioners of having followed "el ejemplo que nos dan las alfombras, los calidoscopios y las corbatas" (II, 408) (the example set us by carpets, kaleidoscopes and neckties). Barrenechea, in a footnote, perceives this as a possible reference to James' *The Pattern in the Carpet*.[12] If this is accepted, we can see the initial reference to James as a signal, hinting at the existence of a hidden configuration in the story. Already, then, the opening paragraph operates in two somewhat different ways.

A futher point concerns the two protagonists, Clara and Marta. It seems likely that the pattern of rivalry between them reflects a wider supposed rivalry between Anglo-Saxons and Latins. There are plenty of allusions of this sort in Borges. One need only instance that of Gentiles and Jews in Hladík's opening dream in "El milagro secreto" or in "Deutsches Requiem". The fact that Clara, who "al fin y el cabo era de linaje escocés" (II, 407) (after all came from a Scottish family), intiates the narrator into enjoyment of James, re-emphasizes her Britishness and at the same time establishes a possible link between her work and that of the American author who, later naturalized British, bestrides in a sense the Anglo-Saxon world. This seems to be the key element: the fact that the tale opens by linking Clara Glencairn and Henry James. The initial reference to her has the effect of privileging her over Marta, so that the reader is warned that it is on her and not so much on the latter that the story centres. At the same time it foreshadows both her superiority at the artistic level and the irony implicit in the rivalry which grows up between the two women.

The next section of "El duelo" consists of two symmetrical paragraphs separated by a single sentence. The first of the two paragraphs deals logically with Clara, supplying details of her personality and life, but it ends with a reference to Marta. The second presents Marta, but it ends with a reference to Clara. The careful juxtaposition of these essentially similar paragraphs preludes the rivalry to come. But already it is the irony behind the situation which is foregrounded before the rivalry as such actually develops. This is a Jamesian aspect of the techninque. Before shifting the focus from Clara to Marta the narrator inserts the notation that the latter was known primarily as the sister of the "brilliant" Nélida Sara. She exists, that is, in the first place, chiefly in relation to someone else.

---

[12] Barrenechea, "Borges y los símbolos", p. 607.

This connects with a fundamental aspect of "El duelo": the fact that, like Fierro and the Negro in "El fin" or Abenjacán and Zaid in "Abenjacán el Bojarí, muerto en su laberinto", Clara and Marta are rivals, one of whom finds her identity in the rivalry itself and has no real existence without it. In this sense, the single-sentence paragraph between the symmetrical presentations of Clara and Marta foreshadows the latter's situation at the end of the tale. More importantly, however, the sentence tells us that the rivalry between the two women is ironic because Marta has in the end no personality of her own. The point is driven home by the second reference to Nélida Sara, which is tacked on to the end of the fourth paragraph without any logical connection to the rest.

By the time we reach this second reference to Marta's sister, the deceptively simple phrase "[Clara] se entregó al ejercicio de la pintura, incitada acaso por el ejemplo de Marta Pizarro, su amiga" (II, 407) ([Clara] gave herself up to the practice of painting, perhaps urged on by the example of her friend Marta Pizarro) no longer relates to a straightforward set of facts. The story which Henry James *perhaps* would not have disdained is that of Clara, who took up painting *perhaps* because of a friend's example, or *perhaps* to be vicariously revenged on the friend's sister, who, "according to report" (i.e. perhaps), had had an affair with Clara's husband. This tissue of suppositions turns out to be the "facts" referred to in the opening paragraph. Even if we discount some of the hypothetical elements, we are left with a rivalry which is at best ambiguous, with Nélida Sara hovering behind it, and at worst ironic, given Marta's lack of personality. To complicate matters further, the surnames, Glencairn and Pizarro, are clearly not chosen at random. They suggest a rivalry which transcends that of mere individuals.

The central section of "El duelo" develops the representative rather than individual aspects of the rivalry. Marta is a figurative, representational painter. She produces scrupulously-correct portraits of bygone notables and unpretentious depictions of local nineteenth-century dwelling-houses. Both her subjects and her techniques are trivial and outdated. In literary terms, she stands for an outworn realism which Borges implicitly associates with Latin traditionalism. Clara is quite different. She produces works which are abstract in tendency but which allude to reality. While the narrator dismisses Marta's work with the reported sneer that she was influenced not by Italian Old Masters but by Italian Old Master Builders, he defends Clara's by sneering in his turn at the dogmatism of the abstract school as a whole. Clara's abstractionism, like Borges's fantasy, is anti-realist, but does not entirely lose touch with reality. In both cases the influence comes from outside the Hispanic tradition.

At this point the narrator's viewpoint alters. Thus far he has presented Clara favourably, as pursuing her art for its own sake, indifferent to sectarian criticism. Now, however, as she achieves her first public success, for reasons extrinsic to the quality of her painting, he intervenes to present both her and Marta slightly contemptuously as mere society ladies, bored with their idle and empty existences and coveting the life of the artist simply as a change from their own. Worse still, Marta is shown defending, not merely realism, but social realism, one of Borges' aversions.

The narrator's second intervention completes his first one and explains its dismissal of the two women as genuine artists. It returns to "Lo esencial" (The essential point) of the crucial first paragraph in order to distinguish between the women's activity as painters, which was trifling and productive of works which "ya nadie miraba" (II, 410) (by now no-one looked at), and the "duelo delicado" (delicate duel) which inspired that activity. It was this silent, loyal, affectionate rivalry which lifted their lives above the mere "conjunto a veces arbitrario de ritos y ceremonias" (II, 406) (sometimes arbitrary set of rituals and ceremonies) of the upper-class life-style. It was this which touched their lives with passion.

The ending, linking the tale to "Los teólogos", "El fin" and "Abenjacán el Bojarí, muerto en su laberinto", reiterates the idea that life, in itself, is mere meaningless succession. As is suggested in "Tlön, Uqbar, Orbis Tertius", men require something, "cualquier simetría con apariencia de orden" (I, 423) (some symmetry with the appearance of order) to give it an appearance of direction. The "symmetry" in this case is the quiet rivalry between the two women. When that symmetry is destroyed, when one of the rivals dies, the life of the other "ya carecía de razón" (II, 410) (now had no *raison d'être*). The picture which Marta paints of Clara, since it is her last, indicates that painting was merely the pretext for living out the rivalry. At the same time, since it follows a style which both admired, it is a reconciliation.

"El duelo" is not primarily about painting. It is about the human need to find finality in existence, to discover a means of imposing the illusion of an order on the otherwise aimless flux of experience. That is why the key sentence is "La vida exige una pasión" (II, 410) (Life demands a passion). The rivalry between Clara and Marta is not merely personal, nor simply artistic; like so much that happens in Borges' better stories, it is seen in an existential context. What we cannot overlook is the fact that Clara finds her existential direction in an activity where she will always remain a mediocrity and in competition with a rival who is not only more mediocre still, but who serves perhaps to conceal the identity of the real rival. In the same way, Marta, who originally only shone in the reflected light of her sister, ends by doing her best work still in relation to someone else, as she produces a portrait of Clara.

"El duelo" is a bitter story despite the softening touches in the final paragraph. It contains gently sarcastic comments on the conventionalities and dilettantism of upper-class life, on the official face of art, on conflicting interpretations of the meaning of art and on the pedantry, provincialism and marginality of the art world in Latin America. But in the end this is secondary. What matters is the way all of this provides a backdrop for the two women's need to convert their mutual attachment to the same hobby into the central fact of their existence. A Marxist critic of the more naïve sort might read the story as a comment on the degradation of art by bourgeois society. But Borges, like James, thinks in terms of the individual and his or her commitment to modes of behaviour which are at once pathetic and ironic. The opening paragraph, as we return to it after reflecting on the rest of the story, no longer seems quite so separate as it did initially.

One of the most unusually structured of Borges' stories is "There Are More Things" (II, 485-91). In effect, the tale is all beginning. It is one long sequence of lead-in followed by the final effect. Commonly, when a story contains a hidden element, this is suggested at the beginning in order to arouse the reader's curiosity and then clarified at a crucial point in the later sequence of events. This point may be at the end, as in "La muerte y la brújula" and most other detective stories, or earlier, as in "El inmortal" when we discover that Argos is Homer, or as in Gabriel García Márquez's "La siesta del martes" when the mourning worn by the mother and daughter is revealed to be connected with the death of an unusual kind of thief. Borges adopts neither of these techniques in this case, but instead makes the preservation of the hidden element into the trick ending. The whole point of "There Are More Things" is that we are not told what it was that the narrator saw when he overcame his terror and did not close his eyes in the final line. The story involves the elaborate creation in the reader of a sense of mystery and horror which is then deliberately left unexplained.

The key word is *"anfisbena"* (II, 490) (amphisbaena), which probably suggested the story. It means a double-ended reptile which can move equally well in either direction, forward or backward. The story seems to be about the threatening presence of some hideous creature, perhaps from outer space, which finds itself trapped on this planet, hiding in a country house near Buenos Aires. Unlike Asterion, who seems to symbolize the evil lurking in man, the terrifying reptile in this case seems rather to symbolize something evil about life, the possibility of the incursion of horror into our everyday existence. In other words, it corresponds to the idea of the labyrinth as a symbol which questions our comfortable assumptions about life's benevolent comprehensibility, but with the additional horror of being alive. A hint about the deeper significance implicit in the presence of such a creature in our world is contained in the reference near the beginning to "esas cosas incompatibles que sólo por razón de coexistir llevan el nombre de universo" (II, 486) (those incompatible things which for the simple reason that they coexist bear the name of the universe). The sentence implies a vision of a cosmos which is the opposite of an ordered, harmonious world created according to divine design. This is the vision vouchsafed to Tzinacán at the end of "La escritura del Dios" and to the narrator of "El Aleph". The horror of that vision, which caused Tzinacán to choose to remain in his dungeon, and the narrator of "El Aleph" to be grateful for being able to forget, is what underlies the evocation of the amphisbaena here. If "There are More Things" is not as successful as the two earlier stories, it is probably because an encounter with a monster is not the same as an abstract vision of the possibly dreadful nature of the human condition. It is a living creature, like Asterion or Melville's Moby Dick, but it does not think or act significantly. It simply *is*, and that is not enough. Hence the interest of "There Are More Things" lies less in the possible meaning (i.e. the question of whether this tale contains another illustration of Borges' well-known assertion that we do not understand reality and that therefore "toda estrafalaria cosa es posible" [I, 179] [any kind of weirdness is possible]) than in the way Borges succeeds in building the story up to its spine-chilling conclusion.

The first noteworthy feature is the curious order of priorities in the opening sentence. The death of the narrator's uncle is the necessary starting-point of the story, since it leaves the mansion he lived in available for sale to Preetorius, who installs the monster in it. It is associated with the first foreshadowing device, the reference to the "hermosas perplejidades" (beautiful complexities) of philosophy. This in turn explains the reference in the title to Hamlet's famous remark to Horatio. The tale will present to the young philosophy student a perplexing experience which no philosophy can explain and which is the opposite of beautiful. But before we make this connection Borges introduces an apparent irrelevance in the second and third sentences: the narrator's realization that the practice of goodness alone can reconcile us to the deaths of others and to our own mortality. In a story which ends with a fantastic vision of evil and danger it is not without significance that the first reflection has to do with goodness in the face of the greatest evil and danger of all: death.

Arnett, the narrator's uncle, is a free-thinking engineer, interested alike in speculative philosophy, theology and fantastic fiction. He and his rigidly ultra-Protestant friend, Muir, function as symbolic representatives of alternative approaches to ultimate why-questions. What is interesting about them is that, though the one is agnostic and the other narrowly Calvinistic, they exist in the tale not as rivals or enemies but almost symbiotically, in friendly collaboration, each needing the other. Their role is to create the abstract context for the story, to act as markers. Philosophy may cast doubt on the reality or the internal coherence of the God-given order postulated by theology, as the references to Berkeley and to "las paradojas eleáticas" (the Eleatic paradoxes) are there to imply (II, 485), but such philosophy itself contains a paradox. It tends to undermine our confidence in our ability to make valid judgements and inter-pretations, but it does so by making use of the very same rational thought-processes whose validity it questions. Theology reassures, but only by an appeal to the supra-rational. In bringing before us Arnett and Muir, Borges balances disquiet and reassurance. But the next clue, the reference to the existence within the universe of incompatible entities (II, 486), breaks the balance and opens the way for the horror of the ending. Horror has no place in philosophy, and in theology is in the end confined to Hell. Arnett and Muir are introduced at the beginning of the tale in order to suggest the inadequacy of their modes of interpreting the universe when it comes to incorporating what is to follow into any scheme of things.

We notice an interesting order of priorities. So far, in contrast to other Borges stories, the introduction makes no attempt to establish tension or arouse curiosity. What it primarily privileges is prefigu-

ration of theme. Only later is the element of suspense introduced
through a series of surprising events: Preetorius buys Arnett's
mansion for twice the normal price; he throws away its contents
regardless of their value; secretly and by night, he has mysterious
alterations made to the house's structure; he installs a new inhabitant;
Arnett's dog is beheaded and mutilated; trees are chopped down;
finally Preetorius leaves the country. There are two distinct elements
of mystery here. One is the indignant refusal by Muir to make the
alterations to the house which Preetorius wanted and the refusal of
the local carpenters to make the furnishings. The other is the
implication that the new inhabitant is responsible for the death and
mutilation of the dog and the destruction of the trees. These motivate
the narrator to begin his "atroz aventura" (II, 487) (atrocious
adventure).

   The adjective "atroz", like "vertiginoso" (dizzying), is a recurrent
word in Borges' vocabulary, almost a call-sign. It alerts us to the fact
that, like those of Lönnrot in "La muerte y la brújula" and Dewey in
"El hombre en el umbral", the narrator's investigation is into a
mysterious aspect of the way things are rather than into a merely
curious set of circumstances. This is immediately confirmed during
his interview with Muir by the latter's strange reference to his refusal
to build either a Roman Catholic place of worship or a dwelling for
the monster. The whole point of the interview with Muir is that the
Scot promises information but, in fact, gives none of any significance, since he does not explain what the "cosa monstruosa" (II,
487) (monstrous thing) which Preetorius wanted built was. All we
perceive is that he regarded it as on a par with a Roman Catholic
chapel: to him, as a rabid Calvinist, an abode of evil. The interview
enriches the mysterious associations surrounding the mansion. It
heightens our curiosity, but not our understanding. The narrator's
subsequent meeting with Iberra (a local tearaway, presumably
belonging to the family mentioned in "La intrusa" and "Milonga de
dos hermanos") is the first of two interludes connected with the
inhabitant of the mansion. He presents physical courage quailing
before the mysterous amphisbaena. But about it he is allowed to be
no more forthcoming than Muir. He does not elaborate on the
"something" which he had come across at probable risk to his life.
Borges is here using the strategy of suppression of essential
information, what Rosalba Campra calls "la falta de enteras
secuencias no sólo útiles sino indispensables para el progreso — y
sobre todo para el sentido — de la acción" (the absence of whole

sequences which are not only useful but indispensable for the progression — and above all for the meaning — of the action).[13] This is a standard feature of fantastic fiction. In this case, evil and danger are suggested but not made explicit. The second interlude, the narrator's premonitory dream, reinforces the first. So far the mysterious presence in the mansion has only been referred to as its "nuevo habitante" (II, 486) (new inhabitant), or by Iberra (II, 488) as "algo" (something) and as "Lo que vi" (What I saw). The narrator himself will follow suit, writing of "lo que verían luego mis ojos" (II, 490) (what my eyes then would behold). But his dream of the Minotaur — "el monstruo de un monstruo" (II, 408) (the monster of a monster) — in its labyrinth prefigures the reptile of "monstruosa anatomía" (II, 490) (monstrous anatomy), the amphisbaena, which we are similarly intended to associate with evil and to imagine returning to its lair as the tale concludes.

It is already clear by this point that what we are reading is a greatly prolonged exposition, a protracted sequence of preliminaries designed to build up mystery and suspense through the systematic suppression of information, first by Muir, then by Iberra and later by Mariani, the carpenter. Each tells just enough to screw up our interest an extra notch. Meanwhile the pseudo-dénouement, which itself will not assuage our curiosity, is being teasingly postponed. Mariani completes the impression already created by Muir and Iberra by implying, while not actually stating, that the furniture which he made for the mansion's occupant was weird, and by actually asserting that Preetorius was insane and that the mansion and its environs are now somehow terrifying. With this, all the opening components seem to be at last in place. But Borges now adds a further significant paragraph, harking back to the title, before finally embarking on the climactic episode. As we have suggested, the narrator is presented as a philosophy student precisely in order to emphasize that the experience which he will undergo will be utterly inexplicable in terms of human reasoning. The last paragraph of the exposition ironically alludes to his repeated reflection that there is no other enigma except that of time, and to his readings of Schopenhauer and Royce. He is, of course, mistaken, as events are about to prove. There is another enigma: that of terrifying evil, which in the systems of Schopenhauer and Royce has no place.

---

[13] Rosalba Campra, "Fantástico y sintaxis narrativa", *Río de la Plata*, 1 (1985), p. 98.

Borges' problem at the end of "There Are More Things" is to convey impressions about the nature of the mansion's hideous occupant without describing it, much less explaining it. The narrator, as he enters the mansion (II, 490), is like Lönnrot entering Triste-le-Roy or Rufo climbing up into the City of the Immortals. Each steps into another dimension of reality, whose nightmarishness is expressed in visual terms. Of the two, the narrator is closer to Rufo. He is vaguely aware of "formas insensatas" (insensate forms) and "cosas incomprensibles" (incomprehensible things) which make him feel himself to be "un intruso en el caos" (an intruder into chaos). In "El inmortal" we learn what the horror and chaos symbolize: the effect of immortality inside time, which would erase all values and meaningfulness. Here we are given the symbol but not the explanation. Campra has suggested that the most symbolically significant Borgesian ending is what might be called the double-take, "en las cuales el desequilibrio parece resolverse mediante una explicación que coloca todo en el paradigma de la realidad conocida, hasta que una inesperada secuencia final pone todo en discusión otra vez" (in which the unbalance seems to resolve itself by means of an explanation which places everything back in the paradigm of known reality, until an unexpected sequence at the end throws everything into question once more).[14] The typical example is "Tlön, Uqbar, Orbis Tertius". In other cases, such as "El jardín de senderos que se bifurcan", the ending is produced by the closing of the frame around the core element of the tale. In each case there is a meaningful interaction between the ending and the earlier part of the story. It is difficult to perceive this in "There Are More Things". The clues which Borges offers at the end (the U-shaped "bed", the V-shaped mirror, the creature's inability to function in our world — it cannot open or close doors —, its "plural" nature) do not seem to add up to a pattern which would either make final sense of the elements incorporated into the long lead-up or precipitate us into unexpected ambiguity.

The story leaves us with a shudder. It is an excellent example, for the most part, of Borges' craftsmanship. But we wonder whether, like Lovecraft, Borges was for once content simply to create a sensation. Lovecraft, like Borges, tended away from a vision of a benevolent universe. But he seems to have been satisfied to evoke fear and horror without necessarily thereby making a comment on the human condition. Borges, on the other hand, usually sees the horror of life in

---

[14] Campra, p. 103.

terms of meaninglessness. Occasionally, as in "Deutsches Requiem" and "La casa de Asterión", he seems to go a step further and postulate a deep dimension of moral evil in man. In "There Are More Things" we seem to catch the implication that the cosmos, which is so mysterious and unknown, may itself include mysterious and threatening forms of evil independent of man. The narrative strategy, a long, slow build-up followed by a fearsome conclusion, seems to be a metaphor of man's fateful will to know — Borges qualifies the narrator's investigation with the adverb "Fatalmente" (II, 487) (Fatally) and the adjective "inevitable" (II, 488) — resulting in a vision of horror. But the symbol which expresses it remains hidden from the reader and is inactive. It is less effective than the City of the Immortals or what "Borges" sees through the Aleph, nor do we see its effect on the narrator as we do that of his vision on Tzinacán in "La escritura del dios". From our point of view, therefore, the interest of this story lies in the contrast between the technique it employs and those we recognize in more successful ones.

The opening strategy of "Tigres azules" (*VA*, 27-42), in which the narrator finds some terrifying stone discs, compares interestingly with that of "El Zahir", which is also about the unexpected finding of something extraordinary. In the earlier story, as we shall see in Chapter 4, Borges introduces the figure of Teodelina partly to distract the reader's attention from the direction the story will eventually take and partly as a parodic prefiguration of the narrator himself. In "Tigres azules" we see in retrospect that distraction is the prevailing element. That is to say, instead of following his habitual practice of using the realistic to lead us gradually into the fantastic, Borges uses a fantastic ploy, that of the existence in India of a blue tiger, to lead us towards an even more fantastic idea, that of the magical blue stone discs. If any proof were needed of the survival of his creative orginality into the very last phase of his writing, it is the ability which he reveals here to give a new twist to his opening strategies. The first paragraph of "Tigres azules" uses the word "tigre" (tiger) seven times, in much the same way that the fourth paragraph of "El Zahir" accumulates references to coins — "monedas", "óbolo", "dracmas", "denario", "piezas de plata", "onzas de oro", "florín" and "luis" (coins, mite, drachmas, denier, silver pieces, ounces of gold, florin, louis) — in order to saturate the text with the same signal. In both cases we absorb the repetition without as yet being aware of its significance. Only later is the symbolic secondary meaning added on.

When we reflect on this opening paragraph we notice two features which gather significance as we read on. The first is the association of the tiger with evil in the very first sentence, only slightly attenuated in the second, where its elegance is still "terrible". When we look back to this from the other end of the tale we can see how the references to Blake and Chesterton portend the atmosphere of the episodes to follow. They are imbued with evil and terror. The second feature is the shift in the third sentence from the tiger as a universal human obsession to the tiger as a haunting presence in the mind of the narrator. Now, the narrator in "El Zahir" is simply a persona of Borges, an example of what Lyon calls his "(Somewhat) Personal Narrator". But the narrator here is quite different. He is a professor of Western and Oriental logic and an admirer of Spinoza. We know from earlier references, notably the one in the opening of "El indigno", what the mention of Spinoza signifies. Spinoza and Leibnitz interested Borges because both philosophers believed in an ultimately harmonious world. For that reason his references to them are always implicitly ironic. Spinoza in particular believed in an ethical world which could be ordered by the mind on rational lines. This is what makes the allusion to him in the opening of "Tigres azules" so important. He is the opposite of the tiger. He stands for a world in which archetypes of evil can be argued away. The tiger's function at the beginning, we soon realize, is to introduce the notion of evil and thus to prefigure the blue stone discs which strike Craigie, the logician, with horror, because of the way they symbolize an unthinkable metaphysical evil, an "obscene miracle". They destroy any possibility of a harmonious conception of the world and, like the City of the Immortals in "El immortal", contaminate with horror the vision we have of the way things are. The function of the references to Spinoza and to logic, on the other hand, is to introduce the opposite notion, that of an orderly, predictable, rational universe. What makes Alexander Craigie the perfect narrator for the experiences which he is to undergo in this story is precisely the fact that he stands between Spinoza and the tiger and is fascinated by both. Characteristically, when he first begins to realize what the multiplication of the discs could mean, he immediately seeks to reassure himself by repeating aloud Spinoza's eight definitions and seven axioms, as if in some way they could defend him from his hideous perception.

Craigie is, of course, a Scot, and like David Brodie in "El informe de Brodie" an Aberdonian to boot. Borges seems to make use of Scottish characters (Alexander Muir in "There Are More Things" is another clinching example) because of the stereotype, created by Stevenson and Barrie among others, which allows him to present them as dour, stern-spirited men whose Calvinistic background and literal-mindedness give them a privileged position as observers of the unusual. Craigie is highly intelligent and his philosophical training renders him able to perceive immediately the frightfulness of what the stone discs represent. A man with a more whimsical, sceptical or frivolous cast of mind might have been able to shrug the realization off or, like the narrator in "El Aleph", rely on the mind's happy ability to forget the impact of disturbing insight. But Craigie's Scottish seriousness and inflexibility, the very qualities which drew him to Spinoza's rather dehumanized system of ethics, make him unable to accommodate himself to what he has stumbled upon.

Once more then, at the end of his creative career, Borges presents us with another of his superbly functional, succinct beginnings. But this does not exhaust his opening strategy, which continues for several pages. It is, in fact, only in the third paragraph that we reach the real ploy, the reference to the possibility of a blue tiger, the search for which leads Craigie to the discovery of the hateful stones. The first two paragraphs, that is, are really devoted to thematic prefiguration and the presentation of a narrator who is exactly suited to Borges' special requirements in this case. But although Craigie is more characterized than, say, the rather featureless narrator of "There Are More Things" or the juvenile story-teller of "La noche de los dones", he has nothing like the allure of the Babylonian in "La lotería en Babilonia" or Asterion. What arouses our curiosity and desire to read on is not the eccentric attraction of this expatriate Scot to tigers and Spinoza, but the reference to a hitherto unknown species of the former perhaps living in the Ganges delta. It is this intriguing possibility that the first two paragraphs, which we did not pause to examine closely on first reading, seem to have led up to. Now the story suddenly takes on the attractiveness of all such tales of search for the exotic (the Yeti, the Loch Ness Monster, or whatever) and our attention responds instantly. But though our realization of it is postponed, Borges is subjecting us to a deliberate fraud. There never was a blue tiger, in the literal sense of the words. We are being led towards a quite different discovery. Nonetheless, the words which give the story its title are not a random choice. We have seen how from the very first the tiger is connected with the ideas of evil and terror. But a blue tiger? In real life it would be a freak, a *lusus naturae* and something hitherto unknown as well. It cannot escape our notice that the real "blue tigers", the hideous discs, are hitherto unknown, evil and terrifying. That is, the idea of a search for a blue tiger is not just a device to arouse our interest in the tale; it also functions as a lead-in to the final discovery. The characteristics of the creature are deftly transferred to the objects Craigie finds.

When, in the third paragraph, he sets out for "cierta aldea muy distante del Ganges" (a certain village far away from the Ganges), the scene appears to be set for a quest story of the type we are familiar with from "El acercamiento a Almotásim" or "El inmortal". In fact, however, Craigie arrives without incident or delay. Nor is the reason far to seek. For the unnamed village and its environs represent anywhere. "India," writes Barrenechea, "with its dual associations of the vast and the chaotic, serves [Borges] as a metaphor of the universe."[15] Not for nothing, she points out, did he write in *Discusión* of "el asiático desorden del mundo" (the Asiatic disorder of the world). But the quest idea is not irrelevant. In a remark quoted by Dauster Borges asserts: "... en los libros antiguos, las buscas eran siempre afortunadas; los argonautas conquistaron el Vellocino y Galahad el Santo Grial. Ahora, en cambio, agrada misteriosamente el concepto de una busca infinita o de la busca de una cosa que, hallada, tiene consecuencias funestas" (in the ancient books, quests always had happy endings; the Argonauts won the Golden Fleece and Galahad the Holy Grail. Now, on the other hand, people find mysterious pleasure in the concept of an infinite quest or the quest for something which, when found, has evil consequences).[16] There is, in fact, as Borges must have known, nothing particularly mysterious about the modern taste for quests which either never end or, as in the present case of "Tigres azules", end in disaster. In literature (beginning with folk-tales, in which quests are an important feature) the object of the quest is usually something that will restore harmony and happiness to an individual or a group. The underlying metaphor is that of recovering meaning and order after they have been threatened or disturbed. This is not a metaphor which commends itself to the world of today, where successful quests have been relegated to popular stories of astronauts and secret agents. When the central figure is a professor of logic, a professional scrutineer of meaning, the quest is bound to fail.

[15] Ana María Barrrenechea, *Borges the Labyrinth Maker* (New York: New York Univ. Press, 1965), p. 29.

[16] Frank Dauster, "Notes on Borges' Labyrinths", *Hispanic Review*, 30 (1962), p. 145.

Craigie is pursuing a chimera; but the end of his pursuit is not simply failure. He does not make the discovery he dreamed of, but a discovery does await him, portended by the reference to the villagers as "poseedores de un secreto que no compartirían con un extraño" (*VA*, 30) (in possession of a secret which they would not share with a stranger). The rest of the first part of "Tigres azules" is devoted to postponing the revelation of the secret which the villagers seek to prevent Craigie from learning. Their hostility completes the metaphor which the story's opening pages have been elaborating. If India symbolizes the mysterious universe, Craigie symbolizes man searching for forbidden knowledge. So long as he confines himself to logic-chopping with his students in Lahore he is harmless and safe. But we know from the example of Lönnrot in "La muerte y la brújula" that the "pure reasoner" is poorly equipped to venture outside the realm of abstract reason, as Craigie is now doing almost as unwisely. For Borges, to come into possession of a secret is to go beyond what mere reason can elucidate, but the effects are nearly always negative. For the discovery of a secret — whether we think of Lönnrot solving Scharlach's cryptic message, Tzinacán reading at last the god's script, a persona of Borges peeping through the Aleph, Paracelsus coming into possession of the magic word or, in this case, Craigie finding the stone discs — is equivalent to acquiring unhappy insight. Death, the will to forget, a sense of resigned futility or the urge to be rid of the tainted treasure — Zahir or magic stone — which is the source of the awareness: these are what the insight brings with it.

Thus the first section of "Tigres azules" in part portends the discovery Craigie eventually makes, but also in part stands in ironic contrast to the rest of the tale. If the original quest for the blue tiger had been crowned with success, it would simply have implied that the processes of nature are more mysterious and astonishing than we think. It would expose our ignorance and thereby shake our confidence, for a time, in the completeness of our catalogue of the denizens of our planet. It would produce a modification of existing assumptions, but it would not seriously call into question our way of looking at the universe. This is what now happens. Borges, in the opening part of "Tigres azules", has led us to expect, at most, a zoological freak (though perhaps more probably a wild-goose chase), but then he presents us unexpectedly with an experience which appears to destroy the very foundations on which we erect our construct of reality. We are faced with a "milagro atroz que socavaba la ciencia de los hombres" (*VA*, 39) (an atrocious miracle which undermined science as men know it). By apparently contradicting in the most radical and disturbing way the argument from design, which sees God as the great Artificer of an orderly universe, it opens the way to a concept of an utterly irrational universe, the creation of a mad demiurge, rather than a beneficent Supreme Being. This is why the village elder, Bhagwan Dass, refuses to touch the stones, preferring death to contact with them. He represents the time-honoured traditional belief that there are mysteries which it is better for man not to meddle with.

In a sense the opening ploy of "Tigres azules" is protracted until after the discovery of the stones themselves. Its function seems to be complete when Craigie recognizes that his find has completely driven his earlier obsession with tigers from his thoughts: "El tigre azul me pareció no menos inocuo que el cisne negro del romano, que se descubrió después en Australia" (*VA*, 36) (The blue tiger seemed to me no less innocuous than the ancient Roman's black swan, which was later discovered in Australia). However, closer examination of the tale's structure reveals that this is not so. Borges goes out of his way to emphasize the shift which takes place at this point:

> Releo mis notas anteriores y compruebo que he cometido un error capital. Desviado por el hábito de esa buena o mala literatura que malamente se llama psicológica, he querido recuperar, no sé por qué, la sucesiva crónica de mi hallazgo. Más me hubiera valido insistir en la monstruosa índole de los discos. (*VA*, 36-37)

> (I reread my earlier notes and recognize that I have committed a grave error. Carried away by the habit of reading that good or bad literature which is improperly called psychological, I have tried to retain — I don't know why — successiveness in the chronicle of my find. It would have been better for me to emphasize the monstrous nature of the discs.)

This paragraph is plainly inserted to act as a signpost in the story, separating the description of the circumstances leading up to the finding of the stones from the development of their frightful meaning. But this separation is more apparent than real; for the very "psychological" element which Craigie affects to regard as having side-tracked him in the first part of his account, quickly reappears in the second part. Indeed, when we look back yet again to the beginning of the story, we see this clearly announced.

What binds together the two parts of the tale are Craigie's dreams. Hence the prefiguring sentences at the end of the first paragraph: "El curso de mi vida ha sido común, en los sueños siempre vi tigres.

(Ahora los pueblan otras formas)" (The course of my life has been ordinary, in dreams I always saw tigers. [Now they are peopled by other forms]). In the second part of the tale we learn what the "other forms" are: they are the stone discs. These recurring dreams — three of the blue tiger, then the one introduced by the sentence "En aquel tiempo contraje el hábito de soñar con las piedras" (*VA*, 37) (At that time I acquired the habit of dreaming of the stones) — not only create a link between the two main sections of the story but also contribute in other ways. The three dreams of the tiger help to stress Craigie's obsession with the animal and hence add verisimilitude to his quest. At the same time they pave the way to the climactic dream which is an important part of the story's symbolic commentary. How is Craigie to convey the full horror of his discovery? In the main he does so by repeatedly making the point that the discs contradict the most simple mathematical assumptions along with the notions of logic and predictability which we derive from them. It is on these last that we found our confidence in an orderly universe, just as we also need for the same purpose the kindred notions of cause and effect, chronological temporal succession and acceptance of the unity of our individual personalities. In other stories Borges had insinuated doubts about these last three supports of our existential confidence. Here he is following suite. But in doing so he is aware that more than just the conscious mind is involved with these doubts. Behind the perplexity lies fear: fear that our ideas of truth, duty and finality are no more than illusions.

Craigie's last symbolic dream or vision of a system of cellars, in which, as in the Spanish poet Antonio Machado's "galerías del alma" (tunnels of the soul), dreadful monsters lurk, expresses the fear that the world may be not merely a prison, as so many Romantic works suggested, but something far worse: a madhouse, presided over by an irrational deity.[17] We cannot overlook the fact that his dream involves the reverse of the process which occurs at the beginning of "El acercamiento a Almotásim". There a spiral metal staircase symbolically led the student upwards from free-thinking, via prayer, to a quasi-mystical experience. But it lacked connecting flights. Here the staircase leads downwards from the world order implied by Spinoza's ethical harmoniousness to a world-view in which "el caos era inextricable" (*VA*, 41) (chaos was inextricable). And the connecting flights are all there. Craigie's nightmare is

---

[17] See poems LXX and LXIII in Antonio Machado, *Obras: poesía y prosa* (Buenos Aires: Losada, 1964), pp. 109, 105.

intended to complement the other descriptions of the hideous nature of the discs into which it is inserted.

So far, then, we have tried to show that the first part of "Tigres azules" is designed both to deceive us about the real thrust of the story and in a subtle way to prefigure it. The discovery is not what Craigie set out to find. Yet ironically it fulfils his quest for something elegant and terrible. The pattern of the story, however, is not yet completed. The description of the development of his realization — at the conscious and subconscious (dream) levels — of the frightful meaning of his find is not in itself a satisfactory climax. The options are madness, death or some form of forgetting on the part of Craigie. Borges, in effect, selects the last, causing Craigie to pray for release to the possibly insane deity who is the creator of the discs. In response the "Ser inconcebible" (*VA*, 41) (inconceivable Being) allows him to rid himself of the evidence, the discs themselves, and thus symbolically to return to the realm of "cordura" (*VA*, 42) (good sense). Craigie is now archetypal man, unable to withstand the sight of the human condition as it actually is. The blind beggar represents Borges taking back the insight his story has offered. But he leaves the warning that rejection of it is "frightful" in the sense, presumably, that it involves a deliberate decision to embrace illusion. For the reader the difficulty of the ending of "Tigres azules" is not that Craigie should be willing to pray to a God who had visited on him the horror of the stone discs, for this can be viewed simply as human weakness. The problem is that Borges, who mocks the idea of a benevolent God in charge of the universe in "La lotería en Babilonia" and elsewhere, seems here to be presenting God as a mysterious being not subject to the laws of this earth rather than as non-existent or maleficent. The "inconceivable Being" who answers Craigie's prayer does not seem to correspond to the creator of the evil discs, unless indeed we are really prepared to see Craigie's final situation without the discs and the insight which goes with them as more "frightful" than it was when he had them.

But for our present purpose what is important is not so much this final paradox as Craigie's basic response to the situation in which he finds himself. He was, as we saw, originally situated between the comforting world of Spinoza's axioms and definitions and the world of the tiger, which is now revealed to be a world without pattern, order or predictability. Having contemplated the latter, he now takes refuge anew in the former. The end of "Tigres azules" harks back to the beginning.

CHAPTER 4

FRAMING DEVICES

The use of framing devices, such as we saw in "La casa de Asterión", is a favourite Borgesian technique. Within his general narrative strategy, these devices form a special group among the various kinds of openings used in the different stories. As a group they are distinguished by their particular functionality in relation to the theme or themes which are to follow. They are differentiated from foreshadowing devices by the fact that the latter are designed to announce the theme, or one of the themes, which is present in the rest of the tale and are, therefore, genuinely part of the opening. Framing devices, by contrast, surround a central core in the tale. In other words, a foreshadowing device normally points forward to a climax at the end of a story, while a framing device encloses the kernel of the tale. As well as providing the opening section, it also provides, or is an important part of, the ending. Borges is a master of the opening gambit; but not all his opening gambits are parts of framing devices. Let us examine some of these.

There is a good example in the spy story "El jardín de senderos que se bifurcan" (I, 463-73). Borges himself mentioned to Charbonnier that the story contains two separate elements: the idea of the world as a labyrinth and the idea of a man killing someone else as a signal to a third party.[1] These are, quite obviously, very different ideas. One is an abstract, quasi-metaphysical notion; the other, as Borges points out, could be an idea for a detective story. Part of the technical

---

[1] Georges Charbonnier, *Entretiens avec Jorge Luis Borges* (Paris: Gallimard, 1967) pp. 131-32.

interest of "El jardín ..." derives from the way Borges contrives to combine the two. There is no question here of foreshadowing. The story of Yu Tsun, the spy with secret military information to be passed to his German masters, Madden, the counter-espionage agent, and the British offensive in Flanders in 1916 in no way portends the meeting and discussion of Yu Tsun and Albert; it simply encloses the latter. What, then, are its functions? The clearest one is plainly that of adding a note of dramatic suspense to the story. The conversation between Yu Tsun and Albert is intellectually interesting but static until Yu Tsun shoots his interlocutor. It is nothing like as memorable as the vision provided by the Aleph in the story of that name, where in consequence Borges needs to introduce only a minor note of suspense. Here in "El jardín ...", the frame of the story is designed primarily to arouse and sustain our curiosity-interest. At the same time it justifies Yu Tsun's visit to Stephen Albert and the murder.

A third function of the frame is indicated by the phrase in the second paragraph: "... mi plan estaba maduro" (my plan was ready). To the habitual reader of Borges it connects with the similar phrase used years later in "Emma Zunz": "... ya estaba perfecto su plan" (II, 47) (by now her plan was perfect). Both Yu Tsun and Emma attempt to impose a pattern of their own on reality. In both cases reality fights back, turning their plan against them in an utterly unpredictable and ironic way. Plans in Borges tend to go wrong: "Las ruinas circulares", "El fin", "El Sur", "El muerto", "Abenjacán el Bojarí, muerto en su laberinto" and other stories readers can think of, as well as the two in question here, are all in different ways illustrations of this. Reality mocks our attempts to encompass it, to shape it to our own ends. Yu Tsun's plan to alert the Germans to the jumping-off point for the Allied offensive in 1916 by killing a man called Albert, the name of the Belgian town, apparently succeeds (though historically it appears that the location was an open secret anyway). But, as his "contrition" at the end indicates, in a deeper sense its success is offset by the tragic irony that he is forced to kill, not just someone (anyone) who fortuitously happens to have the same name as the town, but the one man of all men who had solved the mystery of his ancestor's book/labyrinth. The frame story and the core are not just juxtaposed: they interact ironically. Indeed, the irony is double, because by murdering him, Yu Tsun involves Albert, the code-cracker, in a new coded message.

The first part of the frame ends as Yu Tsun leaves the station at

Ashgrove. But we do not really reach the core section until he arrives at Albert's house. In between there is a lengthy paragraph which merits separate analysis because of the way it provides a critically important series of links between the two. Most obviously, it is designed to announce the idea of the labyrinth as Yu Tsun reflects on the directions he has received to turn left at each crossroads. We notice that what he thinks of at this point is a static spatial labyrinth, like the Library of Babel. But this recalls to his mind the novel written by his great-grandfather Ts'ui Pên, since it is associated with the latter's intention to construct a labyrinth as well. In turn this suggests to Yu Tsun a labyrinth which combines both space and time: "Pensé en un laberinto de laberintos, en un sinuoso laberinto creciente que abarcara el pasado y el porvenir y que implicara de algún modo los astros" (I, 467) (I thought of a labyrinth of labyrinths, of a winding, growing labyrinth which would include the past and the future and which would in some way implicate the stars). This imaginary labyrinth prepares us for that of Ts'ui Pên, the description of which is the crux of the entire story. Yu Tsun's conception here in the linking paragraph is similar to Ts'ui Pên's in its infinite extensiveness and expansiveness, but the essential element is still missing. For so far it seems to suggest only one past and one future, whereas Ts'ui Pên's labyrinth implies innumerable pasts and uncountable futures, all interconnected. Yu Tsun's infinite, but at first sight simpler, labyrinth is a metaphor of time and space still as we normally think of them. Ts'ui Pên's is quite different. Borges leads us towards it gradually, the first step being the simple notion of a maze of country lanes in which, in order to find one's objective, one must always turn to the left.

While this is the paragraph's most important contribution to the overall strategy of "El jardín ...", it is far from being the only one. In an apparently throw-away line, Borges mentions that Ts'ui Pên was murdered by a foreigner. We cannot ignore the fact that this is precisely what will happen to Albert when we return to the final segment of the frame story of espionage at the end. Albert, who has deciphered Ts'ui Pên's novel-cum-labyrinth is in some way identified by that act with Ts'ui Pên himself. His destiny will be a repetition of Ts'ui Pên's, in itself illustrating time's mysterious workings. But the murder of Ts'ui Pên and his own are alluded to by Albert in the core segment with his reference to Fang and his unknown visitor. It is not clear whether this constitutes an actual reference to Ts'ui Pên's novel or is merely an illustrative example of how its technique works, invented by Albert himself. No matter; it clearly connects Ts'ui Pên's death with Albert's. It is tempting to believe that Borges is hinting that Ts'ui Pên's novel forecast both its author's death and that of the eventual discoverer of its secret.

Thirdly, we must notice the equally casual reference in this crucial paragraph to the *Hung Lu Meng*. It is a classic example of an inlaid detail for those with the patience to follow it up. The famous Chinese novel, published in 1791, contains a character whose name is Yu Tsun! This extremely recondite detail may be there simply to underline the fictionality of everything we are reading. But equally, like the appearance of Rocamadour from Julio Cortázar's *Rayuela* in García Márquez's *Cien años de soledad*, it may carry the more disturbing implication of the fictionality of everything and everybody, including ourselves.

An aspect of Borges' technique, that is, is to create a realist-type frame story with direct reference to an actual historical event, the offensive of 1916; inside this he encapsulates a piece of pure fantasy — a chance meeting between the descendant of Ts'ui Pên and the only discoverer of Ts'ui Pên's secret, barbed by the fact that the former must kill the latter. Then, by making Yu Tsun a character from a novel, he collapses the realist frame into the same category as the fantastic core.

Finally, we recognize a familiar Borgesian touch in the description of the countryside through which Yu Tsun passes as he approaches Albert's house. The references to "El vago y vivo campo" (The vague and living countryside) and to "La tarde [...] íntima, infinita" (The intimate, infinite afternoon) recall the vast but "intimate" country-side and afternoon through which Dahlmann passes on his way to the ranch in "El Sur". There, once more, nature is "viva y silenciosa" (I, 533) (alive and silent). The same yellow, circular moon which looked down on Lönnrot as he approached Triste-le-Roy looks down on Yu Tsun. When violence is imminent, the countryside in Borges sometimes becomes charged with a magical atmosphere which is an integral part of the *mise en scène*. Few paragraphs in his fictional work exemplify so well the care with which he assembles elements which refer backwards and forwards, deepening the meaning and anticipating what is to come, as this linking paragraph between the frame and the core segment of "El jardín ...". There is, of course, no comparable one between the core and the second part of the frame, and the slow, carefully-graduated beginning of the story contrasts with the dramatic shift back to the frame at the end.

Borges appeals to quite a different kind of interest in the body of the tale, which incorporates one of his characteristic "What if?" questions: what if, instead of the single, ongoing line of time-progression we habitually envisage, there is a plurality of time-scales existing simultaneously, "infinitas series de tiempos, en una red creciente y vertiginosa de tiempos divergentes, convergentes y paralelos" (I, 472) (infinite series of times, in a growing and dizzying web of divergent, convergent and parallel times)? The notion is not a difficult one to understand. It stems from the recognition, which we all have, that each choice of action which we make involves the rejection of a whole series of other actions which we could have chosen, along with their ever more complex effects fanning out around them. When we act, we eliminate all these alternative possibilities. But suppose it were not so. Suppose that in parallel or otherwise-orientated time-dimensions we decided on other actions, each one different and each one producing its chain of effects. Suppose the present were merely an intersection of these various time-dimensions, all coexisting with one another.

In order to express this concept concretely Borges uses the apparently chaotic and labyrinthine novel of Ts'ui Pên, which has the added novelty of being a (symbolic) labyrinth which not only lost those readers who might have ventured into it, but actually "lost itself", lost its meaning, until Stephen Albert rediscovered its secret. The secret, we now know, is that time may not be linear, as we conceive it to be, moving on from the past, through the present, to the future. It may not even be circular, producing an inescapable and futile Eternal Return, as Nietzsche and, after him, Azorín, Carpentier and Borges among others have at times seemed to believe. It may instead be a web-like structure of coexisting lines of time. To illustrate this further Borges introduces the reference to an excerpt from Ts'ui Pên's novel which tells two different versions of the story of a victorious army (I, 470-71). The text refers to "los divergentes, paralelos y finalmente coalescentes ejércitos" (the divergent, parallel and finally coalescent armies). Lower down, at the crux of "El jardín ...", Albert refers to Ts'ui Pên's concept of "tiempos divergentes, convergentes y paralelos" (divergent, convergent and parallel times). The two sets of adjectives link the excerpt from the novel with its author's notion of time. Ts'ui Pên's novel/labyrinth is a metaphor of what the universe might be like if we were programmed to perceive more than one time-scale. As usual, Borges is trying to shake our faith in our simple, comfortable ways of seeing things.

The shift back from the core to the closing part of the frame occurs dramatically when, after Yu Tsun has finally achieved a vision of innumerable pasts, presents and futures, each containing himself and Albert, the actual single present breaks in, in the shape of Madden, the counter-espionage agent. Yu Tsun's murder of his host at this point links the core of the story to the frame in a dramatic and satisfying way, but also, as we have seen, with profound irony. Whether, as Alazraki argues,[2] the murder negates Ts'ui Pên's notion of time as a network rather than as a line is, in my opinion, not proven. Yu Tsun does not seem to see it that way himself. Apart from referring to the success of his stratagem as "unreal" and "insignificant", he describes his contrition and weariness after the murder as "innumerable". The latter adjective, the last in the tale, strikes us by its oddity, since it normally governs a plural. It is clearly intended to refer back to Ts'ui Pên's postulate, echoed by Albert just before his murder, of "innumerable" futures. It seems as though Borges were suggesting that one act of betrayal somehow contains all other similar actions and contaminates all possible pasts and futures.

Granted, this is not Borges' only allusion to the mysterious relationship between individual events and time. In "Emma Zunz", for example, we read that Emma "understands" (the verb is important — she does not just imagine it, or feel it) that the death of her father "seguiría sucediendo sin fin" (II, 46) (would go on happening endlessly). In a similar but not quite identical way, in "La noche de los dones" it seems that the girl who had experienced the Indian raid "no podía pensar en otra cosa y [...] esa cosa era lo único que le había pasado en la vida" (II, 498) (could not think of anything but that and [...] that was the only thing that had happened to her in her whole life), while in "Avelino Arredondo" Avelino feels that, once he has assassinated the President, "el tiempo cesaría, o, mejor dicho, nada importaba lo que aconteciera después" (II, 524) (time would stop, or rather, whatever might happen afterwards would not matter). As in "El jardín ...", in each of these other cases a unique single incident seems to affect time in its own way. Without negating time's irreversible successiveness, which he had despairingly recognized at the end of "Nueva refutación del tiempo" (II, 405), Borges seems to be ringing the changes on various possibilities, without privileging any one of them.

Despite the unfamiliarity of its central postulate about time, the

_____
[2] Alazraki, *Versiones ...*, p. 105.

actual technique of "El jardín ..." is not unduly complicated. One reason for this is that the frame story and the core of the tale are clearly differentiated and kept substantially separate. In "El Zahir" (II, 77-85) the frame also seems to stand separate from the kernel of the story, but in this case the interaction between them is more subtle. At the same time the core section itself is not a unified entity, since it contains what appears to be an interlude, the narrator's short story, whose function within the strategy of the tale as a whole needs to be noticed. In his remarks to Burgin, Borges characteristically minimizes the role of the frame story (the story of Teodelina Villar, as distinct from the story of the finding of the obsessive, magic coin), restricting it to the familiar ploy of introducing realist-type details in order to facilitate the reader's willing suspension of disbelief at the point where the fantastic is defly introduced: "I can't have the teller of the story buying a packet of cigarettes and getting an unforgettable coin. I have to give him some circumstances to justify what happened to him."[3] Once more this is far from being a full statement of the case.

But before Teodelina is even mentioned, the initial paragraph of the tale constitutes a prologue designed in the first place to arrest the reader's attention with an intriguing opening sentence. This is a favourite procedure of Borges in his earlier stories, notably in, for example, "La lotería en Babilonia" or "La Biblioteca de Babel". But it is one which, interestingly enough, practically disappears after *El Aleph*, to be replaced by more neutral openings, except in the cases of "Guayaquil", where he gently parodies his earlier technique as part of his method of presenting his narrator, and "El libro de arena", where he triumphantly declares the tale to be both fictitious and true. In the rest of the paragraph the technique is to affirm a mysterious link between a coin as common as a British five-penny piece or an American nickel and certain extraordinary and exotic objects. We instantly wish to know what the link is, just as we wish to know how the narrator of "La lotería en Babilonia" could possibly have undergone such weird experiences. Again we notice Borges' mastery of the basic and most difficult techniques of story-telling, in this case, the gripping of interest.

The opening paragraph of "El Zahir" is strikingly similar to that of "El milagro secreto" in that, just like Hladík's dream, the bracketed section which it contains is sandwiched between two sets of realist-type notations. Even more obviously than in the earlier

---

[3] Burgin, p. 44.

tale, this first paragraph introduces the fantastic into the realistic in precisely the same manner that the story as a whole does and thereby begins the latter in a doubly satisfying way. But this bracketed section also has another half-hidden function: that of suggesting a connection with two major religions, Islam and Judaism, and through their common element — monotheism — with Christianity and the theme of the story, the absolute. The conclusion of the opening paragraph completes the titillation of our curiosity by suggesting a further link, this time between the Zahir (whatever it is) and a dreadful change in the narrator, thus engaging our attention in a new, more human direction. The whole beginning of "El Zahir" is exceptionally effective.

The story of Teodelina and the narrator's relationship with her stands in contrast to the corresponding frame story in "El jardín de senderos que se bifurcan". Since the consequences of the narrator's receiving the Zahir are in themselves quite dramatic, there is no need now for the frame to supply an element of suspense. The contrast this time is of another kind. Not much that is helpful has been written about Borges' humour; least of all about its functionality. But a careful survey would reveal that it is rarely present in his stories for its own sake: the passing reference in "La lotería en Babilonia" to "una letrina sagrada llamada Qaphqa" (I, 444) (a sacred latrine called Qaphqa), for example, is an isolated instance. Comparison of cases shows that Borges uses certain well-defined techniques of humour for specific purposes. The gently satirical portrait of Teodelina here belongs to a class of comic descriptions of individuals which includes, among others, Ashe in "Tlön, Uqbar, Orbis Tertius" and Muir in "There Are More Things". It culminates in the portrait of Carlos Argentino Daneri in "El Aleph".

In each case the comic character is closely associated with a serious aspect of the story. Ashe, for instance, provides the clue to the invention of Tlön, while Muir links the idea of an inhabitant of the mysterious house with something monstrous and abominable. Not for nothing is the most extended humourous portrait, that of Daneri, the prelude to the hideous and tragic vision offered by the Aleph. In the case of Teodelina, however much at the "realist" level it might justify the apparent relapse into a form of obsessive mania on the part of the heart-broken narrator, the important feature is not her death. What matter are, first, the tone adopted to give us a portrait of the girl and, second, the implicit parallelism between her obsession and the narrator's. Both closely link the frame to the core of the tale, the first by contrast, the second by similarity. The tone which Borges employs to represent Teodelina functions at one level as a distractor. It operates, that is, like an extended version of the kind of Borgesian joke which is present when Menard is made to publish the exact opposite of his true opinion of Valéry. In the same way, for instance, what is "abominably insinuated" at the end of "La lotería en Babilonia" probably corresponds to Borges' own outlook, while the "eleventh-century heresiarch" of Tlön appears to preach a wholly acceptable doctrine. Similarly, the tone of the satirical portrait of Teodelina in "El Zahir" may mislead the unwary reader into believing that Borges is merely indulging himself playfully at the expense of a typical "professional beauty" as a mere prelude to the serious question of the narrator's obsession. Were this so, the two paragraphs devoted to Teodelina would be no more than an amusing interlude designed to be a sop to the reader before the core story takes over in the fourth paragraph.

In fact, however, once we notice that Teodelina prefigures the narrator as he becomes once he has received the Zahir, the tone assumes a quite different importance. Teodelina seeks "perfection"; she aspires to the "absolute" in a field of human activity — the pursuit of feminine fashions — whose constant mutability and ultimate frivolity preclude any chance of her being able to fulfil her aspiration. She seeks the absolute, that is, in a world which, being pre-eminently subject to time and change, is essentially a world of the relative. We smile tolerantly at Teodelina's worship of fashion, an article of her faith being that a hat which is not a Parisian model is not a hat at all. But Borges is already preparing to turn the tables on any assumption of superiority we may thus make. His whole aim in the core of the story is to suggest that all forms of worship, religious or otherwise, that is, all forms of obsession with the absolute, are as intrinsically comical as Teodelina's. The clue to this aim is not only that implied by her name, which is said to mean a vessel or vague form of God. It is also and primarily in the fact that for the narrator to make fun of her is at the same time to make fun of himself for loving (i.e. absolutizing) her.

On both counts the presentation of Teodelina involves a deliberate parody of the central episode. It is not enough to notice that the narrator offers a comic picture of Teodelina. We have to ask *why* he does so, what is his purpose? Within the *dispositio* of the story as a whole that purpose is eventually to collapse the second part of the tale, the core, into the first part, the frame: to identify in some sort the narrator with Teodelina and each one of us with both of them. The implication is that we are all tempted to absolutize, with the result that the part tends to become the whole and the trivial is invested with transcendental attributes. Hence the references to cult-objects in Islam and Judaism in the first paragraph and the key admission that Zahir is one of the names of God (II, 82), preceded by a reference to its "diabolical" influence (II, 80).

The significance of the first part of the frame story in "El Zahir" is not exhausted by the recognition that Teodelina's absolutization of fashion parodies man's vain and possibly comic aspiration to a transcendental absolute. The parody, we notice, ends ironically. Death briefly brings the perfection which Teodelina had always pursued and permits her to conquer time, forcing it momentarily into reverse. Because of this Teodelina's death is much more significant within the pattern of the story than is presupposed by Borges' suggestion that its main purpose is to justify the narrator's subsequent insane obsession. It interacts with the end of the story, implanting the idea that death alone may bring reconciliation with the absolute.

The last section of the opening sequence of "El Zahir" concerns the narrator's behaviour after his visit to the wake. It is sometimes interesting to notice the manner in which Borges effects the transition from frame to core in his tales. In the case of "El jardín de senderos que se bifurcan", for instance, Yu Tsun's train-journey to Ashgrove links the two parts of the story together. Such journeys are nearly always highly significant.[4] But the shift is re-emphasized by the reference to the labyrinth as Yu T'sun leaves the station: a new concept is suddenly introduced. In "El Zahir" the shift is marked by a notation, not at the beginning of the core section, but at the extreme end of the frame, with the reference to the game of *truco*, which is the very last word in this part of the tale (II, 79). This Argentine card-game is an important symbol in Borges; it stands for chance. If the Zahir symbolizes the absolute, linking this tale with the Borgesian theme (present, for instance, in "El inmortal" and "Funes el memorioso") of man ironically achieving one of his most cherished aspirations, the fact of encountering it by mere chance, underlined by

---

[4] Roslyn M. Frank and Nancy Vosburg, "Textos y contratextos en 'El jardín de senderos que se bifurcan'", *Revista Iberoamericana*, 100/101 (1977), p. 521, observe that "El viaje por tren en la obra de Borges casi siempre implica un viaje a otro mundo, el tránsito al otro lado" (The train-journey in Borges' work almost always implies a journey to another world, the passage to the other side).

the otherwise irrelevant mention of *truco*, automatically degrades it. In the same way Rufo achieves immortality and Funes something like totality of perception purely by chance and unawares. This detail, then, completes the parodic intention of the opening.

The frame story reappears briefly for two paragraphs between the discussion of Barlach's apocryphal book and the climax. But by this time it has changed its function. Instead of parodying the theme of "El Zahir", it intensifies it, by revealing that what the narrator has taken to be a mere fixation is the preliminary to madness. At the same time it prepares the subsequent universalization of the theme — "Cuando todos los hombres de la tierra piensen, día y noche, en el Zahir ..." (II, 84) (When all men in the whole world think, day and night, about the Zahir ...) — before the unexpected final twist in the tale, which identifies the Zahir not only with God, but with all things. Man, that is, is potentially capable of absolutizing anything, including evil, as we know from "Deutsches Requiem".

The frame of "El Zahir", then, is functionally more complex than was the case in "El jardín de senderos que se bifurcan". A third level of complication is visible in "El Aleph" (II, 112-25), where we find not one frame but two, each interacting with the core story, the narrator's encounter with the (possible) Aleph. This duplication is due largely to the fact that "El Aleph" has really three major thematic implications, each quite different from the others. This constitutes a kind of high-water mark of complexity in Borges' fictional writing, from which he has tended to move back in his later stories to a greater thematic simplicity, apparently at least. But, of course, by surrounding the narrator's central experience with both an inner and an outer frame, Borges produces a structural metaphor (of inclusiveness) which to some extent reinforces the Aleph-idea of all-inclusiveness.

The story begins with an arresting anticlimax: the death of Beatriz Viterbo, with whom the narrator had been passionately in love, is followed immediately by a reference to the appearance on the billboards of a fresh set of advertisements for a brand of cigarettes. In another writer this might have been no more than a bitterly ironic opening ploy. But in Borges we are wise to look for more. Man yearns for a fixed principle. We long to think of love as eternal. We instinctively envisage the death of a loved one, as Emma Zunz does, as if it annihilates all other events and will continue to do so. We wish to confer "everness" on emotions, beliefs, events. "El Aleph", with its anticlimatic opening, implacably reminds us that all is change, that nothing is fixed, that reality goes on producing its ever-altering kaleidoscopic patterns despite our pathetic attempts to freeze the temporal flow. The photos of Beatriz in her apartment reinforce this message. They show her in early adolescence, at the time of her marriage and at that of her divorce; they also show her in different poses. Love involves the sense of permanence: permanence of feeling in the lover, permanence of personality in the beloved. But, the photos imply, these are both illusions. We also notice once more the functionality of Borges' humour. Despite the dignity of Beatriz's death, unaccompanied by sentimentality or fear, the portrait of her is first satirical and then degrading. She frequented the *Club Hípico*, not the more exclusive Jockey Club; she holidayed in the commonplace Quilmes, not in more fashionable or exotic resorts; she was, it seems, unfaithful to her husband; she was the writer of obscene letters to her ludicrous cousin, Carlos Daneri. We shall discover the point of this presentation later.

The function of the first frame, then, is to question our illusions of permanence and fixity, preparing us gradually for the vision of a world of chaos which the Aleph will proffer.

Borges has remarked that "el humorismo escrito es un error [...] en el caso de Carlos Argentino Daneri creo que la broma es perdonable porque está incluida en un contexto quizá trágico" (written humour is a mistake [...] in the case of Carlos Argentino Daneri I think the joke is pardonable because it is included in a perhaps tragic context).[5] This remark tells us that the humour of the opening of "El Aleph" is ultimately related to the story's tragic implications; in fact, it acts as a distancing mechanism, as in "El Zahir", encouraging a relaxed response in the reader, out of which he will be unexpectedly jolted by the climax. But humour is also one of the links between the outer frame, concerned with Beatriz, and the inner frame, concerned with Carlos Daneri. Daneri is probably Borges' greatest grotesque. But he is a symbolic grotesque. His presentation rests on two concepts: first, his worship of poetry (his obsession with Paul Fort); second, his sense of modern man's ability to perceive and absorb the whole of reality (his reference to glossaries, timetables, gazetteers, bulletins) and of man's cognate ability to re-express it (the telephone, telegraphs, films and the like). Borges, by contrast, lacks confidence both in our ability to perceive "reality" at all and in our ability to

---

[5] Fernando Sorrentino, *Siete conversaciones con Jorge Luis Borges* (Buenos Aires: Pardo, 1974), p. 79.

communicate it. Critics such as Carlos, Devoto and Paoli have recognized in Carlos Daneri a parody of Dante, and in his poem "La tierra" (The Earth) a parody of the *Divina Commedia* (which includes Purgatory, Hell and Heaven, but not Earth).[6] Dante is the supreme poet of divine order. His poem describes in minute allegorical detail the three realms of the afterlife. Daneri is not a poet at all. His "poem" attempts to describe, in utterly banal realistic detail, the realm of this world, which exhibits no order. We are in the presence of a superb example of functional intertextuality: the greater our familiarity with Dante, the more satirical meaning the presentation of Daneri acquires.

We can now begin to recognize the structural unity of the tale. The first frame portends the Aleph-vision in terms of never-ending temporal change without any principle of stability; in terms, that is, of implicit chaos. The second frame portends the narrator's inability to come to terms with the vision mentally and hence through the medium of words. Daneri functions as a contrastive foil for Borges and his narrator/persona. As we saw, Daneri believes the world to be both readily observable and expressible. The satirical presentation of him signals to us the appropriate reaction on our part.

The centre of the second frame, which is much longer and more developed than the first, is Daneri's "poem". At first sight the description of it appears to be no more than a comic interlude, different only in tone from the discourse on metaphors which is contained in "La busca de Averroes". There Borges rejects the search for novelty; here, the fallacy of "realism". But the description of Daneri's opus is more than a general statement of a literary preference. It interacts in the story itself with the implicit reference to the *Divina Commedia* on one side and with the Aleph-vision on the other. Dante gives us a "divine", meaningful, allegorical vision of the world beyond. Daneri gives us an appallingly trivial and passively realistic vision of the world, seen from the outside, in terms of mere appearances. The Aleph gives us a "true" vision, also of this world. It includes the inside and the hidden as well as the outside and the visible. It reveals, in all its meaningless, hellish unbearableness, the chaos and horror of reality. Thereby it contrasts both with Dante's God-inspired order and Daneri's neutral, documentary observation.

---

[6] See Alberto J. Carlos, "Dante y el Aleph de Borges", *Duquesne Hispanic Review*, 5, no. 1 (1966), 35-50; Daniel Devoto, "Aleph et Alexis", in *Jorge Luis Borges*, ed. Dominique de Roux and Jean de Milleret (Paris: L'Herne, 1964), pp. 280-92; Paoli, esp. pp. 22-26.

At the same time, since Daneri obtains the raw data for his poem from the Aleph, the description of the poem itself prepares us for the introduction of the latter, by virtue of the fact that it "parecía dilatar hasta lo *infinito* las posibilidades de la cacofonía y del *caos*" (II, 118) (seemed to dilate the possibilities of cacophony and *chaos* to an *infinite* extent [italics mine]).

These functions are largely achieved by the middle of the second frame, which consists not of one but of two episodes: the narrator's visit to Daneri in 1941 and the meeting in the saloon bar a fortnight later. The critical question at this point is: what part does this second meeting play in the overall narrative strategy of the tale? It clearly has much less reader-impact than the description of the visit to Daneri's apartment. The additional satire of Daneri's poem is frankly redundant and the reference to Melián Lafinur unnecessarily long for the purpose it serves. But that purpose is important. For the suggestion of Beatriz's adultery with Melián Lafinur brings her into line with Daneri. As he is an anti-Dante, so she is an anti-Beatrice, not merely insensitive to the narrator's adoration and to his creative work, but also morally impure. While through love of Beatrice Dante attains a beatific vision, through love of Beatriz the narrator attains an anti-beatific vision. The alert reader perceives that although the two frames contain different thematic emphases, the contrast between Daneri and Dante, Beatriz and Beatrice establishes a satisfying parallelism which fuses the frames together. Meanwhile, the references to Zunino and Zungri prepare the threat to the Aleph which signals the shift from the two frames to the central episode in Daneri's cellar. A final function of the second frame, which should not be overlooked, is that of degrading the image of the Aleph by making it visible only through a hole in the wall of the cellar, with the viewer in a rather ludicrous attitude. The mockery, that is, extends to the core episode itself and portends the disconcerting suggestion in the postscript that the Aleph of the calle Garay was a false Aleph.

We notice that the two frames both reappear at the end in the postscript, naturally in reverse order. As we moved inward from Beatriz and then Daneri to the Aleph-vision, so now we move outward again from the Aleph and the cellar to Daneri's poem and finally back to Beatriz, whose name is the last word in the tale. The pattern established at one end is symmetrically completed at the other.

With some noteworthy exceptions, such as "Guayaquil", "El Congreso" or "El otro", the narrative strategies in Borges' later stories tend to be less complex than those of *Ficciones* or *El Aleph*. In part, this is because in some of them Borges is concerned, not with the mystery of reality, but with the mystery of the individual human personality, which, as he had written in "Historia del guerrero y de la cautiva", is always "único e insondable" (II, 39) (unique and unfathomable). Such stories — "El indigno", "El duelo", "Avelino Arredondo" etc. — are often broadly realistic in treatment, with no element of fantasy or added complication. In this they differ from "El Sur", for example. There it is certainly Dahlmann's personality which is foregounded, but at the same time the way he acts at the end is typically Argentine (if not Hispanic) and thus greatly extends his representativeness. In addition, we come to realize that the whole story may, in fact, describe a dream or hallucination. If we wish to seek a point of comparison in the earlier stories, we may say that these later ones are more like "Biografía de Tadeo Isidoro Cruz", in the sense that they centre on a single revealing experience or set of experiences. The question is whether they satisfactorily transcend the individual level.

To the reader accustomed to the stories of *Ficciones* and *El Aleph*, the mysteries of the human personality and of human behaviour seem more familiar and less disturbing than, for example, the postulates that evil can have its own saints and martyrs, that the mind creates reality selectively, that life seems to be like a labyrinth without a centre or that time may be an illusion. In order for us to feel that stories which are concerned with character and behaviour are significant in a similar way, the episodes have to be connected with a Droctulf or a Dahlmann, figures who are in some sense archetypes, or with a Cruz, whose character enjoys a special resonance because of his belonging to the Argentine national epic. It is not entirely clear that Fischbein in "El indigno" is in this category, unless we are prepared to see him as an archetypal traitor, a Judas, which the text itself does not seem to endorse. Nor, in spite of the biblical references, do the brothers in "La intrusa" assume a significant degree of universality. Apart from anything else, their behaviour is too barbaric.

"La noche de los dones" (II, 496-500), which is about a young man's first visit to a brothel and his first contact with death, presents the issue rather clearly. If we compare the technique of the story with that, for example, of "Historia de Rosendo Juárez", we see that the pattern is fundamentally similar: a first-person narration of much earlier events in a straight, chronological time-order. In the case of the latter tale, the second narrator is simply presented in the opening paragraph, in terms chiefly of his physical appearance, and he then proceeds to tell the tale. Not so in the case of "La noche de los dones". There the tale begins, after a reference to the place where the first narrator (a boy or a young man) heard what he reports, with a double reference to Plato's theory of knowledge as recollection. The intervention of the second narrator (an elderly man) in turn begins with a reference to Plato's theory of archetypes, which introduces his account of the death of Moreira. At the other end of the story, the first narrator's father interrupts with an indirect reference to Heraclitus' metaphor of time as a river, to which the second narrator replies with a series of considerations which hark back to the beginning.

What we have here is a very foreshortened, almost miniature, framing device. Its function, clearly, is to attach to the story told by the second narrator a wider dimension of human significance, and thus to confer on it a degree of universal relevance. His experiences during the night of the thirtieth of April 1874 are presented as archetypal human experiences, his first real contacts with sex and death, "dos cosas esenciales" (II, 500) (two essential things). The tiny frame into which they are set acts as a commentary, a series of signals to the reader indicating how to decode the inner meaning of the events correctly. The critical question is whether this is all it is: an explicitation-device affixed to the story told by the second narrator.

The story, in turn, is interesting in that, like "El hombre en el umbral", it introduces a third narrator: La Cautiva (The Captive). There is a difference, however. In "El hombre en el umbral" the story told by the old Indian represents the core of the tale as a whole, supplying Dewey with what seems to be the answer to his quest. The use of the triple-narrator method, as we shall see later, is designed to increase the element of ambiguity surrounding Dewey's search for the truth. In "La noche de los dones", however, the function of the third narrator's account is to interact both with that of the second narrator and with the frame. The theme here is not truth, but memory and forgetfulness. This is what is announced in the opening section of the frame. In Borges' fiction, from "Funes el memorioso" on, the paradox of memory is an important theme. On the one hand, as we know from Funes himself and from the last words of the narrator of "El Aleph", total recall would be unbearable: happily, "Nuestra mente es porosa para el olvido" (II, 125) (Our minds are porous with forgetfulness). Memory operates selectively. It assists us to screen out from our consciousness those areas of reality (in this case remembered reality, rather than our ongoing experience of it) which we do not want to incorporate into our comfortable construct: that which protects us against awareness of pure flux and chaos, the "infinito juego de azares" (I, 447) (the infinite interplay of chance) by which we are surrounded. But, on the other hand, memory is the only basis on which we can build a sense of the stability of reality or the continuity of our individual personalities. "Es sabido," Borges wrote in "Historia de la eternidad", "que la identidad personal reside en la memoria" (I, 329) (It is well known that personal identity resides in the memory). Without memory we have no contact with our own pasts. For this reason Borges' attitude to memory is ambivalent. In "El Sur", for example, he creates the powerful symbol of the cat which Dahlmann strokes in the station café, "el mágico animal" (the magical animal) which lives "en la eternidad del instante" (I, 531) (in the eternity of the instant). With no sense of past or future, it partakes of eternity and is compared to a divinity. However, as Borges grew older, his sense of forgetfulness, not so much as a barrier against horrifying awareness, but rather as a bottomless abyss into which all things must fall, seems to have become stronger. Thus he writes in "La intrusa" of "La azarosa crónica de los Nilsen, perdida como todo se perderá" (II, 373) (The chancy chronicle of the Nilsens, lost as everything will be lost); in the opening sentence of "El encuentro" of the triumph of forgetting (II, 389); and in the last words of "Juan Muraña" of "el olvido, el común olvido" (II, 399) (forgetfulness, commonplace forgetfulness). In "Mutaciones" he reflects sadly that "no hay en la tierra una sola cosa que el olvido no borre o que la memoria no altere" (II, 335) (there is not a single thing on earth that forgetfulness does not erase or that memory does not alter). In all this we detect more than a note of personal regret. Forgetfulness is a threat to our very being.

This is the context into which we must set the opening of "La noche de los dones". The references to Plato and to Francis Bacon link memory to knowledge, and ignorance or unawareness to forgetfulness. Their function is to foreshadow the theme. They are a pretext for the second narrator to intervene with the categoric assertion that, while the origin of many of our impressions is inevitably forgotten, certain "essential" experiences endure in the memory. The opening part of the frame, that is, contains a message of reassurance: "... hay otras primeras veces que nadie olvida" (II, 496) (there are other first times that nobody forgets). If this is so, some part of the past remains, some part of the continuity of the personality can be claimed; time is not all-devouring, at least while we live. The affirmation of Schopenhauer which Borges had quoted in "El tiempo circular" — "La forma de aparición de la voluntad es sólo el presente, no el pasado ni el porvenir: éstos no existen más que para el concepto y por el encadenamiento de la conciencia, sometida al principio de razón. Nadie ha vivido en el pasado, nadie vivirá en el futuro; el presente es la forma de toda vida" (I, 368) (The mode of appearance of the will is the present alone, not the past or the future: these exist only for concepts and for the ongoing consciousness, subject to the principle of reason. No-one has lived in the past, no-one will live in the future; the present is the form of all life) — seems a little less frightening.

But Borges presents reassurance only to undermine it. The account of his experiences given by the second narrator begins soothingly, as so often, with realistic-seeming details of time and place. The process of the tale does not really begin until the third narrator, the girl in the brothel, tells her story of terror. And a highly original story it is. The more we look at it, the more we recognize in it one of Borges' most audacious effects. For it is all suspense-creation, with no climax. As the raiding Indians hit the ranch, the story is brusquely interrupted. We are left to infer the outcome from the fact that the girl is called "The Captive". The fact that her story is deliberately left unfinished, frustrating our carefully built-up expectations, compels the question: what is it for?

La Cautiva's narration has a double function. First, it creates a high level of tension, which is then abruptly transferred to the events which begin with the sudden dramatic appearance of Moreira, the famous outlaw, and his gang. But if this were the only purpose, it would have been told without the commentary added by the second narrator. The girl's story parallels his own. Both are accounts of first-hand experiences which are totally unforgettable. The effect created is one of re-emphasis, with the additional linking factor that it is she who provides the second narrator with one of his two "essential" experiences that night: his first experience of the sexual act. The two sets of experiences which make up "La noche de los dones" relate to each other in several ways. The girl's story is one of horrendous violence actually undergone, but not narrated. We only conjecture the outcome (in sexual terms) from the hint contained in her remark that "A las mujeres las llevaban a Tierra Adentro y les hacían de todo" (II, 498) (They carried off the women into the interior and did all sorts of things to them). The boy's story, by contrast, is one in which his sexual initiation is a happy by-product of the goings-on on the ground floor from which he has escaped upstairs. Subsequently he sees violence enacted on Moreira, who is bayoneted to death as he attempts to flee the brothel, now surrounded by police. The girl, that is, suffers terror and violence and is presumably sexually initiated by being vilely abused. The boy escapes violence, except as a spectacle which introduces him dramatically to death, and is even allowed a gratifying form of sexual initiation as a kind of bonus. His story seems to be commenting ironically on hers. Life grants them strangely parallel destinies — the appearance of Moreira and his gang is substituted for the appearance of the raiding Indians at the climax of the girl's story and is obviously intended to be its counterpart — but with very different results. Once more, looking at the two stories together, we see an example of interaction, not just juxtaposition.

The ironic contrast just mentioned does not exhaust the inter-action, nor is it even the most important element in it. What both stories appear to exemplify is the unforgettable nature in each case of the experiences undergone. Although the girl's are horrific and the boy's merely dramatic, both are presented as completely indelible. In a phrase which reminds us of the opening of "Emma Zunz", Borges writes of La Cautiva's story: "... yo sentí que no podía pensar en otra cosa y que esa cosa era lo único que le había pasado en la vida" (II, 498) (I felt that she could not think of anything but that and that that was the only thing that had happened to her in her whole life). But when we look more closely we see that this is probably not the case. Her story is interrupted in the middle by a bystander's question. What is crucial is her response. She appears not to hear the question, but mechanically repeats the sentence which she had just completed, in exactly the same words, before going on. As her tale is interrupted for the second time by the arrival of Moreira, the second narrator drives the point home: "Hablaba la Cautiva como quien dice una oración, de memoria" (II, 499) (The Captive spoke like someone saying a prayer, from memory). The comment is lost at first reading in the excitement generated by the sudden appearance of the drunken brawlers who take over in our minds from the Indians charging the ranch in the girl's tale. But as we reread the story it assumes critical importance when it is reinforced by the second narrator's subsequent admission: "... ya no sé si me acuerdo del hombre de esa noche o del que veía tantas veces después en el picadero" (now I no longer know whether I remember the man of that night or the one I was to see so many times afterwards in the theatre). The reference is to the hugely successful dramatized versions of the death of Moreira staged by José Podestá in Buenos Aires in the mid-1880s and after, using as his source the popular Argentine novel *Juan Moreira* (1879) by Eduardo Gutiérrez (1853-90).

It is this admission that links the second narrator's story both backwards to the girl's story and forwards to the closing part of the frame. He, like her, is perhaps simply repeating what is now no more than a familiar string of words from which all real memory of the actual events has been worn away by time. This is the point of the reference which the first narrator's father makes to "el gran río de esa noche" (II, 500) (the great river of that night), a reference marking the articulation between the end of the core element and the latter part of the frame. The events of the evening had been, in themselves, a "correntada de cosas" (fast flow of things), but the true "great river" which underlies the father's remark is that of time. The remark introduces a contradiction. On the one hand, the second narrator specifically insists that he received an "essential" revelation, something reassuringly unforgettable. But immediately afterwards he takes back that affirmation with the same kind of verbal formula — "ya no sé si ..." (now I no longer know whether ...) — that he had applied earlier to his "memory" of Moreira's face. What is it that he really remembers? Is it his experiences of that night or only the way he has come to put them into words? Explicitly comparing his pseudo-memory with La Cautiva's, he concludes the frame and the story with the sad recognition that it "now" makes no difference who saw the end of Moreira. The story deconstructs its own theme. Its message is identical to that of the end of "El inmortal": "... *ya no quedan imágenes del recuerdo; sólo quedan palabras.* Palabras, palabras desplazadas y mutiladas, palabras de otros" (II, 23) (*now there are no images left in my memory; only words remain.* Words, displaced and mutilated words, words belonging to others). If, as Plato suggested, knowledge is inseparable from memory; if personal identity, too, resides in memory; and if, in fact, our memories are not of true experiences but of the mere words which we apply to them, what becomes of knowledge or identity? Our mode of contact with the world and with our very selves is called into question. Not for the first time in Borges we feel "contaminated with unreality". In "La noche de los dones" we encounter another example of a familiar narrative strategy. The two parts of the core interact both with each other and with the frame to question what we take for granted about the validity of our mental processes.

CHAPTER 5

PIVOTAL EPISODES AND
SHIFTING THEMES

Alazraki's postulate of "el espejo como diseño organizador del
relato" (the mirror as the organizing design of the tale) and his
affirmation that "casi todos los cuentos de Borges presentan un
doble plano, casi un doble fondo, y [...] el segundo de estos planos,
como un espejo, devuelve la imagen del primero, pero invertida"
(almost all Borges' stories are double-sided, almost false-bottomed,
and [...] the second side, like a mirror, gives back the image of the
first, but inverted) represent an undue simplification of Borges'
strategies.[1] To suggest that there is some sort of "common model"
behind all or many of them, what Friedman calls "the same
structuring ur-narrative",[2] is really too reductive. Nonetheless,
Alazraki has shown conclusively that where the model can be
perceived, it is of major structural significance. What follows is that
in some stories which are constructed in this symmetrical way there is
a pivotal episode around which the tale is built.

By far the most obvious example is "Emma Zunz" (II, 46-51), in
which Emma, a working girl from Buenos Aires, appears to revenge
her father's death by means of a perfect crime. Hall, in one of the best
articles on it, has shown that there are half a dozen valid ways of
interpreting this story, which he rightly calls "a *cuento* which is

---

[1] Alazraki, *Versiones ...*, pp. 14 and 41.
[2] Mary Lusky Friedman, *The Emperor's Kites* (Durham: Duke Univ. Press, 1987),
p. 3.

complex rather than simple in its narrative structure".[3] In essence, however, these readings all revolve around one basic question: are we to see the story as "a successful quest for vengeance and poetic justice", which Hall calls "the usual interpretation",[4] or as an ironic treatment of that quest. It may not be irrelevant to recall that, to Burgin, Borges said apropos of this story: "I think there's something very mean about revenge, no? Something futile about it. I dislike revenge."[5] *Prima facie*, these remarks suggest that an ironic treatment might be more likely.

One of the unmentioned features of "Emma Zunz" is that it uses the "mass culture" format of the perfect crime in order to produce a "high culture" ending. In this, of course, its underlying technique is the same as in "La muerte y la brújula", which uses the format of the detective story in a similar way. But there is a difference. The fact that it is the detective of "La muerte y la brújula" who is trapped by the criminal, and not vice versa, leaves no doubt in any reader's mind that the popular format is being deliberately manipulated. Whereas a certain number of critics mentioned by Hall (including Christ, Harss and Wheelock) appear to have overlooked the possible intrusion of irony into the latter part of "Emma Zunz". The key is precisely the pivotal episode. Mass culture trades on built-in reactions. It tends to be reductive, conformist, assertive of received values and hence reassuring. High culture, by contrast, tends towards subtlety, irony, innovation, ambiguity and an interrogative stance towards received values and assumptions. It seems to be the case that in "Emma Zunz", as so often in other stories, Borges induces us to experience a built-in reaction to Emma and her apparent quest for "justice", and then undermines that reaction.

He does so by manipulating our response to Emma and her situation. The special position which "Emma Zunz" occupies in Borges' first two mature collections of stories derives from the fact that for once we are invited to identify ourselves emotionally with a Borgesian character. The second paragraph, with its unusual emphasis on Emma's physical and emotional reactions to the news of her father's death, is designed to produce a response to her which is different from the one we normally experience towards such typical

[3] J.B. Hall, "Deception or Self-Deception? The Essential Ambiguity of Borges' 'Emma Zunz'", *Forum for Modern Language Studies*, 18 (1982), p. 259.

[4] ibid.

[5] Burgin, p. 23.

Borgesian figures as Pierre Menard, Funes or the Librarian of the Library of Babel. They are intended to intrigue us. Emma is intended to move us, through the pathos of her situation and her reaction to it. This is a much more comfortable, familiar and conventional reader-response and for that reason alone should put us on our guard. The two key notations at the beginning of the tale are "ya era la que sería" (she was already the girl she would be) and "el suicidio de Manuel Maier, que en antiguos días felices fue Emmanuel Zunz" (the suicide of Manuel Maier, who in former happy days was Emmanuel Zunz). Their function is to draw us into accepting two implicit assumptions: that Emma's father killed himself, and that she would be a vengeful daughter punishing Loewenthal because of his ultimate responsibility for her father's suicide. We should notice, with Hall, that the first of these assumptions is not necessarily justified by the information which Emma receives and that her informant is, perhaps significantly, called Fein or Fain (= feign). The second assumption which we are tacitly invited to accept is that with the reading of the letter a change *already* takes place in Emma. Our curiosity is aroused; we want to know what that change was. The reference to her "secret" — that Loewenthal had framed her father — adds suspense when we read that it gave her a sense of power.

These elements of curiosity-interest and suspense fulfil a double function in the rest of the tale. Because we want to satisfy our curiosity and maximize our enjoyment of the suspense, we commit ourselves to what seems to be a changed Emma, no longer the drab, insipid working girl, but the girl who is the instrument of justice operating against a wrongdoer. But at the same time this blinds all but the really alert readers to the deeper meaning of the story. Suspense and curiosity are double-edged here. They function both as a bait and as a blindfold. The more we read the story as a satisfying plot, as the description of a perfect crime (or punishment), the less we are motivated to analyse it, with the consequent danger of doing it less than justice.

Borges' strategy is to encourage the reader to allow himself to be carried along by the vengeance plot through references to Emma's plan in paragraphs four and five — "ya estaba perfecto su plan" (her plan was already perfect); "el plan que había tramado" (the plan she had worked out) — and through the suggestion that on putting it into effect she would attain "la simplicidad de los hechos" (the simplicity of the facts). These phrases are designed to suggest that she is somehow in control of events, that she can manage reality, impose a pattern on it, change it by an effort of will. At the same time indications are fed into the narrative which seem to underline the heroism of her decision: she is opposed to violence; her drab, banal life does not prepare her for her role; she is afraid of men; she is timid and pretends amusement at tasteless jokes at her own expense; she is still in her teens. In the light of these we are induced to believe that we appreciate the full enormity — for her — of what she has undertaken to do, and that her scheme is maturing.

But when we examine the pivotal episode, in which Emma sacrifices her virginity with a Scandinavian sailor, we perceive that Borges has taken us in a certain direction only to mislead us. The first clue is the word "caos" (II, 48) (chaos), which is all that remains in Emma's memory after her experience. The second (as we later realize) is the window with the lozenge-shaped yellow panes, identical to those of the house of her childhood and of her parents' married life. The third is the reference in the crucial seventh paragraph to "aquel tiempo fuera del tiempo" (that time outside time), which links the horror of her devirgination to the horror of her father's death. This was similarly outside time and "seguiría sucediendo sin fin" (II, 46) (would go on happening endlessly). The careful time-references to the fourteenth of February, its evening, the night of the fourteenth to the fifteenth, to Friday the fifteenth, to Saturday, the day on which the plan is to be activated, all suggest, like the references to the plan itself, an orderly sequence of days and events moving steadily and inexorably towards the fulfilment of a pre-ordained scheme. But at the critical moment order and predictability dissolve without warning into a "desorden perplejo de sensaciones inconexas" (II, 48) (perplexed disorder of disconnected sensations) which leaves behind only a memory of chaos. Amid this chaotic disorder only one thought surfaces. It connects Emma's devirgination by the sailor with her mother's devirgination by her father. At that point "peligró su desesperado propósito" (her desperate intention was in danger of faltering). Borges' familiar call-sign, the introduction of the word "vértigo" (dizziness) to indicate that we have reached a turning-point in the action, confirms that the factors in play have suddenly undergone an unexpected change. After this pivotal incident nothing in the story is the same.

The technique of the second half of the story is to make it both fit and not fit with the first half. It fits in that Emma carries out her plan and is revenged (though it remains unclear whether her father really did commit suicide and whether Loewenthal was directly guilty of provoking it). It does not fit in that her outlook and motivation have changed radically. Her "desperate intention" has ironically back-fired. The reality on which she thought she could impose her will to be revenged has rebelled. Her revenge is now contaminated by the realization that her father "le había hecho a su madre la cosa horrible que a ella ahora le hacían" (II, 48) (had done to her mother the terrible thing that was now being done to her). In avenging his suicide, if such it was, on Loewenthal, she is at the same time projecting the image of her father on to the victim and avenging her mother's loss of virginity. The pivotal episode, that is, shifts "Emma Zunz" from a mass-culture perfect-crime tale to a high-culture Freudian story with an ironic twist.

That pivotal episodes are commonly associated with a shift towards irony is confirmed by the contrast between "Emma Zunz" and "Avelino Arredondo" (II, 523-27). There is a number of similarities. Each tale concerns a decision to punish what the protagonist perceives as a wrong, a plan adhered to at considerable self-sacrifice and a final violent dénouement. Avelino has in common with Emma his youth, his humble social position and his withdrawn, apparently banal, personality. Like Emma, he has little to say for himself and is at times the butt of jokes by his acquaintances. Like her also, he is a figure of strength of will, not given to going over his decisions in his mind once he has resolved upon a course of action. In both cases, too, Borges interweaves into the commentary a number of reflections on time, which are there to underline the contrast between its inexorable passage, carrying each protagonist towards the imagined act, and the protagonist's changed awareness of time. Both when she learns of her father's death and when she sacrifices her virginity, Emma feels herself to be beyond time, first because the death seems to bring time to a halt and later because the sexual experience seems in its horror to transport her outside time. Avelino, on the other hand, feeling the slow passage of time to be oppressive, seeks obliviousness of time. The toad in his water-trough has the same function as the cat in the railway-station in "El Sur": it reminds us that, however much the stories are concerned with a decisive instant in the lives of the protagonists, our lives are governed by our consciousness of living in successive, ongoing time. Only extreme despair or exaltation can bring a sense of the eternity of the instant.

For our purposes, however, it is not the similarities that matter, striking though they are (even down to the lozenge-shaped window-panes of "Emma Zunz" and the coloured rhombs which Avelino notices). It is the different strategy of the two stories. In the case of "Emma Zunz" Borges twists the story round after the pivotal episode, so that, as we have seen, the ending comments ironically on Emma's original intentions. But in "Avelino Arredondo" he permits his character to carry out his plan exactly as he intended. In place of a pivotal episode he substitutes something quite different: the brief interlude in the bar when a group of soldiers describe how they fired on a gramophone which was relaying prohibited information, and then force Avelino to play the part of a coward. Whereas the episode with the sailor in "Emma Zunz" causes Emma's plan to recoil on her own head, this interlude in "Avelino Arredondo" is carefully designed to interact with the ending. The soldiers, the ignorant agents of a despotic president, attempt to "kill" the truth and only make themselves ridiculous. Avelino, the agent of a moral principle enunciated in his country's national anthem, kills the despot and makes himself into a hero. His quiet acceptance of humiliation in the bar illustrates the sense of purpose which carries him to the outcome. The ironic treatment of Emma's private vendetta is replaced (notwithstanding Borges' disavowal of it in the epilogue) by an approving treatment of Avelino's public-spirited action, with a corresponding radical difference in the patterning of the stories.

Another crucial pivotal episode can be seen in "Deutsches Requiem" (II, 62-68). As we indicate below, the function of the inlaid details in this story is to confirm the religious dimension which underlies it, foreshadowed in the opening. "Deutsches Requiem", that is, has as its macroscopic or multiple subtext the whole of what we know as Lives of Saints. Zur Linde is a parodic or inverted saint, one who sacrifices and mortifies himself for the Nazi ideal as a saint normally sacrifices and mortifies himself for the Christian ideal. This is not to imply that the story alludes to or reflects any single hagiographic work. Insofar as there are microscopic subtexts present they are *The Book of Job* and the Pauline Epistles of the New Testament. The macroscopic does not exclude the microscopic; what it does in this case is to provide the underlying model, the conventional saintly pattern: conversion > trial of faith > martyrdom. The process of conversion is sketched out in the second and third paragraphs of Borges' tale. Zur Linde makes his public profession of faith by joining the Nazi party. He suffers for his faith with the loss of his leg and, a footnote hints, of his virility. He is granted the equivalent of what in the religious life would be a moment of spiritual insight when he realizes that it is easier to die for

the faith than to live it out in all its fullness. With this, the first stage
of his parodic "Way of Perfection" comes to an end.

We now reach the pivotal episode. In almost every well-known
saint's life, after the joy of conversion comes the test. So it is with Zur
Linde. Having mortified himself by accepting, in obedience to the
behest of his superiors, a post which was not to his liking but whose
duties he performs without sinful negligence, he is now deeply
tempted. The double reference to sin in the eighth paragraph
preludes the arrival of David Jerusalem at the concentration camp
which Zur Linde commands. In every saint, the Old Adam, Zur
Linde's Pauline "old man", unredeemed and watchful, awaits the
opportunity to overturn the work of Grace. So in Zur Linde himself
there remains, unsubdued by sacrifice and mortification, what he
calls "una detestada zona de mi alma" (II, 66) (a detested zone of my
soul) which stubbornly resists his ascetic practice of Nazi virtues. It is
his human impulse to surrender to pity and compassion. Until he can
tread it down, just as a Christian ascetic must learn to rid himself of
pride and carnality, he cannot truly follow the Way of Perfection and
advance towards (in this case) the martyr's crown. Zur Linde
survives the test. Overcoming the temptation to show mercy, he
confronts and vanquishes a greater temptation: to allow Jerusalem a
swift and easy death. Wrestling with the unredeemed part of his
nature, he forces himself to use precisely that which attracts him in
Jerusalem — joy in each created thing — to drive the poet to suicide.
"Losing" himself — "... de algún modo me he perdido con él" (in
some way I have lost myself along with him) —, he gains that
"happiness" which he had destroyed in Jerusalem. He is granted a
revelation to recompense his *fortitudo*: that the sacrifice of Germany
in 1945 will be rewarded with the triumph of the values for which
Nazism stood, the triumph of "la violencia y la fe de la espada" (II,
67) (violence and faith in the sword) over "las serviles timideces
cristianas" (II, 68) (servile Christian timidities). He himself can
submit to martyrdom happy in the conviction that a new age has
dawned, of which he was among the conscious precursors.

A later example of Borges' use of pivotal episodes can be seen in
"Historia de Rosendo Juárez" (II, 383-88), in which we hear the
other side of the account of events contained in "Hombre de la
esquina rosada". This is an accomplished story, but one which
ultimately derives part of its interest precisely from its relationship
with the earlier tale; intrinsically it is not fully satisfying. An
examination of its structure clarifies the reason to some extent.

Everything turns around Rosendo's dialogue with his friend Irala, two thirds of the way through. Up to that point the story is a rather picturesque first-person account of the evolution of a young slum tearaway into a hireling of one of the local political bosses, by whom he is employed to intimidate rivals and voters. We notice the similarity between Rosendo's early experiences and those of Otálora in "El muerto". Both are young men from the poor outskirts of Buenos Aires. Each gets involved in a knife-fight, kills his adversary and is protected from the consequences by a local political fixer who recognizes his potential usefulness as a hired thug. But there the similarity ends. In "El muerto", as is characteristic of Borges' earlier stories, Otálora's experiences gradually assume overtones of hubris and irony which confer symbolic meaning on them, lifting them above the level of mere "anecdote" and perhaps relating them to the deeper theme of man's relationship with God. We wait for just such a development in "Historia de Rosendo Juárez", but it does not come. The story relies, like "El indigno", simply on the unexpectedness, in certain given circumstances, of a piece of human behaviour and on the explanation of it, which is implicit in the account offered by the individual involved. Another way of seeing it is by reference to "El Sur". Both Rosendo and Dahlmann are challenged to fight and risk their lives for motives chiefly connected with pride and manliness under the gaze of others. Dahlmann accepts the challenge but in a context which grants his action possible levels of significance which transcend those of a mere act of dignity and courage. Rosendo refuses the challenge with a moral courage which transcends the physical courage he had hitherto needed in order to play the role of a neighbourhood bully, and that is all.

Borges' chief problem, therefore, is to provide a convincing motivation for Rosendo's shift from being a young imitator of Juan Moreira, carried away by the ease with which he had previously killed a challenger and escaped the consequences, to being a man who is mature enough to make a difficult moral decision in front of an excited audience. The story of Luis Irala's death at the hands of Rufino Aguilera, the pivotal episode, performs this function. The double reference to Irala as a true friend is designed to underline the impact of his death. The key question which Rosendo puts to him — "... ¿vas a jugar tu tranquilidad por un desconocido y por una mujer que ya no querés?" (II, 387) (are you going to put your peace of mind at risk for someone you don't even know and for a woman you don't love any more?) — portends, perhaps too clearly, Rosendo's own dilemma shortly afterwards. A feature of the episode is that although Rosendo counsels Irala to ignore public opinion and to abandon the idea of challenging Rufino, he nonetheless feels guilty on receiving the news of his friend's death. There is no obvious reason why this should be so. But the symbolic appendage to the episode, Rosendo's visit to the cock-fight and his bitter reflection on "esos animales [...] que se destrozan porque sí" (those animals [...] which destroy each other for no good reason) clarify the issue. He suddenly sees himself and his fellow bully-boys in the same light as the mindless fighting-cocks, and realizes that they have created the pattern of attitudes which led Irala to his death. The final part of the story shows Rosendo ignoring even the urging of his companion La Lujanera and calmly refusing to accept a drunken challenge. Referring back implicitly to the cock-fight, he remarks: "En ese botarate provocador me vi como en un espejo y me dio vergüenza" (II, 388) (In that idiot bent on provoking me I saw myself like in a mirror and I felt ashamed). Despite his absence of fear he refuses to fight for no good reason and, having achieved a new level of self-awareness, abandons his former way of life.

The striking aspect of the tale, as a Borges story, is the absence of mystery. Seen as a metaphor, it is a relatively simple one of cause and effect: a given experience produces a change of outlook and behaviour in Rosendo. This is not how Borges envisages things in his most striking stories. "Historia de Rosendo Juárez", like nearly all his stories, does up to a point fulfil Cortázar's requirement that a good short story should "actuar en el lector como una especie de *apertura*, de fermento que proyecta la inteligencia y la sensibilidad hacia algo que va mucho más allá de la anécdota" (act on the reader like a kind of *opening*, like a leaven which projects his or her intelligence and sensibility towards something that goes much farther than the merely anecdotic).[6] But it is written affirmatively, not interrogatively. The pivotal episode and the conclusion interact only in so far as the former influences the latter directly, without irony or ambiguity. This is why the story does not seem to reveal Borges at his most creative.

Not unrelated to the question of pivotal episodes is that of shifting themes. In considering the internal patterning of Borges' stories it is sometimes useful to distinguish between those which appear to have a single thematic thrust, however complex the treatment of it may be,

⁶ Cortázar, "Algunos aspectos del cuento", p. 6.

and those in which we notice a subtle transition involving a change of emphasis from one aspect of the original theme to another. Although it is one of Borges' most complicated stories, "Tlön, Uqbar, Orbis Tertius" is very largely in the first category, since it is chiefly concerned with the difference between an idealist conception of the world and our own. How far, at the very end, it suddenly enters the second category, we shall discuss briefly in Chapter 8. On the other hand, "La lotería en Babilonia" and "El inmortal" move almost imperceptibly from one focus to another.

In the prologue to *El informe de Brodie* Borges denies that his stories are fables or parables designed to point a moral or carry a message: "No aspiro a ser Esopo. Mis cuentos, como los de las *Mil y una noches*, quieren distraer y conmover y no persuadir" (II, 369) (I do not aspire to be Aesop. My stories, like those of *The Arabian Nights*, aim to amuse and move and not to persuade). Taken in the context in which Borges places it, that of politically involved literature, there is some plausibility in the statement, though even here few works of literature can escape illustrating, explicitly or implicitly, assumptions which can be interpreted in socio-political terms. But taken more generally, the statement is misleading. Even if they are intended to make us rethink our attitudes rather than change them, many of his best stories express a vision of the human condition which has implications no less easily identifiable because they may not be directly spelled out.

We have suggested that in order to figure forth that vision Borges needed to invent disquieting metaphors. Chief among them is, of course, that of the labyrinth, with its seeming regularity combined with baffling unpredictability. This he was able to project on to the Library of Babel. The Babylonian lottery is another variant, since a lottery combines unpredictability with a measure of organization and control. There is, however, a difference between the Library and the lottery. The former is a spatial metaphor illustrating the infinite recurrence of the same, unchanging pattern. It encourages a search for meaning because of its regularity and repetitiveness. But at the same time it frustrates it, because at the macrocosmic level it has no centre from which it can be perceived radiating outwards indefinitely, and because at the microcosmic level of individual human experiences no comprehensible pattern can be recognized at all. There is a certain element of tension in the story between the Librarian's aspiration to reach the "total book" and his awareness that there is really no possibility of fulfilling it. But this does not greatly affect the structure of "La Biblioteca de Babel".

On the other hand, in "La lotería en Babilonia" (I, 441-47), which describes a sweepstake that comes to involve the whole of life, the metaphor is not that of a static spatial entity which is passively "there" to be explored. The lottery is more like an infinitely complex organism surrounding and enmeshing us, in such a way that every thought and action — or even abstention from them — may have incalculable consequences. To put it another way, it is as if the Librarian, instead of being free to wander safely through the Library of Babel, might find a treasure at the end of one staircase or a torture-chamber awaiting him at the end of another. This alters the metaphor fundamentally. "La Biblioteca de Babel" is about comprehensibility. Its implicit metaphor concerns man's free-ranging thought seeking explanations. In contrast "La lotería en Babilonia" is about predictability. It contains a metaphor of experiences which man is not really free to choose but has to undergo willy-nilly. The introduction of the notion of consequences — possibly arbitrary consequences —, in contrast to the Librarian's freedom to wander where he will unharmed, makes the lottery-metaphor much more relevant to the reality of the human condition than that represented in the Library. Above all, it dramatizes the need to reach an interpretation. The Company which is said to run the lottery is not just a code-book hidden in the centre of the labyrinth, waiting to be found. If it exists, the Company is an active force, dominating every sphere of behaviour and controlling every aspect of happiness and suffering. Hence the tension in "La lotería en Babilonia" between the sense of utter meaninglessness and the desire for an order, however mysterious, is greatly enhanced. This suggests why the story gradually alters its thematic thrust as it progresses.

The two key words in the opening paragraph (I, 441) are "incertidumbre" (incertitude) and "vicisitudes" (vicissitudes). It has been said that the contribution of Ezra Pound and Gertrude Stein to the development of Hemingway's prose was that they taught him what to leave out. Borges also learned what to omit. Here at the beginning of "La lotería en Babilonia" we have no description of the speaker, no awareness of where he is or to whom he is speaking, no background details. Once our attention has been grasped by the speaker's astonishing affirmations, Borges immediately privileges the first theme: life's unpredictability. The crucial second paragraph introduces the metaphor which will be developed in the rest of the tale to figure forth this theme. But before this development begins, the narrator, who is soon to fade into the background as is so often the case, completes his initial functions by already casting doubt, not on his description of the institution, but rather on any general agreement about how to understand it. Disclaiming any knowledge of his own, he emphasizes both that "los magos no logran ponerse de acuerdo" (the wizards cannot manage to agree) and that there exist "veiled men" who presume to utter "blasphemous" conjectures about the institution's workings. These last correspond, of course, to the "blasphemous sect", the "impious ones" among the librarians of the Library of Babel. But there these sceptics were merely a group among others. Here they face the notion of the Company. The key word in the second paragraph is thus "blasphemous". Its function is to convert any discussion about the operations of the lottery into a discussion of the existence of God and of divine Providence moving in mysterious ways. It foreshadows in this manner the second theme of the tale. With it and with the reference to the veiled heretics responsible for the blasphemous conjectures, the exposition may be said to end.

Having thus established the parameters of the tale, Borges proceeds to describe the development of the lottery as an institution in such a way that it turns by graduated stages into a description of the human condition. At first there are only monetary prizes. Then monetary forfeits appear. In the third stage non-monetary prizes and forfeits become the norm. In the fourth stage the requirement to buy a ticket disappears and the lottery becomes secret, free and universal, but obligatory. Everyone, from birth, participates automatically; everyone's life is wholly at the mercy of chance. At this point the main implication of the metaphor seems to have been worked out: the lottery has come to stand for a world in which our experiences are completely unpredictable, in which any attempt to explain them in terms of a comprehensible pattern of causes and effects is doomed to be simply an illusion. But this does not entirely preclude the possibility that the understanding denied to us may be present in the mind of God, for a lottery is, after all, an organized activity. Once the description of the institution is all but complete the story subtly changes course. In the middle of a paragraph we perceive a shift from the theme of life as a lottery to that of the possible existence of an organizing mind, that is to say, of a divine Providence operating through what appears to be mere chance.

This is the pivotal point of the tale. From here on the second part moves off in a new direction, albeit one which develops an aspect of the same metaphor. The Company, which combines attributes of God (all-powerfulness and mysteriousness of operation) with attributes of the Church (the power to issue ambiguous doctrinal statements), assumes new prominence. It offers an interpretation of the lottery in terms of a controlled intervention of chance in "el orden del mundo" (I, 444) (the order of the world). Part of the fearfulness of the lottery-metaphor is thus apparently discounted; we, the readers, momentarily relax. But no sooner has the reassuring concept of an underlying order been enunciated then it is contradicted. In the last stage of the transformation of the original lottery, which only now follows (and we have just seen why), chance is incorporated into the mechanisms of the institution itself. The postponement of the description of the final stage in the evolution of the lottery until after the insertion of the references to the Company and to the concept of order is an aspect of the strategy of the middle of the tale which we cannot afford to overlook. The overlap thus created locks the two parts of the tale together. But quite apart from this, the juxtaposition is in itself significant. The order whose existence is affirmed by the Company is at once discredited. For it is no longer challenged by a relatively simple notion of unpredictability, but by an infinitely complex web of intersecting patterns of chance.

The central section of "La lotería en Babilonia" is critical. For it now relates back to the narrator's posture of ignorance at the beginning of the story and to his reference to those who "blaspheme" against what we now realize are the Company's dogmas. Like the Librarian in "La Biblioteca de Babel", the narrator represents man reflecting on his situation. As the Librarian longs to find the Catalogue of Catalogues, the "justification" for the Library, so the Babylonian, despite his plea of ignorance, seems to accept the hypothesis of the existence of the all-powerful Company, the notion of ultimate order and the idea that "some specialists" are still capable of understanding how the lottery operates. The last stage of the lottery's evolution is in turn encapsulated between a reference to these "specialists" and another reference to "Nuestros historiadores, que [...] han inventado un método para corregir el azar" (I, 446) (Our historians, who [...] have invented a method for correcting chance). We assume that these specialists and historians represent theologians and those philosophers who believe than they can recognize some sort of design in the cosmos and its workings. Since the Company is characterized by "divine" modesty and its functioning is specifically compared in the last paragraph to that of God, we need have no doubt about what it stands for. But even as the narrator accepts the existence of this all-powerful, all-knowing entity, he places himself at three removes from understanding it: the "method" of the historians is only generally trustworthy; its transmission to others includes an element of deliberate deception; and the data on which it is based are unreliable. The whole of the central part of "La lotería en Babilonia", in other words, is deliberately arranged so as to bring into question, not the lottery as a metaphor of man's existence, but the possibility that it could respond to any conceivable order or design.

The proof that the story changes course in the middle is that the climax is not concerned with the lottery at all, but with the existence of the Company. The final question, in other words, is not whether living involves coping with baffling unpredictabilities, but whether any agency exists which organizes them in a way that few can understand but which in reality conforms to a divine plan. We can now see that the basic technique has been to create in the first part of the tale a disquieting metaphor of the world we live in and then to manipulate both it and the narrator who voices it. The aim of the manipulation is to question the main implication of the metaphor itself, the existence of an organizing entity, and thus to qualify it rather radically in the second part of the tale. To this end, the last stage of the description of the lottery introduces a degree of complexity which amounts to infinite chaos. At the same time the narrator's comments are so phrased that they virtually discredit his rather passive and uncritical recognition of the existence of the Company. As was the case with the Librarian of Babel, we accept his description, but not necessarily his own response, which stands for what the Babylonians (i.e mankind) are given to believing in preference to facing the possibility that life may be pure contingency and meaningless chaos.

The "blasphemous conjectures" mentioned at the beginning, the function of which was to portend the second phase of the tale, are spelled out to form the climax. Of the five possibilities considered, only one is consonant with an orderly interpretation of human existence. The other four are variations on the theme of the predominance of chaos, culminating in the postulate that Babylon (i.e. the world in which we live) contains nothing more than "un infinito juego de azares" (I, 447) (an infinite interplay of chance). The original metaphor of "La lotería en Bablionia" is already a disquieting figuration of the way things are. But it is one which admits of an ultimately positive interpretation. Then, by the addition of a further stage of development and a shift of emphasis, it is swiftly converted into an image of total meaninglessness.

The strategy which Borges had employed in "La lotería en Babilonia" re-emerges in "El inmortal" (II, 9-23), which tells of a man who was granted immortality only to find it unbearable. Here once more we have an initial theme — alluded to in the title — which at a certain point begins to be developed in a different, but already foreshadowed, direction.

Epigraphs in Borges' stories, where they occur, are always important indicators, as we can see in the case of "Las ruinas circulares." In "El inmortal" the epigraph from Bacon's *Essays* suggests a static universe like that of the Library of Babel, where everything exists already and for ever, rather than one in a process of constant evolution. Hence it is a universe where change can only mean ultimate repetition, the significance of which will become apparent as we read the first part of the tale. Then, just as "La lotería en Babilonia" introduces the wizards and the veiled men whose unspecified uncertainties and blasphemous conjectures prefigure the second part of the tale, so here Borges introduces the mysterious Cartaphilus instead of beginning the story with the central figure, Rufo, and his first-hand account of his experiences. Like the veiled men whose impious theories, when disclosed, form the climax of the earlier story, Cartaphilus reappears at the end to comment on the meaning of the second theme. In each case an effect is prepared at the beginning which does not reveal its significance until the end. At that point the clues provided by Cartaphilus' name, that of the Wandering Jew traditionally condemned to walk the earth for ever, and by the adjectives "consumido" (dried-up), "terroso" (earth-coloured), "gris" (grey) and "vagos" (vague), which indicate his weariness with what is, in effect, non-being, suddenly assume their prefigurative meaning. We perceive that "Cartaphilus" was more than just the source of the manuscript, but has an essential connection with Homer, Rufo and, of course, Borges. For the time being, however, this is not apparent. As we read Rufo's narration, even those few for whom the name Cartaphilus yields significance merely recognize the appropriateness of the fact that a story about immortality seen as a dreadful burden is transmitted by someone who has been punished by having to bear that very load.

Rufo's story in turn contains its own initial elements of pre-figuration. Colour symbolism, as Natella has convincingly shown, is often of major importance in Borges' fiction.[7] Yellow and red have special prominence. In "La muerte y la brújula", for instance, the wall near which the second murder takes place is painted with yellow and red rhombs; in "El Sur" the change in the colour of the sun from yellow to red prefigures Dahlmann's growing danger of death; in "Emma Zunz", as Emma goes to sacrifice her virginity with the sailor, she sees a window with yellow lozenge-shaped panes which remind her ironically of her childhood home. Here the yellow moon and sand and the red blood-stains on the rider who comes to Thebes seeking the water of immortality signal to us that the quest which Rufo will undertake can have no happy outcome. The hint is repeated when Rufo hears in Rome that "dilatar la vida de los hombres es dilatar su agonía" (II, 10) (to extend the life of men is to extend their agony). But these are not the most interesting foreshadowing devices at the beginning of "El inmortal". For we notice that they refer to the story's first theme, Rufo's quest for immortality. This is what differentiates them from two others. Rufo's first words refer to the river beside which he and the rider are standing. Just as he calls Thebes "Tebas Hekatómpylos", so he calls the river the "Egypt" and not, as we would expect, the "Nile". Only much later do we understand the significance of these Homeric reminiscences.

Thus section I of "El inmortal", though concerned to introduce the search for the waters of immortality, contains clues which, with hindsight, we can see portend the second stage of the tale. For the most part the rest of the section is straight narrative, describing Rufo's expedition across the Western Desert. But it ends with a symbolic dream of a water-jug in the middle of a labyrinth. Our interpretation of the meaning of the symbol changes as the story advances. At first we take it to be an ironic symbol: the water which is perhaps contained in the jug represents the water of eternal life, immortality, which Rufo had despaired of ever finding. Later we realize that it could equally symbolize mortality, which he no less despairingly seeks to recover. Those who have heard Borges say in public appearances, apropos of the afterlife, "I am out for oblivion" may conjecture that release from both mortality and immortality may be the object of desire at the centre of life's labyrinth. At all events, we realize that Rufo's pursuit of an illusion ends in a dream. But he is on the point of learning something about life and reality.

---

[7] Arthur A. Natella, "Symbolic Colors in the Stories of Jorge Luis Borges", *Journal of Spanish Studies*, 2 (1974), 39-48.

At the beginning of section II, "El inmortal" turns into a typical Borgesian "What if?" story. Such stories, which include "Tlön, Uqbar, Orbis Tertius" (What if the world were as the idealists describe it?), "Funes el memorioso" (What if we really had total recall?), "El Zahir" and "El Aleph" (What if we could touch the absolute or view in an instant the whole of creation?) and "El otro" (What if a man could meet his younger self?), are always ironic. Their distant model is the story of Croesus, the story of achieving one's heart's desire only to find it a curse instead of a blessing. To figure forth this irony, Borges' techniques are those of the hidden item of information and anticlimax. In reality both amount to the same, because the hidden element itself produces no more than a delayed anticlimax. The hidden item in this case is, of course, that the troglodytes are none other than the immortals, since the "impure stream" beside which they live is the river of immortality which the Indian horseman had been seeking in section I. The anticlimax occurs in section IV, when Rufo discovers this. But the main anticlimax is his discovery that the supposedly glorious City of the Immortals is, in fact, like a hideous nightmare. A possible strategy would have been for Borges to introduce Rufo directly to the City itself. Instead he chooses to insert a subterranean labyrinth through which Rufo must pass in order to enter it. Why? The function of the underground labyrinth is clearly to contrast with the City above it, while at the same time reinforcing its symbolism. The immortality which Borges is writing about here, personified initially by Carta-philus, is immortality *within time as we know it and within a static universe*. It is not, for instance, Christian immortality, within an eternal afterlife presided over by a benevolent God. It is simply this life eternally prolonged. The subterranean labyrinth represents our life "here below", baffling and frustrating, yet with a hint of design like the Library of Babel. Above all, it has an exit towards which the possible design ultimately leads: death. To move through it from birth towards death is to have at least the illusion of onward direction, perhaps even towards a final explanation. But in the City of the Immortals there can be no illusion of direction. All is reduced to endless circles of futility. The City represents, as Christ puts it, "a world in which there is no meaning and no utterance beyond the cry for death". Murillo agrees.[8] There is a double irony in this part of the

---

[8] Ronald Christ, *The Narrow Act. Borges' Art of Allusion* (New York: New York Univ. Press, 1969), p. 203; Luis Andrew Murillo, *The Cyclical Night. Irony in James Joyce and Jorge Luis Borges* (Cambridge, Mass.: Harvard Univ. Press, 1968), p. 225.

tale. We as readers can perceive the difference between Rufo's two experiences (the labyrinth and the City) while Rufo himself cannot, since he is as yet unaware of his own immortality. But in addition there is the ironic contrast between the City and what Rufo had anticipated (something perhaps akin to Bunyan's City, the City of God, the New Jerusalem).

Rufo's reaction to the City of the Immortals is comparable to Yu Tsun's reaction to his vision of a network of time-patterns in "El jardín de senderos que se bifurcan". As we saw, the latter thinks of "un laberinto de laberintos, en un sinuoso laberinto creciente que abarcara el pasado y el porvenir y que implicara de algún modo los astros" (I, 467) (a labyrinth of labyrinths, a winding, growing labyrinth that includes the past and the future and which in some way involves the stars). In a similar way the narrator in "El libro de arena" feels that the book he has acquired is "un objeto de pesadilla, una cosa obscena que infamaba y corrompía la realidad" (II, 534) (a nightmarish object, an obscene thing which discredited and corrupted reality). The response in each case is one of horror. Likewise, Rufo reflects on the existence and everlastingness of the City as something so horrible that it "contamina el pasado y el porvenir y de algún modo compromete a los astros" (II, 15) (contaminates the past and the future and in some way compromises the stars). The horror is inspired by the notion of the infinite; the infinite, that is, perceived as infinite chaos, meaninglessness without end. A similar vision is implicit in the way Funes is condemned to perceive and remember an infinitude of impressions of reality, as well as in what the narrator of "El Aleph" is permitted to view. Like the latter, Rufo is only anxious to be able to forget it.

This, then, is the first crushing anticlimax of the story. It remains for Rufo to discover that this is precisely the prefiguration of the immortality which he now has to endure. For many writers that discovery would constitute a more than adequate climax to an already highly original story. But between the description of Rufo's experience of the underground labyrinth and the City and his understanding of that experience (which, along with his "return" to mortality, completes the first thematic development of "El inmortal") Borges starts to move the tale in a new direction.

The reference in section III to the "rudimentary troglodyte" who has accompanied Rufo to the city walls marks the beginning of the shift. As in "La lotería en Babilonia", there is a deliberate overlap. Borges does not complete his treatment of the theme of immortality

within time until section IV, which is for the most part made up of
commentary on the impact made by consciousness of being immortal.
But already the foregrounding of the figure of the troglodyte and the
realization that he is none other than Homer (which inserts a totally
unexpected element into the middle of the tale) have introduced a
new theme. When Homer speaks everything in the tale is set for
change. For the moment, however, surprise is all we feel. The full
development is still to come. Meanwhile, Borges rams home the
implications of immortality. Section IV is a development of his
remark in "El otro Walt Whitman", apropos of the world, that "su
misma contingencia es una riqueza" (I, 142) (its very contingency is
an enrichment). It is mortality that confers value on our experiences.
Without the prospect of death, the Immortals, trapped for ever in a
static world, are condemned to undergo, and worse still to repeat
endlessly, every conceivable experience: "... en un plazo infinito le
ocurren a todo hombre todas las cosas" (II, 18) (in an infinite period
everything happens to every man). Without mortality all values are
utterly destroyed: "... toda empresa es vana" (all enterprises are in
vain). All vestige of individuality disappears, since all in the end
participate in the same experiences and think the same thoughts:
"Nadie es alguien" (II, 19) (No-one is anyone). In such circumstances, everything would cancel out: "No hay méritos morales o
intelectuales" (There is no moral or intellectual excellence).

The noteworthy feature of most of section IV of "El inmortal" is
the sporadic shift from first-person singular narration to an inde-
terminate first-person plural narrator. To the reader this presents no
problems. It could imply that Rufo is merely reporting Homer's
account of immortality, offered from the standpoint of one of the
Immortals speaking on behalf of the rest. Equally the switches back
to the first-person throughout the section make it seem possible that
Rufo, when he speaks as "we", is gradually identifying himself with
the Immortals, whose ranks he has now joined. This leads us to the
assumption that the first-person singular narrator of the following
section V is still Rufo, whose circular destiny, after many centuries,
brings him back to the Red Sea area where his tale began and permits
him to recover his mortality. But we are in for a surprise, for in a
footnote this section is attributed to Cartaphilus. He in turn casts
doubt on the single identity of "Rufo" at any point, adducing as
evidence the adjective "Hekatómpylos" applied to Egyptian Thebes,
the use of the "Egypt" for the Nile, the words taken from Homer
which Rufo speaks when he drinks the water of immortality and

finally the "remorse" he appears to feel in the City of the Immortals (which we know to have been suggested and planned by Homer). But this is not all. Towards the end of section V Cartaphilus refers to "un hombre de letras, ganoso (como el autor del catálogo de las naves [i.e. Homer]) de mostrar vocablos espléndidos" (II, 22) (a man of letters, anxious [like the author of the list of ships] to bring out splendid words). This ambitious man of letters is, of course, none other than Borges himself, the author of "El inmortal". Finally, Cartaphilus asserts categorically: "Yo he sido Homero" (I have been Homer).

What does all this mean? It means two very different things. First, that Homer, Rufo, Cartaphilus and Borges are in some sense one and the same; that there is no such thing as individual personality. In several of his essays, notably in *Historia de la eternidad*, Borges had entertained the idea that "la historia universal es la de un solo hombre" (I, 368) (the history of the universe is that of a single man) and Emerson's notion that all the books ever written are emanations of the same universal mind. In other words, not content with questioning one of man's deepest wishes — to be spared death —, Borges in the second part of "El inmortal" questions one of our deepest convictions, that of our individual identity. This second theme is prefigured during the development of the first and, in fact, is used to provide its surprise climax, with the startling revelation that "Argos" is Homer. Then, after an interlude of commentary, the second theme takes over completely and a new "What if?" question is implicitly posed: what if our sense of individuality is merely a delusion?

But there is another side to the question of the meaning of the second theme. How does it relate to the question of immortality? Here we see another example of Borges' "double-take" endings. For if there is no individual identity, if, as Borges has suggested, space and time are possibly illusions and there is only an eternal present occupied by a single mind, of which we are merely manifestations, then it follows that we are in a sense immortal already. No sooner do we begin to congratulate ourselves on not sharing the fate of Rufo and Cartaphilus than we are induced to wonder whether that fate is not, in fact, ours in any case. Suddenly the suggestion is silkily advanced that the theme of the first part of "El inmortal" actually touches our own human condition. We instinctively reject the suggestion, but not before we have been forced to take it into consideration. Even as we do so, Borges slips in another postulate

which turns into the climax of the story as a whole and which
undermines it completely. This is the postulate that in the last resort
the two disquieting themes which have been submitted for our
attention are merely forms of words, conventional signs on pieces of
paper which, when articulated, become language, "un mecanismo
arbitrario de gruñidos y de chillidos" (II, 179) (an arbitrary
mechanism of grunts and squeals). How can any of this tell us
anything about reality, when "la realidad no es verbal" (II, 168)
(reality is not verbal)? With this conclusion the double-take becomes
a triple-take!

We can now see that in terms of technique there is a clear line of
development from a story like "La forma de la espada", through "La
lotería en Babilonia", to "El inmortal". In the first, as McGrady has
shown, Borges uses a technique of foreshadowing clues to indicate
progressively to the alert reader that the narrator is, contrary to
appearances, Moon himself.[9] In "La lotería en Babilonia" the
technique is developed so that indicators in the first part of the story,
instead of merely foreshadowing a trick ending, point towards a
second theme which eventually grows out of the first. In "El
inmortal" the technique reaches a peak of complexity. The story is
introduced by a narrator who adopts the stance of a mere presenter,
translator and (in the conclusion) commentator of a second narration,
attributed to Cartaphilus. The latter similarly translates and comments on the narration of Rufo, whom he identifies with Homer and
Borges. Meanwhile, a footnote identifies Cartaphilus with Rufo. The
result is that a series of clues in the earlier part of the tale, this time
specifically listed by Cartaphilus at the end, portends the second
theme. This, however, is now no longer just an outgrowth of the first,
but interacts with it in an unexpected way before Borges produces a
final anticlimax by undercutting language itself.

"Veinticinco agosto 1983" (*VA*, 11-18) offers another variant. At
first reading, it seems to be a kind of mirror image of "El otro". In the
latter the older "Borges" meets his younger self. In the former it is the
younger figure (relatively speaking) who is present in some sense at
his future suicide. Like "El otro" the story is very complex. It
illustrates the opposite intention to that stated in the prologue to *El
informe de Brodie*, where Borges had alluded to his desire to write
"direct stories". It involves at least three different themes: dream

---

[9] Donald McGrady, "Prefiguration, Narrative Transgression and Eternal Return
in Borges' 'La forma de la espada' ", *Revista Canadiense de Estudios Hispánicos*, 12, no.
1 (1987), 141-49.

versus reality, the possibly illusory nature of time and space, and the perhaps equally illusory nature of our belief in the unity of our personalities. As so frequently, Borges' aim is to undercut our most tenaciously-held assumptions about the nature of the real and about ourselves. These are assumptions which tend to have in our minds the status of basic intuitions. It is on them that, for the most part unconsciously, we found our sense of belonging to a world which our minds seem programmed to understand and cope with. A great deal of modern fantasy literature, in Spanish America notably that of Borges and Cortázar, is deliberately aimed at challenging what Hume calls "humanly desirable myths of meaning"[10] in order to test our intellectual complacency. "Veinticinco agosto 1983" is probably the last major story by Borges to incorporate this aim. The problem, in terms of narrative technique, is to combine the three themes in such a way that they reinforce one another.

The opening of the tale is once more masterly in its simultaneous use of foreshadowing, irony and suspense. Just as "Tlön, Uqbar, Orbis Tertius" begins with a mirror, this story begins logically with a clock. Like the orchestral conductor measuring out tempi near the beginning of Alejo Carpentier's *Los pasos perdidos*, it is a symbol of man's sense of understanding and controlling time. In both works that understanding and control are subverted, and with them our comfortable confidence in our ability to arrange sense-data and events in time-order and thereby into chains of cause and effect. Without this we cannot feel really at ease. As we read the story for the first time we are unaware of the subversion to come. It is only on subsequent rereadings that we notice the hint of irony in the apparently unambiguous time-notation. The same applies to the narrator's mention of the place in which he finds himself and his relief at being in a familiar environment. As we read on we find that his assumptions and feelings are sadly misplaced. He is not where he has the impression of being. Finally, when he enters what we realize is a hotel, the mirrors in the lobby reflect the plants in the lounge. But this reflection of reality, we presently discover, is only apparent. There is no such reality to be reflected, either because the hotel may have been demolished or because in any case the "reality" is merely that of a dream. Once more the significance of the reference is for the moment hidden, though habitual readers of Borges are likely to have been already alerted. The rest of the story will suggest that if the

---

[10] Kathryn Hume, *Fantasy and Mimesis* (London: Methuen, 1984), p. 25.

"reality" reflected in the hotel mirrors is illusory, so too perhaps is the mind's reflection of reality, including that of the self. At the end of the first paragraph, surely one of Borges' most effective and compact short-story openings, the theme of the reality of the self is suddenly foregrounded. Our curiosity is instantly aroused by the narrator's discovery of his name freshly written in the hotel register. All the themes of the remainder of the story are implicitly announced in this opening paragraph. At its climax our attention is riveted by a mysterious and intriguing detail. In retrospect, having finished the story, we can see that Borges' order of priorities, which places the prefiguration of the themes even before the creation of the suspense, is in itself a signal to the reader, telling us something about how to read (or better, how to reread) what originally lay ahead.

The first phase of the story, which ends when the older "Borges" implies his suicide by indicating with a gesture the empty bottle on the bedside table, fulfils two basic functions. Firstly, the hint contained in the signature in the hotel register is developed into the theme of the double. As in "El otro", this symbolizes doubt about the unity and continuity of the human personality over an extended period of time. Our acceptance of the reality of ourselves is one of the basic supports of our acceptance of the reality of others and thereby (since consensus is an important factor in making any decision about it) of the reality of what appears to surround us. Hence, any attack on the reliability of the intuition we possess of the self is potentially deeply disturbing. Both Robert Louis Stevenson and Miguel de Unamuno knew it before Borges. Balderston, in his book on Stevenson and Borges — and especially in Chapter 4: "Más allá del dualismo" (Beyond Dualism), which incomprehensibly makes no mention of "El otro" — fudges the issue. Since he perceives it in Stevenson in terms of two characters — Jekyll and Hyde — who are actually one, he fails to realize that in Borges what is equally important is the notion of one character who is actually converted into two by the passage of time. The implied result is the same — "la inexistencia de cada uno" (the non-existence of each of us), as Balderston puts it —,[11] but the impact on the reader is far greater, since time passes inexorably for all of us, carrying off our former selves. The cases Balderston cites — Droctulf and the Captive, Abenjacán and Zaid, Juan de Panonia and Aureliano — involve

---

[11] Daniel Balderston, *El precursor velado: R.L. Stevenson en la obra de Borges* (Buenos Aires: Sudamericana, 1985), p. 121.

characters with whom we have far less in common than with the first-person narrators of "El otro" and "Veinticinco agosto 1983".

The second function of the opening sequence of the latter story is to dramatize the encounter between the narrator and his older self by situating it just after the older man has swallowed a mortal dose of the substance which will bring about his death. The imminence of the demise of the octogenarian "Borges" adds an element of suspense and perhaps also of pathos, which is absent from "El otro". The knowledge that the subsequent dialogue prefigures, not merely the narrator's future life, but also his stoical, emotionally detached death, is a very important factor in our response to the story. Suicide is nothing if not a negative comment on existence. The death of the narrator's older self — his own future willed self-destruction — inevitably carries with it the idea of growing indifference to, or disgust with, life in the labyrinth. We are reminded of "Utopía de un hombre que está cansado" (II, 531-35), which also ends with suicide, and of Borges' comment on the honesty and melancholy which characterize it in the epilogue to *El libro de arena*.

The first section of "Veinticinco agosto 1983", then, associates ontological doubt — insecurity with regard to the self — and suicide. Readers of Unamuno's *Niebla* will recall a similar association in that novel, though we cannot be quite certain whether in that case Augusto Pérez actually killed himself. What is important is that both writers saw a possible relationship between the two. The difference is that Unamuno makes his point at the end of the novel, while Borges makes his at the beginning of his tale. Thus before the "older" Borges is allowed to die, the whole idea of suicide on metaphysical grounds has to be reinforced in order to attenuate the reader's natural resistance to it. In "Utopía de un hombre que está cansado" Borges uses other means, granting his people of the future a vastly prolonged natural life, while at the same time suggesting that, as in the case of the troglodytes in "El inmortal", this leads to a growing sense of unhappy awareness which gradually erodes the impulse to go on living. Agheana's interpretation of "Utopía de un hombre que está cansado" is falsified, among other reasons, by his determination to see the picture which the narrator carries away with him as a symbol of hope.[12] Given the solitude and aimlessness of the lives of the individuals in that story, we have no difficulty in accepting their refusal to have more than one child and their eventual rejection of

[12] Agheana, pp. 232-36.

life. They are quite different from us, as the whole of the dialogue in the story emphasizes, but in "Veinticinco agosto 1983" the octogenarian "Borges" belongs to the familiar here and now. Hence we need more to convince us that his action is justifiable.

The second sequence of the story reinforces the first in two different ways. On the one hand, we are given to understand that the origin of the present situation of the two characters is to be found in a story roughed out much earlier in the very hotel of which the narrator is dreaming. In that story a "Borges", younger than either of those whom we have just met, imagines his own suicide in room 19 of the same building. The idea of "life" allowing itself to be contaminated by "literature" and the consequent implication of the unreality of the former produce an extremely interesting use of *mise en abîme* with unusual causal implications. On the other hand, the second sequence of the story suddenly undermines our sense of time and space. The narrator believes himself to be in 1960 and in Adrogué, where the draft of the earlier story has been written. His older self, however, asserts that the hotel has long been demolished, that the time is 1983 and that the place is Borges' home in the calle de Maipú in Buenos Aires. Logically speaking, that is, the old man, as he drifts into death in Buenos Aires, is visited by a younger self who is under the illusion, suggested by an earlier piece of writing, that the visit is taking place in Adrogué. But the crucially important point is that the story is told, not from the point of view of the older man, but in the first person, from the standpoint of the younger figure. This is precisely so that the reader can participate fully in his growing realization that he is utterly mistaken in his assumptions with regard to time, space and the unity of his personality. It is the life-threatening impact of this realization on the narrator, and through him on us, that constitutes the reinforcement of the theme of the "double". The occurrence at the end of the second sequence of the phrase "somos dos y somos uno" (we are two and we are one), echoing the phrase from the first sequence "somos dos y somos el mismo" (we are two and we are the same), indicates clearly the relation of dependence of the two sequences. To lose confidence in our ability to know where, when and who we are is to take a long step towards losing confidence in the value of life.

The third sequence in the tale deals ostensibly with the future literary career of the younger "Borges". Its true theme is, of course, the futility of literary creation. This is seen as simply another of the "misfortunes" (which include loneliness and blindness) still in store for the younger figure. Travel, it is implied, will provide a welcome distraction. But movement through space cannot alter the misfortunes characteristic of the human condition. The key sentence is the one containing the reference to Keats, "cuyo nombre, como el de todos, fue escrito en el agua" (*VA*, 15) (whose name, like that of all of us, was written on water). The water is that of the river of time, which washes away all things, including literary achievements. It is not failure to produce a masterpiece which has led the older "Borges" to his decision to kill himself. Rather it is awareness of the pointlessness of having done so, along with age and the growing sense it brings of life's repetitiousness, which became "uno de los caminos que me llevaron a esta noche" (*VA*, 16) (one of the roads which have led me to this night). Here we have the second stage of the process of intensification designed to ram home the motivation for the suicide which creates the story's dramatic effect.

We perceive a difference between the two stages. The references to time and place are in the end references to abstractions. The real punch of the story grows out of the idea that even in our own lifetimes we possess no enduring self. We are "one" with ourselves in a crude sense. But we are also "two" in the sense that we are different from any of our past selves. This, the aspect of the tale which is related to the self, not to time or space (though both are involved with it), is the true source of the story's disturbing nature. In the second stage an important element in the reinforcement process is that what is emphasized is the futility of the narrator's own life-work. We are all subject to the threat of the possibly illusory nature of time, space and ourselves; but we are not all the major writer whom the narrator is represented to be. Denial of the ultimate validity of literary creation strikes more directly at him than was the case in the story's first stage.

The process of coming closer to the focalized individual is completed in the last stage of the story, which ends with the death and disappearance of the older "Borges". The ultimate cause of his suicide is revealed to be his conscious abhorrence of much of his own self. To ontological insecurity, doubt about the correspondence of our sense-impressions to anything beyond them and even the futility of creative effort, is finally added the realization that the double is not simply a former or future self, and not (as in Stevenson) a morally different self, but that it may become a caricature — or perhaps an unbearable revelation — of the real nature of the present self, a reflection in time's ironic mirror of those aspects of our personality which we have secretly come to detest.

The quotation from Virgil's *Aeneid* alluded to at the end of the story — "Noctes atque dies patet atri ianua Ditis" (Night and day the door of darkest Dis stands open) — brings "Veinticinco agosto 1983" to a close on the same note as "Utopía de un hombre que está cansado". The narrator is left momentarily contemplating what is both the fulfilment of a story written years before and the pre-figuration of his own suicide twenty-three years later. Had the story been told from the viewpoint of the older "Borges" as a third-person narrative, this would have been the uncanny aspect: a suicide, on his deathbed, is permitted a last dream in which to reveal to a younger self the latter's future life and melancholy destiny. Even taking into account the dream element, this would be a simple metaphor of determinism. But the story we are reading is focalized on the younger man. Where is he? He believes himself to be in Adrogué, but the actual suicide appears to be taking place in Buenos Aires. When is he dreaming this experience? He believes the year to be 1960, but he has been projected into 1983. Who is he? He believes himself to be an autonomous being, but it is clear that he is inseparable from his older self. Above all, what is happening to him? He cannot merely be a figure in the older man's dying dream-fantasy; for, if that were so, he would disappear at the instant of the latter's death, just as Averroes does at the end of "La busca de Averroes". Nor is it intended to be wholly convincing to take the story as a dream in the narrator's mind. For if so, why should he get the place wrong? And why should each of the two figures in the tale stubbornly insist that it is he who is dreaming the episode? As the story itself tells us: "... lo fundamental es averiguar si hay un solo hombre soñando o dos que se sueñan" (*VA*, 14) (the fundamental thing is to find out if there is one single man dreaming or two who are dreaming each other). The only possible answer is also given us: "Somos dos y somos uno" (*VA*, 14) (We are two and we are one). Each is simultaneously dreaming the other; hence the discrepancies. But each is part of the same man. Instead of a metaphor of determinism what we have is a metaphor of the incomprehensible and illusory nature of reality, whether psycho-logical or external to our own minds. Life is a dream — our experiences are all dreams, so the final climactic sentence of the story tells us — but it is a deeply baffling dream.

CHAPTER 6

INTERLUDES AND INLAID DETAILS

We saw, in an earlier chapter, that a feature of Borges' earlier tales was a lack of interaction among the different segments of the stories. Subsequently we recognized a noteworthy example of interaction in that which exists between the frame story and the core element in certain of the mature stories. The opposite of framing is, naturally enough, the incorporation into the text of passages which allude to the meaning of the story by which they are surrounded. That is to say, just as frames interact with what they enclose, incorporated features interact with what encloses them. Let us look at some examples.

Interludes

One of the more elusive aspects of Borges' narrative strategy is his use of interludes. The difficulty for the reader is the same as in the case of framing devices: we remain unsatisfied until we have worked out a connection between the interlude and the theme. A typical instance is presented by "La busca de Averroes" (II, 69-76). At the surface level the story is about Averroes trying to understand the meaning of the terms "tragedy" and "comedy" inside a culture, Islam, which had no conception of drama. At a broader level the story could be regarded as containing a metaphor of the difficulty for each one of us of breaking out of our construct of reality. Related to these others, there is another meaning more directly relevant to Borges himself as the writer of the tale.

The structure is comparatively straightforward. The problem is posed to Averroes early, as he prepares his commentary on Aristotle.

Later he is offered two clues to the answer: the children acting out a little scene in the street outside and a description by a traveller, Abulcásim, of a theatrical performance in China. But Averroes, trapped inside his own culture, which he is convinced is all-encompassing, is unable to see that these clues point to the solution of his difficulty. For him Islam is a construct which he accepts uncritically, but which betrays him because it is reductive and lacks the concepts which he needs. So far, we meet with no major difficulty. If anything, we recognize that the difficulty presents itself to Borges as the author: how is he to postpone the second clue offered to Averroes so that it does not tread too rapidly on the heels of the first? For this would trivialize the tale and cast doubt on the intelligence of the protagonist. In fact, Borges introduces an interlude of discussion between the mentions of the first clue and the second, while a further interlude of discussion separates Abulcásim's account of the Chinese playhouse and Averroes' return home after hearing it. What is the function of these two passages?

We notice that the first interlude is linked to the beginning of the tale by Averroes' interest, not so much in Aristotle as in Plato. In the course of writing a minor polemical work, he argues that God knows only the archetypal — "las leyes generales del universo" (II, 69) (the general laws of the universe) —, not the individual. For him, it is as if the divine mind contained only platonic Ideas, not their particular manifestations in everyday reality. In this first interlude he also thinks of the original of the Koran as the platonic Idea of the Koran. By contrast, the second interlude is linked to the end of the story, since it is concerned with the repetition or reuse of poetic tropes, in this case a simile. At the end Borges' narrator explains that he has chosen the story of "La busca de Averroes" in preference to other similar stories of vain quests, because it is more "poetic". It would seem to follow that the function of the first interlude has to do with the presentation of Averroes, while that of the second has to do more with Borges' reflections on himself as the narrator of the tale.

The first interlude opens with an irony. Challenged to affirm or deny his belief in the existence of a species of rose whose petals display a verse from the Koran, Abulcásim, the traveller, prevaricates. But Averroes dismisses the notion with polite incredulity. Borges craftily associates Averroes' scepticism on this point with that of Hume, who preceded Kant in casting doubt on the adequacy of our mental categories for understanding reality in any depth. The irony lies in the fact that Averroes is able to bring a pre-Humeian scepticism to bear on this case of superstition, but is unable to bring it to bear on the supposed all-inclusiveness of the culture within which he lives. He rejects a lesser superstition, only to accept unconsciously a greater one.

The second part of the first interlude reveals that Averroes is doubly at variance with Aristotle, part of whose teaching is that there is no true science other than that which is concerned with individual phenomena. By denying knowledge of these last to God, and by admitting that the original of the Koran, the ultimate source of all Islamic knowledge, is something like a platonic Idea in God's mind, Averroes is adopting a stance which not only prevents him from recognizing the meaning of the clues which are offered to him, but also precludes him from understanding why he is unable to move towards such a perception. He is in the paradoxical position of trying to understand Aristotle and prepare a commentary on his work from a standpoint which is in complete defiance of Aristotle's own views.[1] His position is a metaphor of human intelligence in general as Borges sees it. For our minds are not only limited by our specific culture, but may well be trying to decipher a world which they are not, as it were, "programmed" to comprehend. The interlude functions, then, as a commentary on Averroes' difficulty, expanding its significance to include not only cultures other than Islam, but also possibly the inherent limitations of the human intellect itself.

The second interlude introduces a concept which is dear to Borges and fundamental, as he has often stressed, to his evolution as a poet. That is, his discovery, after his early avant-garde phase, that the pleasure of poetry does not reside in its power to astonish the reader with novel and unexpected images. Rather, Borges came to believe, there is only a handful of enjoyably familiar metaphors, on which poets ring endless changes. Thus, what characterizes great poetry is not renewal, but subtle repetition, linking images with earlier associations connected to them. The function of this second interlude is to prepare the tale's conclusion. There a narrator who is indistinguishable from Borges himself completes the circle of reasoning which the story contains. Averroes' vain attempt to understand Aristotle's ideas about theatrical genres offers a metaphor of man. He is imprisoned within the bounds of his contemporary culture, as well as possibly within the bounds of inherent mental

---

[1] See Jaime Rest, *El laberinto del universo: Borges y el pensamiento nominalista* (Buenos Aires: Fausto, 1976), esp. pp. 54-58.

categories which do not correspond to the reality outside the mind. Borges' vain attempt to understand Averroes is a repetition of that metaphor, and it gathers poetic force from its association with the earlier one.

The structure of the tale, then, is: introduction > problem > clue > first interlude > clue > second interlude > false solution > conclusion. The interludes function as specific commentaries on features of the story and contribute additional depth of meaning.

A similar technique is used in "La escritura del Dios" (II, 86-90). Like "Funes el memorioso", "El inmortal" and "El Aleph", it is a tale of ironic wish-fulfilment. In each of these stories the central character enjoys the gratification of one of man's deepest desires — total recall, everlasting life, the vision of all things — only to discover that the gift is, in fact, a curse. Tzinacán, like the "Borges" of "El Aleph", is granted an anti-beatific vision; like the "Borges" of "El Zahir", he comes into possession of the absolute. In each case the result is horror. The existence of this group of stories illustrates Borges' often repeated remark that he had only a few stories to tell; they are all, in this case, variations of the same story of the vanity of human wishes. If accepted, this casts doubt on the suggestions, by Pérez and Sosnowski for example, that the ending of the story can be read in a positive sense, as signifying pantheistic union with the cosmos, or a successful search for the divinity.[2] A positive interpretation of Tzinacán's vision destroys the irony of the story. More convincing is the view of Barrenechea and Christ that Tzinacán's perception is crushing because it is a perception of futility.[3] But in what sense? The clue is to be found in "La busca de Averroes" when the Arab philosopher discovers his own unreality in the face of "lo crasamente infinito, [...] el mero espacio, [...] la mera materia" (II, 73) (the crassly infinite, [...] mere space, [...] mere matter). Similarly what crushes Tzinacán is a vision of the futile infinity of time and space symbolized in its circularity. This is why he sees it as a wheel (turning for ever, but going nowhere). The total lack of purposiveness revealed by the vision destroys any possible object which the deciphering of the God's script might have had.

What is the function, within this scenario, of the interlude: Tzinacán's enigmatic dream of dreams within dreams and suffocating

    [2] Alberto C. Pérez, *Realidad y suprarrealidad en los cuentos fantásticos de Jorge Luis Borges* (Miami: Universal, 1971), p. 166; Saul Sosnowski, "'The God's Script': A Kabbalistic Quest", *Modern Fiction Studies*, 19 (1973), 381-94.
    [3] Barrenechea, *Borges the Labyrinth Maker*, p. 89; Christ, *The Narrow Act*, p. 200.

grains of sand? Sosnowski interprets the dream as relating to a non-human world; but this seems arbitrary. Alazraki suggests that the content of the dream bears little relation to the rest of the story;[4] but this would be a contradiction of Borges' normal practice, since everything in his tales is meaningful. Three features characterize the interlude. The first is its position immediately following Tzinacán's clearest expression of his aspiration (II, 88). He longs for one single divine word in which all is enunciated but — and this is crucial — carrying with it "la plenitud": total fulfilment. The second factor characterizing the interlude is the contrast between it and the newly-defined aspiration of the Aztec priest. The aspiration is expressed as the outcome of conscious rational reflection; the key words are "Consideré [...] Consideré [...] reflexioné" (I considered [...] I considered [...] I reflected). The interlude, however, involves something neither rational nor conscious. It is a dream; in fact, like dreams in Borges generally, a vision: essentially the same vision as the one which now follows and is its conscious form. Thirdly, Tzinacán's happy return from it to his prison-cell, which he blesses because it is less frightful to be there than to dream, prefigures his decision at the end of the tale to remain in prison rather than pronounce the phrase which he has deciphered.

The interlude is thus the crucial point in the strategy of "La escritura del Dios": the point at which longed-for plenitude is replaced by horror, at which the will to perceive meaning and purposefulness gives way to the perception of meaningless futility. We are told specifically that *"lo infinito [...] es el número de los granos de arena"* (II, 89) (*the infinite [...] is the number of the grains of sand*). The grains of sand in turn symbolize the infinite regression of dreams within dreams which is the true description of man's never-ending attempts to confer meaning on his experience. The interlude, that is, is an expanded version of Averroes' reaction to the "crassly" infinite: a sense of his own unreality. Its function is to point up the irony of the tale: what the rational mind deludes us into comfortably accepting is negated by a deeper level of perception. It comments on the aspiration expressed in the preceding paragraphs. At the same time it is designed to prevent the climax of the story, the anti-beatific vision, from contradicting too brusquely and clumsily the promise of plenitude proffered by the hope of a divine answer to human

---

[4] Jaime Alazraki, "Estructura y función de los sueños en un cuento de Borges", *Iberoromania*, New Series, 3 (1975), 9-38.

aspiration. Like the interludes in "La busca de Averroes", it is both meaningful in itself and structurally important; but not in quite the same way. For the former story belongs to the class of those in which there is a certain shift of emphasis (in this case, from the situation of Averroes to the cognate situation of the narrator). The two interludes, with their separate functions, underline the shift. By contrast, "La escritura del Dios" belongs rather to the category explored by Alazraki in the above-cited article, in which the later part of the tale contradicts, distorts or inverts the beginning. In both categories the critical moment is the transition.

One of Borges' later stories, "El Evangelio según Marcos" (II, 424-29), also contains a baffling interlude. In the tale a young man on a farm is taken by a peasant family, the Gutres, to be a sort of Christ and is crucified by them. In the interlude a virginal young girl who lives with the Gutres comes to Espinosa, the young man, the night before his crucifixion and sleeps with him. Borello, in his excellent article on the tale, describes it as representing "una de las mayores dificultades interpretativas del cuento" (one of the greatest inter-pretative difficulties of the tale).[5] "El Evangelio según Marcos" is largely a deliberate parody of the New Testament account of Christ's passion. The key sentence in it is Espinosa's reflection:

> ... los hombres, a lo largo del tiempo, han repetido siempre dos historias: la de un bajel perdido que busca por los mares mediterráneos una isla querida, y la de un dios que se hace crucificar en el Gólgota.
> (II, 427)

> (... men, down through time, have always repeated two stories: that of a lost ship seeking a beloved island amid the Mediterranean seas, and that of a god who has himself crucified on Golgotha.)

In this archetypal story, that is, there are two elements: one Christian, one classical. The classical one comments ironically on the Christian one. The suggestion is that all men seek a haven, a refuge from the endless, aimless journey of life, symbolized by the wanderings of Ulysses. They seek, in other words, something that confers purposiveness and direction on what is otherwise mere movement. As we have seen, they may find it, like Asterion and Zur Linde, in conscious adherence to a principle of evil. Alternately, they may find it in acceptance of a divinity and its dictates. The implication of "El Evangelio según Marcos" is that, in the latter case,

---

[5] Rodolfo Borello, "El evangelio según Borges", *Revista Iberoamericana*, 100/101 (1977), p. 511.

man is impelled to degrade and destroy that which promises fulfilment. It is also implicit both that the divinity itself is the creation of man's aspiration to transcendence and meaningfulness, and that whatever incarnates or manifests the divine collaborates passively in its own destruction (the form of words "has himself crucified", rather than, say, "whom they crucify", seems significant).

As Borello rightly indicates, Borges' strategy here is to allude to similarities between Espinosa and Christ while at the same time preserving the fundamental differences which generate the tale's savage irony. The most basic of these differences concern Espinosa's beliefs and his sexuality. He is a freethinker, who at first reads the Bible to the Gutres as a kind of experiment. More especially he accepts carnal relations with the girl who comes to him. Wheelock suggests that Borges is deliberately reducing the incident to the level of "the human sacrifices of primitive peoples".[6] The girl offers herself as if Espinosa were the victim of an Aztec ritual killing, before which the individual chosen for immolation was granted a period of luxury and sexual gratification. Borello stresses the ritual aspect of the girl's behaviour and offers a variety of human and allegorical motivations for her action, including the hypothesis that she may in some way symbolize the Holy Spirit. This last seems rather far-fetched.

What we must notice is that the incident is the last significant event in the tale before the crucifixion itself. It climaxes the ambiguous presentation of Espinosa. To appreciate its importance we need only consider what the effect on the tale would have been if Espinosa, instead of accepting the girl's sacrifice of her virginity, had gently and delicately declined it. The balance of Christ-like and non-Christ-like aspects of his presentation would have been upset and the irony of the concluding episode of crucifixion would have been seriously compromised. It is because the presentation of Espinosa finishes on an all-too-human note, rather than on one of idealization, that the ending achieves its full impact. At the allegorical level, on the other hand, we notice that Espinosa both commits the sin of Adam and

---

[6] Carter Wheelock, "Borges' New Prose", in *Prose for Borges*, ed. Charles Newman and Mary Kinzie (Evanston: Northwestern Univ. Press, 1972), p. 365. David T. Haberly, in "The Argentine Gospels of Borges", *Bulletin of Hispanic Studies*, 66 (1989), 47-54, a fascinating article, relates the interlude to the fact that the Gutres are cattlemen and suggests that "it is to improve the breeding stock that the family's daughter is sent to mate with Baltasar" (p. 52). But as breeders they would know that one contact would probably not be enough and in any case it hardly fits with the Gutres' identification of Baltasar with Christ.

redeems it, which relates him appropriately both to the humanity and to the divinity of Christ. Finally, since the tale is connected with the theme of eternal repetition, in this episode Espinosa may be seen as a "God" impregnating a virgin and thus symbolically begining the cycle again. However we interpret it, the interlude is of key importance.

In an article on another late tale, "El Congreso" (II, 469-84), which describes an attempt to create a body which would be representative of the entire cosmos, Cortínez identifies "tres escenas, narradas morosamente, sin relación directa con el asunto central" (three scenes told quite slowly, with no direct relevance to the central issue).[7] Later he specifies: "Me refiero a los episodios con el cuchillero frente al burdel, las breves vacaciones en la estancia de Glencoe y los amores de Ferri en Inglaterra" (I refer to the episodes with the knife-fighter in front of the brothel, the brief holiday on Glencoe's ranch and Ferri's love-affair in England).[8] His conclusion is that "Los tres episodios sirven un mismo propósito: mostrar en acción a los dos personajes principales, revelar sus respectivos temples anímicos" (The three episodes serve the same aim: to show the two principal characters in action, to bring out their respective personality traits).[9] Cortínez, that is, relates the three interludes essentially to the major characters of "El Congreso". His argument is cogent, based as it is on Borges' own confession that he was better at imagining plots than at delineating characters and that here he needed the interludes in order to bring the main characters alive. Cortínez challenges us to ignore these interludes and thereby recognize how much weaker the characters of Ferri, the narrator, and Glencoe, the leading spirit of the enterprise, are without them. No doubt. But his remarks do not directly address the content of the interludes themselves. Nor do they take into consideration the order in which they appear. When these are examined, it seems possible, as in other stories, to relate them to the theme of "El Congreso" quite as much as to the characterization.

The episode outside the brothel in the calle de Junín stands apart from the other two and is granted slightly more prominence, while the second and third interludes appear to complement each other. To understand their function we must first glance at the tale's thematic

[7] Carlos Cortínez, "Hacia el éxtasis: 'El Congreso' de Borges", *Hispanic Review*, 54 (1986), p. 313.

[8] ibid., p. 320.

[9] ibid.

content with which they interact. Early on we pick up the crucial reference to John Wilkins, recalling that Pierre Menard had studied him and that Borges devotes an essay to him in *Otras Inquisiciones*. Wilkins' aim was to overcome the arbitrary connection between the linguistic sign and its referent, that is, to systematize the expression of our perceptions of reality by means of an artificial language. In Borges' essay, this endeavour first provokes his ridicule and then leads to some of his clearest and most unambiguous statements about man's inability to classify reality, since we do not know what "the universe" — the reality of ourselves and our surroundings — is. The reference to Wilkins, then, prefigures the "revelation" granted to Glencoe at the climax of the story. He, like Wilkins, had harboured the illusion of reducing the universe to a "representative" Congress. But time brings him the recognition, long vouchsafed to Borges, that reality is totally heterogeneous and eludes all systematic classification.

The end of "El Congreso", it is worth emphasizing, does not contradict the end of "El Aleph". The happy band of individuals, who symbolize their endorsement of Glencoe's revelation by driving round Buenos Aires revelling in the variety of sights and sound which it offers, do not contemplate the whole of reality. Their protective screening-mechanism is not, as was the case with the narrator in "El Aleph", suddenly converted into a tragic vision of all things. Hence their song. The abandonment of the attempt to systematize and classify reality is attended with a sense of release and euphoria. But the only remaining choice is to recognize that, behind the richness and variety of what the group sees during its drive, lies mere chaos. Here we may recognize the relevance of the first interlude. Just as the writers of the Generation of 1898 in Spain questioned everything except the ethical criterion, so Borges questions our most cherished assumptions, but excludes from his questioning the value of courage. The importance of the calle de Junín episode, in which the narrator defies a dangerous bully, lies in the implication that *even if* (as the members of the Congress discover) we live in a world which our minds cannot enclose — and which may be no more than "un infinito juego de azares" (I, 447) (an infinite interplay of chance) —, courage remains an absolute. We may temporarily screen out awareness, as the members of the Congress do in their moment of joy at the end, but when blind chance puts us to a test and the insight against which we have shielded ourselves is reaffirmed, courage is our chief resource. This is how the first and most important interlude is to be read *vis--vis* the full significance of the ending.

To suggest, as Wheelock does, that this and the other interludes in "El Congreso" are superfluous is to be over-hasty.[10] More especially as Borges highlights the first interlude by alluding to it in the very first sentence, when Alejandro Ferri is at pains to disclaim the glorious and warlike associations of his given name and surname. Why else should the tale begin this way? Why else at the end of the first paragraph (always so important in a Borges story) should the author deliberately bring together chance and courage, if not to hint at the significance of the interlude to come? It thus interacts both with the opening and the close of the story. Ferri's act of courage, thrown into relief by Eguren's pusillanimity, is an event amid the blind flux of other events; but it is one which Borges deliberately privileges. And not just for what it tells us about Ferri.

The other two interludes seem to function reciprocally. The first, the visit to Glencoe's ranch in Uruguay, stresses primitivism, masculinity and solitude. The second, Ferri's trip to London and his encounter (in the British Museum!) with Beatriz Frost, has associations of culture, femininity and the love-relationship which for a time conquers solitude. It is hard to avoid the conclusion that the Uruguayan episode alludes to America, while the London one alludes to Europe. Inevitably the grand old theme of the struggle between civilization and barbarism in Latin America hovers in our minds. Can we discern a relationship between these two carefully paired interludes and the rest of the story? Although they concern Ferri, while the revelation at the end is granted to Glencoe, we must view all three interludes as in some way forming a commentary on the latter's moment of insight. We have seen that this is possible in the case of the calle de Junín episode. In that of the other two interludes the clue seems to lie in their central events. In the first we learn of the "cambio total que se había operado en don Alejandro [Glencoe]" (II, 477) (the complete change that had come about in Don Alejandro). In the second, as Ferri is vainly seeking an appropriately universal language for the Congress, he falls in love. Each event is unexpected and faintly ironic. The man of thought who appears to have evolved the abstract intellectual concept of the Congress suddenly reveals himself as a patriarchal rural landowner. Ferri, sent on an intellectual mission, experiences the revelation of love and sexual fulfilment, a strikingly rare experience for a Borgesian

[10] Wheelock, "Borges' New Prose", p. 388.

character. In one case strength of character and in the other the overwhelming impact of love are set beside mere intelligence. On the ranch the symbol of this last is the grotesque amphitheatre (never to be used or even completed) a-building in the empty landscape. In London its symbol is the grotesque pseudo-language conceived by Wilkins. Each satirizes intellectual constructs and the abstractionist tendency behind the postulate that a classification of the real can be based on the notion of archetypes. While it may be granted that the story might have been more satisfying if the narrator, with whom we are more identified, and not Glencoe, had been the recipient of the final revelation, it nevertheless remains true that each of the two paired interludes contains a "revelation" which indirectly prefigures the climactic one.

Inlaid Details

A second important incorporated feature in some of Borges' short stories is the use of "inlaid details". At the beginning of "El inmortal", for instance, the narrator, as we have seen, refers to the city of Thebes in ancient Egypt as "Tebas Hekatómpylos", and a little later calls the Nile the "Egypt". At the end of the story a narrator, who is at once the same and subtly different since he now incorporates the experiences of later incarnations, explains that for a Roman such as Marcus Flaminius Rufo these terms would be anachronistic. They are, in fact, characteristic, not of the speech of a tribune in Diocletian's army, but of the terminology used by Homer. Their function at the beginning of the tale is to suggest from the outset what we learn to be the case at the end: that Rufo and Homer (together with Cartaphilus and Borges) are one and the same. They are, in short, details of the kind that Borges specifically referred to when, in an interview with Irby, he remarked that "La muerte y la brújula" and "El jardín de senderos que se bifurcan" contained "muchas cosas (many things) 'worked in, inlaid'".[11] Christ defines them as details which "correspond to other details and therefore in a certain sense predict or predetermine subsequent events".[12] That is, we recognize in them major details which have been deliberately introduced, like the interludes, in order to perform a special function

[11] Irby, *Encuentro con Borges*, p. 26.
[12] Ronald Christ, "Forking Narratives", *Latin American Literary Review*, 7, no. 14 (1979), p. 57.

in relation to the story's meaning or its structure. As the word "inlaid" implies, they are usually half-hidden and designed not to attract attention at first sight. Only on a second or subsequent reading do we usually perceive their importance. It follows, therefore, that the ones mentioned above are unusual in that they are explained. Normally we have first to recognize them (as belonging to a different category from other details) and then to evaluate their function for ourselves. It is a task which requires nice discrimination, especially since, as Klein has pointed out, there are occasional details (such as the torture of the red-haired slave girl by black-haired ones in Averroes' harem) which appear to be deliberately intended to look like inlaid details but which probably do not function as such.[13]

In certain cases repetition assists us in recognizing Borges' intention. This is the case with a class of inlaid details which function as signals to the reader to arrest his attention. The most common of these is the use of the words "vértigo" (dizziness) or "vertiginoso" (dizzying), one of which tends to appear whenever we reach a crucial passage in a given story. Early examples of the latter occur in *Historia universal de la infamia* when it is used to describe the story of the New York gangs described at the beginning of "El proveedor de iniquidades Monk Eastman" (I, 265), the plains of Arizona in "El asesino desinteresado Bill Harrigan" (I, 271) and the desert of Khurasan in "El tintorero enmascarado Hákim de Merv" (I, 285). These uses of the word prefigure the description of Babylon in "La lotería en Babilonia" as "un país vertiginoso donde la lotería es parte principal de la realidad" (I, 442) (a dizzying country where the lottery is a major part of reality) and Ts'ui Pên's conception of time in "El jardín de senderos que se bifurcan" as "una red creciente y vertiginosa de tiempos" (I, 472) (a growing, dizzying web of times). Probably the first real use of "vértigo" to draw attention to the importance of an event in a story is in the phrase "sentí un vértigo asombrado" (I, 412) (I felt an astonished dizziness) which describes the narrator's reaction to looking through *A First Encyclopaedia of Tlön, Vol. XI* in "Tlön, Uqbar, Orbis Tertius". The word reappears at the climax of "La forma de la espada" in the phrase "a través de negros corredores de pesadilla y de hondas escaleras de vértigo" (I, 489) (through dark nightmarish corridors and deep dizzying stair-cases). In "La muerte y la brújula" the word "vertiginoso" marks the

---

[13] Lucy B. Klein, "Los falsos indicios en la narrativa de Jorge Luis Borges", *Symposium*, 28, no. 2 (1974), 146-53.

beginning of the climax, when Lönnrot is overpowered and disarmed by Scharlach's bodyguards (I, 502). In the second and third paragraphs of "El Sur" (I, 530-31) Dahlmann's entry into and exit from the sanatorium are each associated with three words: "coche" (car), "destino" (destiny) and "vértigo" (dizziness). "Destiny" and "dizziness" are again associated with each other at the end of "El muerto" as Otálora reaches the height of his hubris (II, 28). In the pivotal episode of "Emma Zunz" Emma surrenders to "vértigo" (II, 49). Tzinacán's realization in "La escritura del Dios" that the God's writing can probably be perceived in any created thing is likewise accompanied by "vértigo" (II, 87), as is the wizard's realization of his unreality in "Las ruinas circulares" (I, 439) and the narrator's terrible vision in "El Aleph" (II, 122).

In a similar way the number 1001 tends to recur significantly with associations of unreality: thus, Ashe's volume of the First Encyclopaedia of Tlön has 1001 pages, while Dahlmann carries with him to the South the 1001 stories of *The Arabian Nights*. In "Las ruinas circulares" a bird-call summons the wizard to his task, and in "El Evangelio según Marcos" and "Veinticinco agosto 1983" a bird-call precedes the deaths of Marcos and the octogenarian "Borges". These recurrences are more than simply verbal tics and the habitual reader of Borges comes to recognize them as call-signs identifying important moments in the development of a story.

In other cases the inlaid detail is a one-off effect. We may instance the iron staircase which the student climbs at the beginning of "El acercamiento a Almotásim". Deliberate mention is made of the fact that several of its flights are missing. Why is this so and how does he get to the top? Oddly, no explanation is forthcoming. I have tentatively suggested that, since the tower is obviously symbolic (it is both circular and connected with death), the stair is probably symbolic too.[14] It seems to prefigure the mystical quest on which the student is about to embark. The quest begins with a rational decision: the student "Piensa" (Thinks), "Arguye" (Argues) and at length "Resuelve" (Resolves). Thereafter this "freethinker" unexpectedly resorts to prayer! Reason has led to faith and faith to the mystical quest. But the missing flights in the staircase which led the student to his point of departure seem to suggest that this apparently consistent upward progression involves movements between levels — the rational, the spiritual and the mystical — which are not, in fact,

[14] Donald L. Shaw, *Borges: Ficciones* (London: Grant and Cutler, 1976), p. 20.

readily connected to one another. In a rather similar way the Janus-faced statue in the garden of Triste-le-Roy, which Lönnrot notices near the end of "La muerte y la brújula", is there to alert the reader to the ambiguity of his situation as the pursuer pursued and to the deeper ambiguity expressed in the two names Lönnrot and Scharlach. Occasionally, too, Borges uses tiny inlaid details almost jokingly, as when, for instance, he contrasts the courageous *A*benjacán with the cowardly *Z*aid or the *A*leph with its destroyers, *Z*unino and *Z*ungri, and Daneri's ineffectual lawyer, *Z*unni. Likewise, the fact that the three female figures associated with the memory of Pierre Menard are called respectively *B*achelier, *B*acourt and *B*agnoregio tells us that initially in the story in question Borges is gently pulling our legs.

At the beginning of "El indigno" and "Historia de Rosendo Juárez" there is a curious similarity. In the first we read: "El café ha degenerado en bar" (II, 377) (The café has degenerated into a bar); in the second: "... el almacén [...] ahora es un bar" (II, 383) (the store [...] is now a bar). The detail might pass unnoticed if it were not for the repetition in contiguous tales. As it is, it takes on significance, since each story is about unexpected change. In "Historia de Rosendo Juárez", the reference stands alone, introducing an otherwise flat description of Rosendo, the principal narrator. In "El indigno", on the other hand, it is amplified by two further references. One is to what was once a traditional open vestibule giving on to an inner courtyard, but which is now blocked up and leads only to a lift. The other is to the replacement of Fischbein's bookshop by an antique shop. The amplification is functional. It still emphasizes unexpected change, but highlights that it is change for the worse. The key word is "degenerated": the "degeneration" of the café into a mere bar prefigures the moral degeneration of Fischbein. The inlaid detail, which we recognize when it reappears in the next story, is part of an opening strategy which symbolically announces the theme of "El indigno" before introducing Fischbein or adding the circumstantial information which sets the scene for his confession. The question arises as to why Borges left the similar inlaid detail at the beginning of "Historia de Rosendo Juárez" unamplified, although its function is identical. Clearly he did not wish to repeat the effect too obviously. But perhaps there is also another reason. Fischbein's treachery is more striking, less clearly motivated and hence probably less credible to the average reader. In any case, other things — chiefly entertainment value — being equal, such à reader normally prefers stories of moral elevation to those of moral degeneracy. It is, therefore, appropriate that the prefiguration of the latter should be more emphatic. In essence, however, the technique is plainly the same.

A more significant example is that of the mysterious book in "La Biblioteca de Babel" which the Librarian classes along with the others as "un mero laberinto de letras" (I, 457) (a mere labyrinth of letters"), but whose penultimate page is unexpectedly found to contain the phrase "Oh tiempo tus pirámides" (Oh Time, thy pyramids). This is almost a quotation from the third stanza of Borges' own poem "Del infierno y del cielo", which was written in the same year that "La Biblioteca de Babel" appeared (1942). The poem's first stanza suggests that when the Last Day comes and the dead are raised they will find no Hell in the traditional sense. The second stanza similarly suggests that there will be no Heaven either. The third stanza resolves the mystery:

> cuando el Juicio retumbe en las trompetas
> últimas y el planeta milenario
> sea obliterado y bruscamente cesen
> ¡oh Tiempo! tus efímeras pirámides,
> los colores y líneas del pasado
> definirán en la tiniebla un rostro ...[15]

> (when the Judgement resounds in the last trumpets
> and the age-old planet
> is obliterated and suddenly cease to exist
> Oh Time! your ephemeral pyramids,
> the colours and lines of the past
> will define a face in the dusk ...)

For the righteous, contemplation of that face (which may be one's own) will be paradise; for the evil-doers, hell. In the poem the inference is clear. The pyramids, being among man's oldest monuments, symbolize that which triumphs over time. But in the eye of eternity, of infinite time, they are merely ephemeral. In "La Biblioteca de Babel" Borges removes the adjective (which gives the game away) and leaves the enigmatic phrase. But the inference remains: the infinite swallows up the finite and renders it unreal. Earlier Borges had written in "La perpetua carrera de Aquiles y la tortuga": "*infinito*, palabra (y después concepto) de zozobra que hemos engendrado con temeridad y que una vez consentida en un pensamiento, estalla y lo mata" (I, 192) (*infinite*, an anxiety-producing word [and later concept] which we have rashly engendered

---

[15] Borges, *Obra poética, 1923-1977*, p. 185.

and which once allowed into a thought explodes and kills it). In "Avatares de la tortuga" he repeats that it is "un concepto que es el corruptor y el desatinador de los otros" (I, 199) (a concept which undermines the others and makes them look silly).

Why does Borges introduce into "La Biblioteca de Babel" this very oblique reference to the horror of the infinite by means of an inlaid detail? It has to be related, first, to what follows and, secondly, to the story's ending. What follows is the reference to somewhere in the Library (i.e. the Universe) where the librarians (i.e. people) have renounced any attempt to find an explanation for it and, like their equivalents in "La lotería en Babilonia", accept that the cosmos is no more than "un infinito juego de azares" (I, 447) (an infinite interplay of chance). The last paragraph of the story begins with the sentence "Acabo de escribir *infinita*" (I, 462) (I have just written *infinite*), which suggests that the Library/Universe is infinite and that its only conceivable principle of order would be some form of cyclic recurrence, endlessly (and thereby futilely) repeating itself. The enigmatic inlaid detail, when followed up, leads us to the central inference of "La Biblioteca de Babel": that infinitude in time and space mocks any attempt to understand it from the standpoint of a historical moment: "... toda reducción de origen humano resulta infinitesimal" (I, 460) (any diminution whose origin is human turns out to be infinitesimal). This, ironically, is the "solution", fraught with "tragic projections", to the problem of "uniformity/disconnectedness" which the Librarian had promised in the third paragraph of the tale.

Another illustrative case is that of "Deutsches Requiem". We saw earlier that Zur Linde represents directly, in terms of human experience, what Asterion represents symbolically: a being who has embraced evil, violence and murder as a way of life, not because he is some kind of satanic figure, but because he needs something around which to structure his existence. Unable to find it in a conventional pattern of belief, he finds it in an unconventional one: Nazism. In the third paragraph of the tale he states: "Antes, la teología me interesó, pero de esa fantástica disciplina (y de la fe cristiana) me desvió para siempre Schopenhauer, con razones directas; Shakespeare y Brahms, con la infinita variedad de su mundo" (II, 63) (Previously, theology interested me, but from that fantastic discipline [and from the Christian faith] I was turned aside for ever by Schopenhauer, with direct arguments; by Shakespeare and Brahms, with the infinite variety of their worlds). But this leaves a blank in his mind, which

Nazism fills. He embraces Nazism as a counter-religion to Christianity. At this point, Borges' problem is how to suggest to the alert reader that Zur Linde's story contains a parody of Christian belief without trivializing "Deutsches Requiem" by making the point too explicitly. In Chapter 3 we saw that the epigraph taken from the Book of Job and the reference to Zur Linde's forbear, the theologian and Hebrew-scholar Johannes Forkel (possibly a Jew), constitute a foreshadowing device. Now we notice another technique.

We have already seen that if stories such as "Funes el memorioso" and "El inmortal", in which a boon turns into a curse, are modelled ultimately on tales like that of Croesus, "Deutsches Requiem" follows a different, but equally familiar model, that of a Life of a Saint. Zur Linde is an inverted saint and martyr. He dedicates himself ascetically to evil, mortifying and overcoming what is good in his nature, just as other men had dedicated themselves selflessly to the holy life, treading down and rooting out systematically whatever in their sinful nature was an impediment to following the way of perfection. Zur Linde's development follows the classic stages of the consecrated life: conversion, temptation, martyrdom and apotheosis. It is to this aspect of the story that the inlaid details refer. They involve the instinctive use by Zur Linde of vocabulary and concepts associated with religion: "vocation", "justification", the idea of "new men" and finally his most explicit identification of Nazism with religion when he reflects that, in his own case, "Morir por una religión es más simple que vivirla con plenitud" (II, 64) (To die for a religion is simpler than living it to the full). The climax of this pattern of inlaid details comes with his affirmation that "El nazismo, intrínsecamente, es un hecho moral, un despojarse del viejo hombre, que está viciado, para vestir el nuevo" (II, 65) (Nazism, intrinsically, is a moral fact, a stripping-off of the old man, who is corrupt, to put on the new one). This, in fact, is a half-concealed reference to the Pauline calls to divest ourselves of sin and be renewed in Christ. Thus in *Colossians*, 3.9 we read: "You have put off the old nature with its practices and have put on the new nature", and in *Ephesians*, 4.22: "Put off your old nature which belongs to your former manner of life and is corrupt". Barrientos in particular notices the biblical subtext here but fails to see how the Pauline references supply the ultimate clue to the inner meaning of the story.[16]

---

[16] Juan José Barrientos, *Borges y la imaginación* (Mexico City: Bellas Artes-Katún, 1986) p. 86.

McGrady has shown that "La casa de Asterión" uses biblical references as inlaid details in a very similar way.[17] In the first case the sentence "Cada nueve años entran en la casa nueve hombres para que yo los libere de todo mal" (II, 54) (Every nine years nine men come into the house so that I can deliver them from all evil) contains an implicit allusion to the Lord's Prayer ("Deliver us from evil"), which McGrady interprets as referring in this case to life in general. In the second case we read: "Desde entonces no me duele la soledad, porque sé que vive mi redentor y al fin se levantará sobre el polvo" (Since then solitude does not pain me, for I know that my redeemer lives and at last he will stand upon the earth). Like the epigraph in "Deutsches Requiem", this is an allusion to a famous verse of the *Book of Job* (19.25). In our opening chapter we attempted to show that the story is not concerned with life in general, but with the life of evil, the life of the moral monster. The point of comparison is not "El inmortal", as McGrady contends, but "Deutsches Requiem". Be that as it may, what is to be emphasized is that the technique employed not merely suggests a biblical subtext, but ironically inverts the traditional implications of the words used.

A later example of the use of inlaid details is to be found in "El otro duelo", which tells of two peasant rivals who carry their rivalry right up to the instant of their deaths. At first sight the story appears to contain no more than a macabre anecdote. In general Borges disliked the tendency in Argentine literature to over-idealize the gaucho (and in this case his successors in the countryside). Part of the motivation for his attribution of physical courage and a sense of honour to the dwellers of the slum suburbs of Buenos Aires is the desire to offset the traditional attribution of these qualities chiefly to men of the pampa. At the surface level "El otro duelo" belongs to his tendency to demythicize the latter, which we also recognize in the Uruguayan episode in "El Congreso", the gently satirical comment on paintings of gauchos in "El duelo", and the presentation of the Gutres in "El Evangelio según Marcos".

The two protagonists, who live in the period of the decline of the original rural economy and, of course, are not "true" gauchos, bear no comparison with, for example, the patriotic heroes of Leopoldo Lugones' *La guerra gaucha*. Borges insists that "El concepto de patria les era ajeno" (II, 413) (The concept of the fatherland was foreign to them); that they view killing with indifference and that

[17] McGrady, "El Redentor ...", pp. 533-34.

they lack enough imagination even to experience fear or pity. They are at the opposite extreme from Ricardo Güiraldes' Don Segundo Sombra and the stoical, taciturn, but great-hearted gaucho cowhands with whom he lives and works. They are mere primitives, dominated by petty rivalry and hatred. The climax of their presentation is the incident in which Cardoso begs as a favour to be allowed to cut the throat of a prisoner in order to enjoy a novel sensation. The ending of the story seems to be no more than an illustration of the idea that those who live barbarously may in the end die barbarously. In outline, the pattern of the tale appears to be not unlike that of "El asesino desinteresado Bill Harrigan" in *Historia universal de la infamia*. As in his case, the death of the two rivals is appropriately related to their lives and provokes in the reader only a slight shudder of uneasiness at the reactions of the onlookers.

But as we suggested in relation to *Historia universal de la infamia*, the principal difference between the stories which it contains and the later stories is that the latter carry implications which are all but absent in the earlier ones. In the case of "El otro duelo" these implications seem to be related to those of "El fin", "Abenjacán el Bojarí, muerto en su laberinto" and "Los teólogos". The clue is provided by the sentence "Sin sospecharlo, cada uno de los dos se convirtió en esclavo del otro" (II, 412) (Without suspecting it, each of the two turned into the other's slave). What Borges seems to be saying is that there are cases in which the only way a man can find his identity is by rivalry with another. The concept is related to that most difficult and disquieting of his ideas: the non-existence of the individual personality.

"El otro duelo" hints at this idea. The two peasants, Cardoso and Silveira, have no real identity in the story apart from their long-standing enmity. But whereas in the above-mentioned tales on this theme one of the rivals survives the other, in this case their lives are snuffed out together. The ending, that is, constitutes an ironic comment on the rivalry in the body of the story rather than a development of its now familiar implication. As in other instances, we feel disappointed: until we notice the inlaid details. One of these occurs in the second paragraph: "Hablamos, como siempre, de la entreverada historia de las dos patrias" (II, 411) (We spoke, as always, of the intermingled histories of the two fatherlands). Not, we notice, "of the two countries". This is the first clue to the tale's other deeper implication. Since the narrator's interlocutor, Reyles, was a Uruguayan, the "two fatherlands" in question are Uruguay and

Argentina. As the story advances, this tiny clue allows us to postulate
a parallel between the "intermingled histories" of the two countries
and the rivalry between Cardoso and Silveira. Like the two countries,
their farms are contiguous. As in the case of the two countries, their
quarrels are over trifles, their mutual hostility a sign of rudimentary
civilization. Yet part of the national identity of each fatherland is
derived from its confrontations with the other.

The second inlaid detail appears in the sixth paragraph. The dog
which belongs to Silveira and which Cardoso poisons is called
"Treinta y Tres" ("Thirty-Three"). The reference is, of course, to
"The Immortal Thirty-Three" who in 1825 crossed the River Plate to
begin the movement which liberated Uruguay from Brazilian
domination. Nothing in a Borges story is ever there just by chance.
The name of his dog is there to identify Silveira (as in a sense does his
slightly Brazilian-sounding name) with Uruguay, and thus Cardoso
with Argentina. It is now that the final episode in the story can
assume its full significance. "El otro duelo", that is, alludes not only
to individual identity, but also to national identity. The futile rivalry
of Cardoso and Silveira, who have no identity apart from each other,
alludes to the futile rivalries of Spanish American countries which
are, in fact, much more alike than different. The death of the two
antagonists, each still trying pointlessly to outdo the other, alludes to
the danger of such inter-American rivalries, which threaten both
countries involved, as we see from historical examples like the Pacific
War or the Chaco War. Such an interpretation, based as it is on inlaid
details, does not exclude one based on the absence of individual
identity; it simply extends it. In addition, once we perceive the
hostilities of Silveira and Cardoso in the context of collective
contention, it is not a large step to thinking of them in the context of
the civil war between Uruguay's "White" party and its "Red" one in
the early years of this century, one more instance of futile and
ultimately destructive rivalry.[18]

[18] Borges' comments on "El otro duelo", in *Borges on Writing*, ed. Norman Thomas
di Giovanni, Daniel Halpern and Frank MacShane (New York: Dutton, 1973), pp. 15-
52, are not very helpful. However, he does remark in passing: "Naturally, this story is
wound up with the history of Argentina and of Uruguay" (p. 52).

CHAPTER 7

NARRATORIAL STANCES

From his earliest stories in *Historia universal de la infamia* Borges confronted the problem of authorial authority. Alicia Rivero Potter traces the process of declining confidence *vis-à-vis* the text on the part of some twentieth-century Spanish American authors, showing that it reached a peak towards the end of the Boom with some of the later works of Fuentes and especially with Sarduy.[1] Her chapter on Borges, however, is disappointing. It fails to focus directly on the technical point at issue and concerns itself instead largely with Borges' attitude to inspiration. The real ground was broken in 1973 by Lyon, who, although he does not deal directly with the idea of authorial authority, shows that Borges succeeds both in assuming it and undermining it at the same time, in "El impostor inverosímil Tom Castro" especially. The narrator "knows all the details yet casts doubt on the truth of many things he brings up". Lyon argues that here Borges developed for the first time a narratorial stance which he was to use frequently in the rest of his tales, that of "a type of intruding, non-dramatized, often distant yet familiar first person narrator".[2] The posture is that of a non-omniscient teller of the tale, who often concedes that his account may have been affected by time, lapses of memory, incomplete information or subjective reactions,

[1] Alicia Rivero Potter, *Autor, lector* (Detroit: Wayne State Univ. Press., 1989).

[2] Lyon, pp. 365, 364. Lelia Madrid (who, interestingly enough, does not mention Lyon's indispensable article) attempts, in the second part of her *Cervantes y Borges: la inversión de los signos* (Madrid: Pliegos, 1987), esp. pp. 99-135, to reduce all Borges' narrators to one — unreliable — model which reflects the unreliability of language. Her views are interesting and provocative, but in the end reductive.

while at the same time retaining some sort of hold on the events with which the story deals. Often the narrator, prominent at the beginning of the tale, fades into quasi-anonymity once he has served his purpose, which varies from tale to tale.

The overriding purpose of these first-person narrators is, of course, to invite suspension of disbelief by creating an impression of candour and plausibility. They function as "authenticating devices". At the same time their appearance marks Borges' deliberate avoidance, in contrast to the stance which he sometimes adopts in tales which he chooses to tell ominisciently, of any assumption of privileged vision or insight. This use of the first person is a narratorial stance which parodies or negates the realist tradition of pseudo-objectivity. As we know from "El arte narrativo y la magia" (I, 163-70), what Borges dislikes is the "straight" realist-type story governed by a "causal process" which pretends to be able to show how each event was motivated or came about. For him, such stories project a simplified and ultimately falsified metaphor of life, screening out its mystery and suggesting that it is tidier and more comprehensible than it actually is. Instead of endorsing such a picture of reality, Borges commonly parodies or undermines it. However, he is making fun not just of the "realist" literary convention, but of what underpins it, namely confidence in an explicable universe.[3]

In reality, even in *Historia universal de la infamia*, the narratorial voice is slightly more complex than Lyon suggests. By assuming the role of a mere intermediary, retelling in Spanish stories which already exist in some other language, the narrator obtains a large measure of liberty which he exploits in various ways. If in "El inverosímil impostor Tom Castro" he chooses to show his hand, combining apparently factual information with a deliberate reminder to the reader that "his" (the narrator's) Tom Castro is merely a figment of his imagination, elsewhere the situation is different. The fact that he can write in "El atroz redentor Lazarus Morell": "Copio su narración" (I, 251) (I copy his narrative), in "La viuda Ching, pirata": "Copio algunos artículos" (I, 261) (I copy some articles) or in "El incivil maestro de ceremonias Kotsuké no Suké: "Sigo la relación de A.B. Mitford" (I, 277) (I follow the narration of A.B. Mitford) actually allows Borges all the freedom of an omniscient narrator. We do not know whether the details he mentions at any point are his own inventions or are taken from works which he has

---

[3] See Robert Magliola's perceptive discussion of this point in "Jorge Luis Borges and the Loss of Being", *Studies in Short Fiction*, 15, no. 1 (1978), 25-31.

consulted. But in between the confessed inventor of an imaginary Castro (a "phantom" in spite of being based on historical facts) and the narrator who refers us to sometimes imaginary printed sources as a guarantee of his reliability, there is a shadowy third figure. His voice is heard conjecturing what is presumably not in the sources (or else it would be stated as a fact): "Es verosímil suponer que Morell se negó a la placa bruñida" (I, 247) (It is a likely assumption that Morell denied himself to the polished plate); or more especially inserting authorial commentary of his own, as when reference is made to "El Destino (tal es el nombre que aplicamos a la infinita operación incesante de millares de causas entreveradas)" (I, 256) (Destiny [such is the name we apply to the infinite unceasing operation of thousands of intermingled causes]), or when a distinction is made between "our" hoodlums and those of New York (I, 265), or again when, along with the suggestion that Billy the Kid was the most feared man on the Western frontier, the idea is mooted that he was also probably the most lonely and dehumanized of the frontiersmen (I, 274). In the case of "El incivil maestro de ceremonias Kotsuké no Suké", indeed, such intrusive authorial commentary is even used as the conclusion. This is more than Lyon's "background presence"; it is a hangover from past authorial authority which Borges never entirely relinquishes.

In a later article than Lyon's, Costa takes up the issue afresh with regard to three crucial stories which mark the transition from *Historia universal de la infamia* to *Ficciones*. He points out that we can postulate a clear line of development from "Hombre de la esquina rosada", through "Pierre Menard, autor del *Quijote*", to "Tlön, Uqbar, Orbis Tertius". The first of these tales is a "direct" one in which the narrator is neither a detached voice nor a mere participant in the action, but the actual perpetrator of the assassination of Francisco Real. The second tale employs a narrator who is still an "involved participant" to the extent that he is "an enraptured admirer of the preposterous Pierre Menard", and whose comments and discourse are manipulated so as to create an ironic discrepancy between his outlook and that of Borges, such that the alert reader "realizes that the speaker is someone other than the author". Finally, in "Tlön, Uqbar, Orbis Tertius", "the Narrative 'I' now belongs to someone very much like the signatory of the piece, Jorge Luis Borges".[4]

---

[4] Costa, pp. 194-95.

This suggests that we can situate Borges' narrators along a spectrum which starts from true, impersonal, omniscient narrators, such as those of "El Sur" and "Emma Zunz". Next come a variety of what Lyon calls "personalized yet unrestricted" narrators, like those of "Funes el memorioso" or the "Borges" of "El Aleph", whose degree of involvement or participation in the story varies considerably. Finally we reach a category of narrators like those of "La lotería en Babilonia", "La Biblioteca de Babel" and "La escritura del Dios", who — at first sight anyway — are quite unlike Borges himself and whom we may term "independent" dramatized narrators.

Omniscient narration usually presents little that is of interest so far as the narrative voice is concerned, unless we can in some way distinguish between the "tone" of the narrative and the broader question of its style. This is not normally the case with Borges. Hence the primary technical consideration with the stories which he tells omnisciently usually concerns their general structural arrangement. It is perhaps worth noting that there are remarkably few omniscient stories in *El informe de Brodie* (only "El Evangelio según Marcos") and *El libro de arena* (only "El espejo y la máscara"), although they had occurred quite frequently in *Ficciones* and *El Aleph*. Whether this is in any way meaningful is open to question. It does seem, however, that with age Borges became more inclined than ever to foreground the fictionality of what we are reading. So much so that "El soborno" actually begins with the words "La historia que refiero ..." (II, 517) (The story which I relate ...), as if to forestall any impulse on the reader's part to confuse it with an account of observed reality.

In fact, omniscient narration presents critics of Borges with the same sort of problem that his careful craftsmanship does. How can we reconcile the depiction of a vision of reality which presents it as chaotic and labyrinthine, with the fact that it is contained in stories which reveal an exceptional degree of formal unity and coherence? It is trifling to respond that we are in the presence of metaphors of the triumph of the "order" of Art over the disorder of life. However much Borges may have longed to write "the poem" which would justify his existence once and for all, he does not seem to have believed for a moment that aesthetic values provided a valid response to metaphysical problems. We are simply faced with a paradox. Similarly with his assumptions of authorial omniscience. For this is essentially connected with the reassuring notion that the world of observed phenomena, including human motivation and behaviour, is explicable, at all events to the privileged vision of authors. This, too, is a notion which Borges certainly did not endorse. So, here we have another paradox. On the one hand, Borges was perfectly clear that reality is mysterious. More than that, he recognized that there was no ultimate relationship between mere words and things, whether or not the latter can truly be said to exist, which is another question. In a sense, then, literature is not about reality, which is not verbal, but is an addition to reality. Yet at the same time (despite some ill-advised critical attempts to do so) it is idle to deny that Borges believed that literature could tell us something meaningful about life and reality, that it could make statements about something other than itself — and, indeed, that he was prepared to assume on occasion the mantle of omniscience to express some of his most important insights.

With this we may turn to some tales in which he adopts a stance of modified omniscience or, as he says in the prologue to *Elogio de la sombra*, tends to "simular pequeñas incertidumbres, ya que si la realidad es precisa la memoria no lo es" (II, 351) (simulate small incertitudes, since if reality is precise, memory is not). Thus, for example, in "El muerto" the body of the tale is recounted entirely omnisciently. With phrases like "Lo inquieta algún remordimiento, eso sí, de no extrañar a Buenos Aires" (II, 25) (He was worried by a certain remorse, undoubtedly, because he did not miss Buenos Aires) or "Otálora comprende que es una broma" (II, 27) (Otálora understands that it is a joke), we find ourselves, so to speak, inside Otálora's mind to a degree that it is clearly impossible to attain in everyday life. And yet, at the beginning, Borges writes: "Ignoro los detalles de su aventura; cuando me sean revelados, he de rectificar y ampliar estas páginas" (II, 24) (I do not know the details of his adventure; when they are revealed to me, I shall have to rectify and expand these pages). It is not quite clear which details have been withheld, if on occasion the narrator has access even to Otálora's thoughts.

This exemplifies Lyon's statement that in certain cases the first-person narrator — initially emphasized in "El muerto" by the phrase "quiero contarles el destino de Benjamín Otálora" (II, 24) (I want to tell you about the destiny of Benjamín Otálora) — afterwards can be seen to have "slipped into anonymity". A more curious example is "La intrusa" (II, 373-76), which marked Borges' return to short-story writing after a gap of thirteen years. A feature of the telling of the tale is that, although it deals with a clash of emotions in each of the Nilsen brothers, there is no direct expression of interior tension in either of them. There is no dialogue as such. The most we are told is that quarrels between the brothers occurred but were not in appearance about the woman, Juliana, whom both of them shared, and that only the briefest discussion preceded her sale to the brothel. The brothers are presented as inarticulate and in any case unwilling to admit the degree of their emotional involvement with the woman, even to themselves. Thus, it is their behaviour, their actions, which are the measure of their emotions. Psychological commentary is reduced to a minimum. Nevertheless, albeit vestigially, it is there. The narrator steps out of his role of reporter of mere events, or of hearsay, or of what the neighbourhood could and did notice, and makes statements which go beyond what an outside observer could normally know: for example, that both men felt humiliated by their love for Juliana. His voice here is the same "third" narrative voice, speaking with virtual omniscience, that we hear occasionally in *Historia universal de la infamia*, "El muerto" and elsewhere.

What is striking in "La intrusa" is how it contradicts the voice which opens the tale. The very first word — "Dicen" (They say) — presents the story as mere hearsay. The first adjective — "improbable" — casts doubt even on the hearsay evidence. The rest of the first paragraph tells us, in addition, that the narrator himself only heard the story at fourth hand, though later he had some apparently independent confirmation of it. In the third paragraph the effect of the first one is expressly re-emphasized when the narrator paradoxically calls on "what we do not know" to buttress our understanding! A series of veils has been deliberately interposed between the reader and anything about to be narrated. The pattern is respected in the first part of the story, where the narrator presents as facts only what onlookers could have seen or known, or collective responses: "El barrio los temía"; "El barrio [...] previó ..." (II, 374) (The neighbourhood feared them; The neighbourhood foresaw ...). But, after the reference to the brothers' "latent rivalry", the narrator's voice begins to hover uneasily between omniscience and qualified knowledge — "Fue entonces, creo ..."; "Acaso, alguna vez, se creyeron salvados"; "Parece que Cristián le dijo ..." (II, 375-76) (It was then, I believe ...; Perhaps, now and then, they believed themselves saved; It seems that Cristián told him ...) —, with the former predominating. Even at the climax the narrator professes some uncertainty about the direction in which the brothers set off in their cart with Juliana's body, but, nonetheless, he tells the rest of the final episode with confident authorial authority. The tone of the ending is thus very different from that of the opening, and it is not clear, here or elsewhere, what we are to make of the contrast.

The narrator begins by denying knowledge of who originated the tale and pointedly all but excludes Eduardo. Yet the details of the ending could presumably only have come from the latter. This being so, the obvious choice for narrator would seem to have been Eduardo himself. But Borges evidently wished to distance the narrative voice from participation in the events, while at the same time granting himself the option of telling certain parts of the tale as if the narrator had actually been, not only present, but privy to the characters' inner reactions. This might have been more justified, perhaps, if the intention had been to tell the tale from a hostile moral standpoint. But, in fact, despite the brothers' revolting actions, moral commentary is as minimal as psychological commentary. It is reduced to the three adjectives "sórdida" (sordid), "monstruoso" (monstrous) and "infame" (infamous). These remove any suggestion of moral complicity between the narrator and the brothers. But they do not alter the fact that the story is told from the standpoint of comprehension of their outlook and sympathy with their sacrifice, rather than criticism of their behaviour.

A different process is visible in "La busca de Averroes", where once more the body of the story is told omnisciently, but this time Borges destroys the illusion at the end by intervening in the first person to stress once more the fictionality of the tale — "En la historia anterior quise narrar el proceso de una derrota" (II, 76) (In the foregoing story I wanted to narrate the process of a defeat) — and to comment both on the writing of it and on one of its major implications. Something similar occurs at the end of "Avelino Arredondo". It begins with a familiarly-phrased rotund statement — "El hecho aconteció en Montevideo, en 1897" (II, 523) (The event happened in Montevideo, in 1897) — and continues with an accumulation of descriptive details of Arredondo's behaviour in his self-imposed solitude, as well as of his thoughts and emotions. None of them, plainly, could have been accessible to direct observation. Either some form of first-person confession, as in "El jardín de senderos que se bifurcan", or third-person omniscience are the obvious options. Borges chooses the latter, but at the end writes: "Así habrán ocurrido los hechos, aunque de un modo más complejo; así puedo soñar que ocurrieron" (II, 527) (This is how the events must have occurred, although in a more complicated way; this is how I can dream that they occurred). Borges first disclaims the omniscience which he has assumed throughout the tale, but claims at least verisimilitude. But then he undermines even this by the use of the verb "dream". The implication is perhaps not that the story (which is based on a historical event) is in some way false, but rather that all human behaviour is ultimately mysterious or that Borges has allowed himself to idealize Arredondo's motivation and behaviour while inwardly realizing that, given human nature, such idealization borders on fantasy. In the cases mentioned, the stories clearly could have been told from end to end as omnisciently as "Emma Zunz" or "El Sur". What is important is that Borges, in these instances, rejects that option. He either forewarns the reader that his assumption of authorial authority is fraudulent or else deliberately destroys the illusion at the end.

An interesting variant is "El hombre en el umbral" (II, 106-11). Although this is not one of Borges' more memorable stories, its use of three narrators is almost unique in his work. At the centre of the tale is an event: in India the corrupt and cruel judge, Glencairn, is himself being judged and condemned to death by his victims. An old Indian is recounting a version of the circumstances to Dewey, a British official, at the very moment that the trial is being conducted nearby. We know this to be the case because, just before the end of his account, the old man is able to alter his assertion that the trial lasted at least nineteen days, to the statement that is lasted exactly nineteen days. He has learned, that is, from a passer-by that Glencairn has just been executed. Dewey in turn tells the tale to the narrator, who tells it to us, the readers. The question which arises is: why do we need this last narrator? What would the story lose without its first paragraph?

The opening paragraph contains a reference to an Indian dagger, which then serves to introduce Dewey, and two very familiar Borgesian ploys. A variant of the first — "Mi texto será fiel" (My text will be a faithful one) — had appeared already in "Funes el memorioso", where the narrator had similarly declared that he would report "truthfully" his dialogue with Funes, and will reappear later, for example, in "La intrusa", where the expresion is "with probity" and in "Undr", where the narrator affirms his version of Adam of Bremen's story to be "worthy of belief". The second ploy denies any intention of dressing up the tale with fictitious, circumstantial (i.e. pseudo-realist) or exotic details. This, too, is not unlike statements made at the beginning of "El muerto" and "El duelo". Both ploys, in effect, amount to pleas for a suspension of disbelief on the reader's part. But suspension of disbelief in relation to what? Not to a first-hand account by the narrator himself, but in this case to the fidelity of his account to Dewey's account. What seems to be another authenticating device turns out to be authenticating only a version of a version. The function of the third narrator, the narratorial voice in the opening paragraph, seems to be that of prefiguring ambiguity under the guise of unadorned accuracy.

This fits in well with the rest of the technique of "El hombre en el umbral". Its deep theme seems to concern Eternal Return. The old Indian appears to be relating a series of events which had taken place many decades previously, but, in fact, he is relating events which are culminating as he speaks, though the clue to this, mentioned above, can easily be overlooked. Once we notice it, however, we are slightly bewildered. We seemed to have "cracked" an aspect of the tale's technique. This is something which in Borges usually brings us a step nearer to some aspect of the tale's meaning, as in "La muerte y la brújula", for instance, when we notice that Scharlach and Lönnrot have names which refer to the same colour. But in this case picking up the clue leaves us bereft of the deep theme of Eternal Return which we had earlier been inclined to posit. As in the first paragraph, Borges has left us guessing. We have to look for another clue.

Not for the only time, Bickel's article, with its emphasis on the order-versus-chaos duality in Borges' work, comes to our aid.[5] Glencairn has imposed an order on the tumult and upheavals of an Indian city, but his was a false order, based on corruption and tyranny. After a while his victims rebel and kidnap him, not only because of his crimes, but also because he has betrayed their feeling that life under the law is better than disorder. With the rebellion, disorder breaks out again, not in the rebellion itself (which requires the orderly co-operation of thousands of the oppressed), but in the "justice" which is now turned against Glencairn. The enormous jury contains Moslem scholars, jurists, Sikhs, Hindus, monks of Mahavira, fire-worshippers and Negro Jews; anyone, that is, except Glencairn's peers. All, moreover, are described as "senseless", while the judge is a lunatic. It is not wholly clear what Borges is suggesting here. But the story does seem to carry the possible implication that in human affairs we swing from the imposition of an "order" which is arbitrary and erratic, inspiring no confidence, to acceptance of the rule of chaos. Some of Borges' best-known remarks concern our inability to

[5] Gisèle Bickel, "La alegoría del pensamiento", *Modern Language Notes*, 88 (1973), 295-316.

understand the world outside ourselves or, indeed, to comprehend our own minds and motivations. We just do not know enough about the way things are to find any true "order" in the universe.

What has this to do with the narrators? The pattern of the tale is that the old Indian gives Dewey an "explanation" which is essentially ambiguous: true in one sense, false in another, it is a metaphor (like Dewey's search through the labyrinthine city with its plethora of false informants) of our inability to reach significant truth. Dewey recounts the circumstances and the "explanation" (apparently much later) to the actual narrator. The best the latter can hope to do is to stay close to his recollections of Dewey's narrative. We are, in other words, at two removes from a "truth" which in itself was partially a deception intended to placate Dewey until the execution was accomplished. The similarity to the opening of "La intrusa" is not casual. It seems likely that we are in the presence of an extended metaphor, this time connected with the pursuit of knowledge, of explanation. The structure of "El hombre en el umbral" — a tale within a tale within a tale —, like the structure of "La casa de Asterión", and the fact that when we reach the centre we reach only ambiguity, seem to offer the clue to the story's deep theme which initially eluded us.

Not all of Borges' narrators by any means are personal. Some of his most interesting ones are not. Among these are the narrators of "La lotería en Babilonia" and "La Biblioteca de Babel". Both are quite extraordinary figures. The former makes a "hurried statement" to an unknown group of listeners addressed as "ustedes" (you) in an unidentified seaport; the latter writes in the back of a book an "epistle" which he regards as already existing somewhere in the Library. The contrasting use which Borges makes of these two narrators makes the former worth a glance because of the light that can be shed on the more developed function of the Librarian.

The narrator in "La lotería en Babilonia" corresponds, at a more fantastic level, to the model described by Lyon. Prominent at the beginning, he fades into impersonality in the middle until he intervenes typically to qualify the reliability of his account with the remark: "... yo mismo, en esta apresurada declaración, he falseado algún esplendor, alguna atrocidad. Quizá, también, alguna misteriosa monotonía" (I, 446) (I myself, in this hurried declaration, have falsified some splendour, some atrocity. Perhaps also some mysterious monotony). He is, in fact, part and parcel of the story's opening strategy. As in "La casa de Asterión", our curiosity is artfully aroused by overhearing a mysterious voice making a series of astounding statements in a completely undramatic tone. But once that effect has been created and its purpose achieved, it is quickly abandoned. The Babylonian becomes a largely neutral reporter. He is involved with his description of the way Babylonian society works since he has experienced the impact of the lottery on his own life: he is, or was, inside the context of that society and, as he insists in the second paragraph, took it utterly for granted. This is a very significant hint to the reader that he, too, takes the world too much on trust and is about to have that trust questioned, but it is the only hint of its kind that the Babylonian drops. In the rest of the tale the pattern of expression moves from first-person testimonial verbs — "he conocido"; "he sido declarado"; "sé que" (I, 441) (I have known; I have been declared; I know that) — to "Mi padre refería" (II, 442) (My father recounted) and soon to the impersonal "Nadie ignora que"; "Algunos moralistas razonaron"; "hay que recordar que"; "es fama que" (II, 443-46) (No-one is unaware that; Some moralists argued; one must remember that; rumour has it that), culminating at the end in the completely detached rehearsal of possible explanations, none of which the narrator himself endorses.

Both the lottery and the Library are in the clearest sense metaphors of human existence. But in the case of the lottery the Babylonian accepts it impassively in spite of its obvious injustice and cruelty. There is no sense of protest, alarm, hope or despair. The tone is flat and controlled. When the Babylonian reports a view, he is offering an aid to understanding, not a criticism. Much of the success of "La lotería en Babilonia", in fact, stems directly from the contrast between the matter-of-fact way in which the narrator tells the tale and the implications of the tale itself.

It is quite different with "La Biblioteca de Babel". Here critical emphasis on the elucidation of the metaphor of reality presented by the Library and its inhabitants has deflected attention from the role and function of the narrator. In answer to Roffé's question: "¿Vd cree que la visión del mundo como un caos es el tema de 'La Biblioteca de Babel'?" (Do you think that the vision of the world as chaos is the theme of "The Library of Babel"?), Borges replied: "Es lo que siento desgraciadamente, pero quizás sea secretamente un cosmos, quizás haya un orden que no podemos percibir; en todo caso debemos pensar eso para seguir viviendo" (Unhappily, it is what I feel, but perhaps secretly it is a cosmos, perhaps there is an order that we cannot perceive; in any case we should think so in order to go on living).[6] Gisèle Bickel, as we have just seen, long ago commented perceptively on this fundamental dualism of Borges' outlook, which swings between accepting chaos and postulating a secret order governing reality. This is what lies behind the narrator's stance in "La Biblioteca de Babel". Unlike the narrator of "La lotería en Babilonia", who is outside Babylon, distanced from it mentally and emotionally uninvolved, the Librarian is inside the Library, close to death after a life of futile peregrinations but, as his "prayer" near the end reveals, desperately anxious still to find some ultimate truth so that "tu enorme Biblioteca se justifique" (I, 461) (thy enormous Library will be justified).

What we find here is not an objective, still less a sceptical narrator. Borges has elaborated a suitable metaphor of a problematic world through his initial description of the Library, in which the architectural pattern and the order of the shelving are counterbalanced by the chaotic incoherence of the books' contents. His next problem is to manipulate the narrator so that the latter's account of the reactions of the inhabitants to their situation both presents a line of argument and at the same time invites us to criticize or reject it. We, the readers, however, are intended to recognize that the Librarian's own outlook and aspirations reflect human delusions which are just as open to question as those which he reports. The contradiction inherent in the Library metaphor is compounded by the contradictions in the narrator's response to it. Uniquely in Borges, the narrator of "La Biblioteca de Babel" is presented as a kind of gently parodic Everyman whose view of life is fraught with errors, illusions and vain hopes similar to those he sees in his fellows.

The process of identifying him with archetypal man is part of the opening strategy of the story. In this case there is no "special effect" pursued at the beginning. The description of the Library itself is sufficiently strange and fascinating to engage our curiosity while at the same time it establishes the theme: the Library as a metaphor of the world. We notice that this description comprises two paragraphs. But they are not successive. The first insists on order, repetition, unchanging pattern. The key words are "invariable" and "identical". On the other hand, the third paragraph, which continues the opening description, insists on chaos, the key expression being "disconnectedness" in contrast to "uniform" a few lines earlier. In between,

⁶ In *Espejo de escritores*, ed. Reina Roffé (Hanover, N.H.: Ediciones del Norte, 1985), p. 11.

man, the Librarian, has already begun his quest. He seeks "a book", perhaps "the catalogue of catalogues", only to discover a tragic enigma. So that even before he has completed his first description of the Library, Borges has already indicated man's yearning for a meaning behind the regularity, a convincing argument from Design to a Designer. The incorporation into the initial account of the Library itself of the quest for an explanation of it symbolizes man's immediate, instinctive need for some kind of certainty.

Here and hereafter, the Librarian has three distinct roles as narrator: he describes the Library; he presents reactions to it on the part of other inhabitants; and he presents his own reactions. We are invited, as in the majority of Borges' best stories, to decipher the metaphor and decide for ourselves what the relationship is between the Library and life as we experience it. To stimulate us to respond to the invitation, the narrator introduces us to a series of interpretations which represent standard ways of cracking the metaphor. Like the beliefs of the inhabitants of Tlön, they tend to be gently mocked; that is, they are offered as options which we are intended to reject. Where we recognize a typically Borgesian ploy is in the way the Librarian, by reporting critically the opinions of the other inhabitants, implicitly sets up his own judgement as the standard. This tempts us to overlook the ambiguity of his own outlook. It is by noticing this that we can perceive how Borges has manipulated him to create a characteristic double-take: the Librarian rejects or questions certain responses to the way the Library is, but we in our turn are invited to be alert enough to reject or question his response.

The process begins in the first paragraph when the Librarian affirms his disagreement with the commonly-held view that the Library/Universe is finite. He insists, here and at the end, that it is interminable (that is, infinitely extensive in space) and eternal (that is, characterized by infinite duration in time). Other hypotheses are mentioned slightly dismissively: that of the idealists, who "Razonan que es inconcebible una sala triangular o pentagonal" (I, 456) (argue that a triangular or pentagonal room is inconceivable), which is self-contradictory and plainly intended to raise a smile; that of the mystics, which the narrator regards as a mere metaphor; that of certain sceptics, which he suggests is a half-truth. These introductory hypotheses are not dwelt upon. But in the middle of the story, when we reach more instinctive human reactions, we are given more details. These may be humorous, as in the case of the passage written in a Baltic dialect of a Spanish American Indian language (with classical Arabic inflections!). They may be dramatic, as in the case of the fanatical seekers of Vindiction (personal salvation?) and the destructive Purifiers, or again, merely pathetic, as in the cases of the Inquisitors and the believers in mere chance. These references to trends of outlook in the Library allude satirically to aspects of religious, philosophical and scientific enquiry. They point explicitly to the uselessness of seeking any ultimate understanding of the universe.

But even as the Librarian describes these trends, he himself clings to a set of propositions (albeit described as dreams or elegant hopes) that are no less typical of the lengths men will go to in seeking to avoid this conclusion. On the one hand, the elements of predictable order in the Library/Universe lead the Librarian to postulate an Artificer, God, but a God who is not necessarily responsible for the existence of the only life-form present in the Library, man. It hardly needs to be pointed out that such a God would be a very strange divinity indeed, and quite the opposite of the Christian God who, according to Scripture, made the world for mankind. On the other hand, the Librarian persists, in the face of all the evidence that "nadie espera descubrir nada" (I, 459) (no-one expects to discover anything), in holding the belief that somewhere, somehow, the contents of the Library's books can be shown to make sense. We may take it that the "naturaleza informe y caótica" (I, 457) (formless and chaotic nature) of these contents *vis-à-vis* the regularity of the Library's architecture and arrangement implies that, although there may be elements of apparent design in the physical universe (above the level of subatomic physics, drift phenomena and the Uncertainty Principle), there is none in our lived contact with it. The chaotic content of the books seems to correspond to Unamuno's concept of "niebla", the vision-obscuring mist of everyday experiences with which we are enveloped. The fact that all the books contain the same letters, punctuation and spacing, together with the fact that there is no "disparate absoluto" (I, 461) (absolute absurdity) — that is, the fact that we all experience the world more or less in the same, but never identical, terms and that, for instance, there are no effects without causes — leads the Librarian to assert categorically that, though it has never been found so far, there must be a meaning in them. Finally, though he regards the Library/Universe as infinite and eternal, he does not regard it as wholly limitless, since there is a finite number of combinations of twenty-two letters, full stops, commas and spaces. His answer appears to be that this vast combination repeats itself for ever cyclically.

What ultimately shows his hand are his references to the "divine" Library, with its "divine" staircases and its "divine" disorder. The repetition of the adjective cannot but be meaningful. The Librarian, like Borges, like Everyman, has an unconquerable longing for an answer to his ultimate why-questions. The Library is an extended metaphor of the Universe seen in terms of an enigmatic combination of regularity and chaos. At the centre of the metaphor, the point at which the regularity breaks down, are the individual books. The metaphor tells us that we are all human, as the books are all books. We find ourselves side by side in the same universe with its reliable predictabilites (fire always warms, the sun always rises in the East and so on), just as the books find themselves in the regular hexagons of the Library. But the contents of our lives, our own inner experiences, are in fact a jumble of sense-impressions, different in every individual and irreducible to any immediately comprehensible pattern. But the metaphor does not present itself. It needs a presenter and commentator, the Librarian. When he describes the Library he represents man contemplating the universe. When he describes the books, he represents man contemplating the endless variety of individual human experiences. When he suggests explanations, he represents man's attempts to understand the physical universe and the human condition. The interest lies in the interrelation between the narrator and the metaphor. In the former we perceive a determination to impose order and meaning on a universe which the metaphor itself, and the failure of the reported attempts to explain it, tell us resists any such imposition. It is not merely the inadequacy of the explanation which the Librarian reports, but the obvious discrepancy between his own account of the Library and his attempt to explain it that reveals Borges' desire to bring us to a clearer awareness of the ambiguity of reality and to warn us against trying to explain it away. Even the Librarian is made to recognize at the end that his anguished prayer for all to be made plain is merely one of the Library's infinite contents and that the refutation of any basis for that prayer is another. Worse still, both the prayer and the possible reasons why it cannot be answered may be connected with a "universe" which is a mere linguistic construct, one of many possible and different ones. Nowhere else does Borges universalize and involve his narrator to quite the same extent as he does in "La Biblioteca de Babel".

If, as was contended earlier, Borges with age tended to forsake to some extent the abstract mysteries of time, reality and the organization of the universe for the more familiar mysteries of human behaviour, the reason was probably that "esa perplejidad, que me ha acompañado a lo largo de la vida y que hace que muchos de mis propios actos me sean inexplicables" (*VA*, 79) (that perplexity, which has accompanied me throughout my life and which causes many of my own actions to be inexplicable to me) increased as he became older. When we look at the relevant stories we notice two things. The first is that stories involving some element of cowardice, treachery, weakness or cruelty predominate over those which emphasize courage or nobility of mind. The second is that very frequently Borges uses first-person narration in the case of the former. It is not his invariable rule. "El muerto", for example, is told omnisciently so as to allow the death of Otálora to become the natural climax. But it is the case, for instance, in "El jardín de senderos que se bifurcan", "La forma de la espada", "La casa de Asterión", "Deutsches Requiem" and "Guayaquil". In each of these instances the first-person "confession" confers additional credibility on the story. In the case of the minority of stories in which characters are shown behaving in a courageous or noble way, such as "Biografía de Tadeo Isidoro Cruz" or "El Sur", third-person narration avoids any danger that the character involved may sound self-satisfied. The outstanding exception is, of course, "Historia de Rosendo Juárez", where the first-person narration is required by the storyteller's supposed intention to "set the record straight" and by the fact that only he, and not the bystanders, regards his behaviour as justified.

Probably the story which contrasts most sharply with "Historia de Rosendo Juárez" in the category of first-person narratives in which the narrator is not a persona of Borges or a representative of Everyman is "El indigno" (II, 377-82). It tells of a Jewish informer who betrays the leader of a local gang of criminals to the police. Critical remarks about it have hitherto not been entirely helpful. One might instance Barrenechea's suggestion that its secret theme is "La eterna lucha del hijo que mata al padre" (The eternal theme of the son who kills the father).[7] Wheelock offers another interpretation, in which Ferrari, the victim, is seen as "a subverted Christ-figure" and Fischbein, the informer, as a modern Judas. However, he goes on to write: "One does not know who betrayed whom, who is really judged

    [7] Ana María Barrenechea, "Borges y la narración que se autoanaliza", in her *Textos hispanoamericanos* (Caracas: Monte Avila, 1978), p. 141.

unworthy and unworthy of what."[8] This is a perceptive comment. If we are to take "El indigno" as containing any reference to a biblical subtext, the fact that Ferrari is a petty criminal who partially corrupts his young disciple alters the entire perspective from one which has to do with Eternal Return to one which involves an element of ironic parody.

For this reason it is probably more prudent to see the story as one which illustrates a theme originally incorporated into Argentine literature by Roberto Arlt in 1926 with his novel *El juguete rabioso*. Possibly influenced by Dostoyevsky, Arlt introduced into the end of the novel the concept of self-discovery via self-degradation, as the hero, Silvio, betrays his best friend to the police. Something similar surfaces again in Juan Carlos Onetti's *La vida breve* (1950), in which the central character, Brausen, finds his identity through contact with a semi-prostitute and as the accomplice of her killer. A more recent example of the way this theme has become naturalized into Argentine fiction is Luisa Valenzuela's short story "La palabra asesino" in *Cambio de armas* (1982). The heroine, a cultured, intellectual woman writer, falls in love with a cold-blooded criminal and former drug-addict, who is responsible for at least two killings. She, too, makes important self-discoveries in this situation. It is perhaps noteworthy that all three stories are told really from a first-person perspective, even though Valenzuela's narrator uses an assumed third-person stance.

As in "Historia de Rosendo Juárez", which is placed next to it in order to accentuate the contrast, the first-person narration is introduced by a familiar pseudo-"Borges" who figures as the original narratee. In each case, as we saw earlier, virtually the same inlaid detail, the change of status of the locale, is used to prefigure the shift in the behaviour of the protagonist. But in "El indigno", not content with amplifying it by using two similar examples, the latter leading us to Fischbein's own shop, Borges reinforces it with a reference — later seen to be ironic — to the "complexities and discords" which "enrich" the Jewish personality. This does not complete the contribution of the opening paragraph. The references to Spinoza and the Cabbala are also highly relevant. The "fantastic theory" of the former suggested, in effect, that a system of ethics could be worked out and presented deductively, through a series of theorems, which would thus rule out any element of subjectivity. This plainly

---

[8] Wheelock, "Borges' New Prose", p. 364.

constitutes ironic comment on the behaviour to which Fischbein confesses, which is quite clearly irreducible to any such system. On the other hand, the Cabbala symbolizes for Borges one of the more fantastic of human attempts to pierce the mystery behind reality. The reference to it is made here to remind the alert reader that the mystery remains and, in the concrete instance, that Fischbein's story ultimately defies explanation. We simply do not understand certain aspects of human motivation.

With this in mind we can turn to Fischbein's narration itself. Precisely what constitutes its most salient characteristic is the absence of clear motivation. The whole technique of the story is the opposite of that used in "Historia de Rosendo Juárez". There, as we saw, the key element is the sudden achievement of self-awareness, Rosendo's acquisition of the ability to see himself "as if in a mirror" as a direct consequence of his recent experiences. In "El indigno", on the other hand, what we never learn is why Fischbein's sense of not deserving Ferrari's trust and friendship leads him to betray the gang-leader to the police. His narration consists of a series of descriptions of incidents, along with a parallel set of intercalated reflections. In principle, these reflections, which make up Fischbein's own commentary on the incidents, ought to explain the selection and significance of them. In practice, this is not the case. Once more the parallel with "Historia de Rosendo Juárez" is instructive. In his interview with Irala Rosendo listens to the latter's account of his private situation and comments on it in a way which prefigures his own future decision. After the death of his friend he visits a cock-fight and again comments on it in a way that indicates his growing awareness of the shift which is taking place in his outlook. Finally, he is challenged by El Corralero and, before refusing the challenge, he reflects on the confrontation in such a way that we, the readers, understand quite clearly what his motivation was. "Historia de Rosendo Juárez", that is, incorporates a clear-cut pattern of causal explanation supplied by Rosendo himself in connection with his behaviour. Precisely the opposite is the case with "El indigno."

The arrangement of the incidents in the story follows a straight-forward pattern. There is a rising sequence beginning with Ferrari's quiet, unaggressive assertion of his territorial control when it is implicitly questioned by the appearance of a newcomer of his own kind. The lonely, insecure, adolescent narrator finds in him a personality-ideal, a role-model, the "hero" he needed. The second incident, in which Ferrari intervenes between some louts and the narrator's womenfolk, reinforces the impact of the first and brings about Fischbein's incorporation into Ferrari's gang. The climax of the sequence is the latter's remark that "para mí, entonces, era un dios" (II, 380) (for me, then, he was a god). A page later Fischbein is at Police Headquarters betraying Ferrari's plan for a break-in at a factory. The result is Ferrari's death. This falling sequence balances the earlier rising one. When we reflect on this symmetry we realize that what is missing is the kind of pivotal episode which would motivate Fischbein's treachery. In place of it we find simply a description of the preparations for the factory break-in. This is, in effect, a test for Fischbein. By forcing him to recognize that Ferrari has genuinely accepted him as a fully-fledged and trusted member of the gang it crystallizes his dilemma. Ferrari's words — "Sé que te portarás como un hombre" (I know you'll behave like a man) — leave him no further room for manoeuvre: he must either live up to them or betray them. They bring him face to face with his real self, just as the fight between the posse and Martín Fierro does in the case of Cruz in "Biografía de Tadeo Isidoro Cruz", where Cruz deserts his own men and goes to the aid of the outlaw whom he and they have been hunting down. But the words do not produce an explicit description from their hearer of a moment of self-insight. We are thus thrown back on Fischbein's other inserted remarks for any possible clarification.

To have cast the story in the third person would have made some allusion to Fischbein's motives all but unavoidable. Thus, for example, the realization by Cruz of his motives is heavily emphasized by the five-fold use of forms of the verb "comprender" (to understand) which immediately precedes his shift of allegiances and change of sides in the fight. There Borges had little choice. The incident he was describing was well-known and Cruz's motives were readily imaginable by readers of *Martín Fierro*. Borges' task was to amplify the context, add circumstantial details and render Cruz's thoughts more explicit than in the poem. There is no great element of potential mystery in the decision of a former outsider and ex-criminal to come to the rescue of one of his own kind, even if in the meantime he has turned to law-enforcement. The choice of third-person narration was logical.

Fischbein, on the other hand, specifically uses his confession paradoxically to emphasize that he has no explanation to offer: "No sé cómo explicarle las cosas" (II, 379) (I don't know how to explain things to you); "La amistad no es menos misteriosa que el amor o cualquiera de las otras faces de esta confusión que es la vida" (II, 380) (Friendship is no less mysterious than love or any of the other faces of this confusion which is life). His attitude towards his own actions is overtly contradictory. On the one hand, he asserts that he felt uneasy at his lack of remorse at the time. Yet he had expressed the hope to the police-officers that his behaviour would be punished by his own murder. He asserts: "... ahora no me arrepiento" (now I feel no repentance). Yet he has kept the story secret even from his wife and his remark that "Mientras dura el arrepentimiento dura la culpa" (While repentance lasts, guilt lasts) suggests that his other remarks in this connection contain an element of bravado and repressed guilt. Indeed, it could hardly be otherwise. The suggestion is reinforced by his incidental use of the phrases "para desgracia de los dos" (II, 378) (unhappily for both of us) and "Ojalá nunca lo hubiera hecho" (II, 379) (Would to God I had never done so), referring to his getting to know Ferrari. By using the first-person form of narration Borges is able to let Fischbein adopt this highly ambiguous stance. Its object is clearly to complement the author's view that we do not understand external reality and must accept "La imposibilidad de penetrar el esquema divino del universo" (II, 224) (The impossibility of penetrating the divine scheme of the universe), with the view that we do not understand the inner reality of ourselves either: "... los hombres gozan de poca información acerca de los móviles profundos de su conducta" (II, 248) (men enjoy little information about the deep motives of their behaviour).

We are, of course, at liberty to treat the story, not as implying the mystery of the personality, but as a psychological tale in which we are invited to perceive behind Fischbein's profession of incomprehension an explanation which he himself is repressing. Such a reading would presumably lead to seeing Fischbein as an individual with such an active sense of inferiority and such a negative self-image that the friendship of a greatly admired person placed an intolerable psychological strain on him. Such a strain could have the effect of virtually compelling him to bring it to an end by means of an action which would reinforce his own self-contempt. The objection to such an approach is not that it implies a clearer knowledge of the character's personality on the part of the reader than on the part of the character himself. Such clearer knowledge on the reader's part is normal in psychological narratives and is part of their appeal. The real objection is that it would attribute to Borges the intention to offer us a case of psychological deformity which he implicitly understands and about which he provides sufficient data, albeit somewhat ambiguously, for us to figure it out. This is a possible but improbable reading of "El indigno", where the mystery seems intended to remain a mystery, as in "Abenjacán el Bojarí, muerto en su laberinto". In any case, the first-person narration is still crucial, since it is clearly more satisfying for the character in question to reveal to us, in spite of himself, the real cause of his behaviour, than for an omniscient author to drop the hints.

Perhaps the most humanly complex and interesting of Borges' non-self-reflecting narrators is the unnamed professor of History who tells us the story of his renunciation of an important professional mission in "Guayaquil" (II, 416-23). As is normal in Borges' best fiction, the tale contains suggestions of several possible interpretations. The most obvious one is indicated by the narrator's reflection near the end: "En aquel momento sentí que algo estaba ocurriéndonos o, mejor dicho, que ya había ocurrido. De algún modo ya éramos otros" (II, 421) (At that moment I felt that something was happening to us or, rather, that it had already occurred. In some way we were already others). The inference is that the scene in the professor's house in Buenos Aires is somehow a re-enactment of the famous and mysterious encounter between Bolívar and San Martín at Guayaquil in July 1822. To some readers this may of itself provide a satisfying understanding of the tale. But others will feel conditioned by earlier stories to expect more than just the repetition of a crucial historical episode in more banal circumstances. In fact, a second approach to the story's meaning is offered by one of the narrator's earlier remarks. Referring to some words of his adversary, Zimmermann, he declares: "... eran ya la expresión de una voluntad [...] el poder estaba en el hombre, no en la dialéctica" (II, 420) (they were already the expression of a will [...] the power was in the man, not in his dialectics). Zimmermann confirms the narrator's opinion in nearly identical terms: "Dos hombres se enfrentaron en Guayaquil; si uno se impuso, fue por su mayor voluntad, no por juegos dialécticos" (II, 421) (Two men confronted each other in Guayaquil; if one of them imposed himself it was because of his greater will, not because of dialectical games). We seldom meet such re-emphasis in a Borges story. Zimmermann's next words — "Como usted ve, no he olvidado a mi Schopenhauer" (As you see, I have not forgotten my Schopenhauer) — make it clear — perhaps too clear — that, more than with the idea of Eternal Return, we are here concerned with the triumph of the individual will. However, despite

Borges' admiration for Schopenhauer, his favourite philosopher, this is not an idea which he fully accepts. Courage and ethical principle may support us in our hesitant pilgrimage through life's labyrinth, but strength of will, individual self-assertion, is not a significant factor. In "Emma Zunz", to remind ourselves of only one example, Emma's determination to impose her will on reality produces very ironic consequences for her. Life, for Borges, is too unpredictable and baffling for will-power to operate effectively in most cases.

The reader long exposed to Borges' writing may well suspect, therefore, that the unusually explicit emphasis on Schopenhauer and the will is a diversionary tactic intended to lead us away from the real point of the story. We can recognize another possible clue. There is no better way of misleading than to deceive with the truth. Schopenhauer seems, in fact, to be the presiding presence in the story, but not because of his advocacy of the individual will in the sense referred to above. Rather it is because of his idea that we all will our own fates: "Nuestro maestro, nuestro común maestro," Zimmermann reminds the narrator at the story's climax (II, 423), "conjeturaba que ningún acto es involuntario. Si usted se queda en esta casa, en esta airosa casa patricia, es porque íntimamente quiere quedarse" (Our master, our common master, conjectured that no act is involuntary. If you stay in this house, in this elegant patrician residence, it is because inwardly you wish to stay here). He adds ironically: "Acato y agradezco su voluntad" (I bow to your will and am grateful). The true key to the story, in other words, may well be Borges' remark in "Nathaniel Hawthorne": "Schopenhauer ha escrito, famosamente, que no hay acto, que no hay pensamiento, que no hay enfermedad que no sean voluntarios" (II, 186) (Schopenhauer has written, in a famous phrase, that there is no act, that there is no thought, that there is no illness, which is not voluntary).

What this suggests is that the narrator is not simply overborne by Zimmermann's irresistibly superior will; he obscurely wishes to be pushed aside by his rival. He collaborates in his own failure. Here we have a third level of meaning, less philosophical, less voluntaristic, but more psychological. The interest of the story technically lies in the strategy that Borges uses to suggest that the narrator, and hence by implication San Martín, contributed to his own defeat. The story, in other words, may really be concerned with the enigma of the personality and once more with Borges' assertion that we know very little about the deeper springs of our behaviour. As Zimmermann puts it: "... el misterio está en nosotros" (II, 421) (the mystery is in ourselves).

Wheelock proposes a different explanation still.[9] He, too, sees that "The will in question in 'Guayaquil' is not Zimmerman's (sic) imposed upon the narrator". But he goes on to argue that the narrator wills his own defeat "for a cause". He deliberately refuses the mission which he had been offered, involving the authentication and publication of a supposed letter by Bolívar about the meeting in Guayaquil, because he does not wish to "repeat Bolívar's error" of saying anything at all about the encounter with San Martín. He wants to "preserve the mythic ambiguity" of the meeting, to retain its "suggestive indeterminacy". The weakness of this explanation lies in Wheelock's misunderstanding of a somewhat sophistical argument of Zimmermann's intended to provide the narrator with a face-saving reason for opting out of the contest. The German scholar argues that the document with which the mission is concerned may be apocryphal and in any case will be likely to give only Bolívar's side of the story. The narrator, as a San Martín specialist, would be wiser to avoid the risk of attaching his reputation to a possibly fake letter and to wait for Zimmermann's publication of it in order to discuss its contents from a Sanmartinian position. There is no justification for Wheelock's assertion that if the narrator published a commentary "the effect will be deadly". To compound his error, Wheelock offers a quite arbitrary interpretation of the second of two parables told by the narrator. In this tale within a tale, two Celtic bards are engaged in a song-contest. When the first has finished a lengthy song, the other merely puts aside the harp and rises. His mere gesture causes his opponent to concede him the victory. This hardly seems to mean only that "the best song remains unsung". How do we know it would have been the better song? All we know is that the first bard abandoned the contest without an explanation. We can only infer his motivation by reference to the narrator's, which it is intended to parallel. The question is: on whose side is Borges, the narrator's or Zimmermann's? Does the story really leave us, as Wheelock would have us believe, with the sensation that the narrator sacrifices himself simply in order to preserve an ideal of historical ambiguity?

The use of the first-person narrator is crucial. It is by describing the event in his own words that the narrator accuses himself through his tone and manner. At the same time the use of the first person focuses

[9] Wheelock, "Borges' New Prose", pp. 379-81.

our attention squarely on him. For Schopenhauer, the opposite of will-power is analytical thought, leading to excessive self-awareness. The unduly reflective man will always will his own destruction. From the opening of the tale the illustration of this is a prime function of the first-person form. The first paragraph announces, with a rhetorical over-accumulation of negatives, the narrator's renunciation. The second paragraph shows him immediately pausing to reflect on the first. He begins by excusing its pomposity on the grounds that it reflects the "monumentality" of the style of another historian; but then he justifies it by asserting that he wished to add a note of pathos to the description of a banal episode. Meanwhile, his use of the words "penoso" (painful), "confesar" (confess) and presently "ingratas" (unpleasant) contradicts the implication of "baladí" (trifling). Borges, that is, arranges the first paragraphs so that we can perceive that, psychologically speaking, the narrator is experiencing sensations of shame and humiliation which he tries to defuse by unsuccessfully minimizing their cause, by transferal (patronizing Korzeniovski, the other historian, who stands in for Zimmermann) and by pretending that the tone of pathos is assumed, when the feeling behind it is plainly all too real.

Secondly, and once more in contrast to Wheelock's interpretation, he twice insists in the opening paragraphs: "Referiré con toda probidad lo que sucedió" (I shall report what happened with complete probity) and "... quiero dejar escrito mi diálogo con el doctor Eduardo Zimmermann" (I wish to leave a written account of my dialogue with Dr. Eduardo Zimmermann). He does, that is, exactly what San Martín abstained from doing. His inability to imitate the hero's silence is, in retrospect, one of the pointers to his unconscious self-presentation as weak and self-deceiving. By writing this confession he identifies himself with Bolívar and does what (in the story) San Martín's adversary had so unwisely allowed himself to do. To cap it all, he later speaks of burning the manuscript, but — since we are reading it — he evidently cannot bring himself to do so. He cannot resist the masochistic urge to expose his own debility.

His presentation of Zimmermann continues the process of unconscious self-accusation under the guise of self-excuse. Despite the patronizing references to Zimmermann's work as "sin duda benemérita" (II, 417) (doubtless commendable) and to the immigrant scholar's "exodus" and "migrant activities", what comes through is Zimmermann's fidelity to his race (he defended "Semitic" Carthage) and political courage (he attacked Hitler's histrionics). A clear indication that Borges is manipulating the first-person form to reflect adversely on the narrator is the way in which the latter is made to refer to Heidegger, the only major intellectual to support Hitler openly, as the "venerado existencialista" (venerable existentialist) and to regard as decisive his "refutation" of Zimmermann based only on newspaper headlines. Indicative of the same process is the tone of irritating superiority which Borges causes the narrator to adopt towards Zimmermann with respect to the latter's height and appearance, his taste in clothes, his pronunciation of Spanish and his gestures. The impression we are intended to get is that of a man who is compensating for his own insecurity with false pride.

This is precisely what Zimmermann intuits and exploits. The striking effect in the middle of the tale is the way in which Borges shows the narrator losing his duel with Zimmermann without abandoning his assumed stance. The interest of the description of events lies less in Zimmermann's tactics than in the narrator's revelation of his own abject surrender. Zimmermann does not bully him. Instead he offers the narrator two alibis or excuses for renunciation which, we discern through the latter's own account, his false pride and insecurity impel him to accept instead of brushing them aside. Fearful that his reputation might be compromised, he grasps at the suggestion that the Bolívar letter might be a fake, while pride in his Argentine ancestry causes him to bow to the view that his role should be that of commenting on the letter from a Sanmartinian standpoint while at the same time imitating his national hero by renouncing mere ambition.

In the latter part of the story Borges inserts the apparently casual reference to the Golem to suggest that, just as the Golem is a parody of man, so the narrator is a parody of San Martín. It is an inlaid detail, an additional clue to how the story should be read. Of the two parables mentioned by the narrator the first is the less important. It seems designed to stress the parallelism between the historic Guayaquil meeting and the encounter between the narrator and Zimmermann. The second reflects, but does not explain, the narrator's renunciation. We do not know whether the emphasis is on the second bard's symbolic gesture or on the first singer's acceptance of defeat. Again what is important is that the narrator himself tells the parable and, in his own words, appears to interpret it in terms of Zimmermann's success and his own defeat. Clearly Zimmermann's superiority of will is an important factor. The choice of a first-person narrator may simply be an obvious device to underline the irresistibility of that force. But another way to read the story is as a disguised alibi which the narrator constructs for himself to excuse, and thereby reveal, his own willed subservience.

CHAPTER 8

CLOSING STRATEGIES

The one kind of ending we do not and cannot expect to meet in a Borges story is the kind which illustrates "poetic justice" or in some similar way offers a comforting view of the way things are. On the contrary, what we learn to expect at the end of a typical Borges story is often something quite unforeseen. Just as he excels at creating the intriguing opening, so Borges is a master of the unexpected ending. Nor is this at all surprising, given his conception of the world as full of ironic unpredictabilities, on the one hand, and, on the other, his tendency to mock, subvert or betray expectations which he himself has earlier encouraged in the reader. In a certain number of cases where the story seems to have fulfilled our expectations, as when, for example, Emma Zunz revenges herself on Loewenthal or when the Negro kills Martín Fierro in "El fin", we may discover that a twist has been added which ironically alters the original perspective.

Not all such endings have been found by critics to be completely satisfying. In the case of "Hombre de la esquina rosada", for instance, Alonso long ago suggested that the inclusion of the last few sentences was a mistake, since there were already enough clues in the tale to make it clear that the narrator was responsible for the death of Leal.[1] I have myself suggested that "Tres versiones de Judas", which identifies Christ with Judas, is open to similar criticism. It begins in the format of pseudo-article in a learned magazine reviewing the work and ideas of a Scandinavian writer, Nils Runeberg, and is largely written in a detached scholarly tone, but it undergoes an

[1]Alonso, p. 350.

unfortunate alteration at the end. The mode of presentation changes abruptly from that of a scholarly account to that of a short story with an omniscient narrator. Runeberg no longer "suggests", "observes", "goes on", "argues", but "intuited", "understood", "felt", "remembered". Borges is no longer pretending to rehearse evidence; he is making direct statements about Runeberg's inner experience. The shift from a pseudo-expository style to full assumption of authorial authority is an ending device whose possible effectiveness must be set against the loss to the story's unity of technique.[2] For his part, McGrady, while praising "La forma de la espada" as a "profound detective story" which is "elaborated with the same care and ingenuity that characterize the later Borges", nonetheless asserts that "it remains true that by specifying the solution to the central mystery of his tale, Borges deprives the careful reader of the pleasure of unravelling that problem for himself".[3]

In the last resort these conclusions reflect the taste of the critics in question and it is for the reader to decide whether to agree with them. But two considerations are relevant. The first is that while Borges' stories are, as their narrative strategies and thematic complexities reveal, written with the "careful reader" in mind, they are not written exclusively for such an élite audience. Indeed, the fact that "Hombre de la esquina rosada" appears to have been partly misunderstood by some critics, let alone careful readers, might seem to indicate that the elucidation at the end was advisable. Secondly, McGrady refers to "the lesser pleasure of going back and picking out the clues" after enjoying the story for the first time.[4] But this may not be a lesser pleasure; it may be a bonus. It is arguable that precisely the impulse to perform this operation on the reader's part is what makes many of Borges' stories so enjoyable. In any case, we cannot exclude the view that, for alert readers, some of the clues will have been picked up in the course of the first reading and, as we suggested was the case with the identification of Asterion as the Minotaur, the reader in question has the pleasure of seeing his or her suspicions confirmed at the end. What really distinguishes "Hombre de la esquina rosada" and "La forma de la espada", in respect of their endings, from "La casa de Asterión" is something else which shows Borges' development as a short-story writer in the interval. "Hombre de la esquina rosada"

[2] Shaw, *Borges: Ficciones*, p. 54.
[3] McGrady, "Prefiguration ...", pp. 148, 147, 146.
[4] ibid., p. 142.

alludes to a familiar and fairly simple dichotomy: that between moral and physical courage. "La forma de la espada", as McGrady illustrates, alludes to something less familiar and less simple: the fundamentally Borgesian idea that "cualquier hombre es todos los hombres" (I, 488) (any man is all men). For its part, "La casa de Asterión" alludes to two even less immediately recognizable concepts: that of evil as an existential construct and that of an inverted Christ-figure as an ironic Redeemer. In other words, although in each case the ending makes explicit something hinted at before, when we go back over the stories again what we then find is increasingly "profound" in McGrady's sense.

Barrenechea has noticed another of Borges' closing strategies: "Es muy usual en Borges (en el Borges de *Ficciones*, de *El Aleph* o de los ensayos de *Otras inquisiciones*) el presentar primero una historia extraña y 'verdadera' (por ejemplo, 'La otra muerte') y desplegar al final un abanico de hipótesis explicativas, entre las cuales, a veces, se privilegia una" (It is very usual for Borges [the Borges of *Ficciones*, of *El Aleph* or of the essays in *Otras inquisiciones*] first to present a strange and "true" story [for example, "The Other Death"] and at the end to open out like a fan a series of explanatory hypotheses, among which sometimes one is privileged).[5] As well as "La otra muerte" she mentions "La busca de Averroes". We should prefer to add "Deutsches Requiem" and "La lotería en Babilonia". In each of these stories Borges uses a somewhat similar method of bringing them to a close. What makes them different from the stories we have just been discussing is the avoidance of any kind of surprise or ironic twist at the end. Instead there is a very direct and explicit connection between the theme and the ending in each case. "La lotería en Babilonia" is an extreme example. This is a story in which, as we saw, there is an unobtrusive transition from one thematic aspect to another, that is, from reality seen as a lottery to the question of a possible guiding power which manipulates the prizes and the forfeits. The final paragraph of the tale elegantly reverses the thrust (I, 447). Its first and last words — "La Compañía" (The Company); "un infinito juego de azares" (an infinite interplay of chance) — reassert the basic antinomy around which the story revolves. But in addition the passage from one (mentioned at the beginning of the last paragraph) to the other (climactically positioned) underlines the meaning of the story as a whole. The ending, that is, is confirmatory,

---

[5] Barrenechea, "Borges y la narración que se autoanaliza", p. 132.

not subversive, of what seems the most likely reading of the story. In contrast to "What if?" stories like "Tlön, Uqbar Orbis Tertius" or "El Aleph", whose endings we examine below, "La lotería en Babilonia", like "Deutsches Requiem", is ultimately built around a statement (respectively that the world is more likely to be governed by chance than by divine design; that Nazism may have indirectly triumphed despite its apparent defeat). The rehearsal of a series of hypotheses, as noticed by Barrenechea, suggests a certain ambiguity. But the privileging of one has the contrary effect. To that extent the two above-mentioned "statement" stories constitute a special category in Borges' fiction.

One is tempted to suggest that a more characteristic Borgesian closing strategy is the "double-take" ending, such as we find in "El Aleph", "Tlön, Uqbar, Orbis Tertius" or, *pace* Barrenechea, "La busca de Averroes", in which a further disturbing element is added, as if as an afterthought, to what seemed to be the original conclusion. After the first interlude in the latter tale, Averroes hears mention of the Great Wall of China, which suggests to him the idea of the infinite and causes him to feel himself to be unreal. At the climax of the story, when he has written his erroneous conclusion, he looks in a mirror and disappears. He is *in fact* unreal, since the "Averroes" of the story (significantly referred to in inverted commas in the last line of the text) is merely a figment of Borges' imagination. The last few lines of the tale return to the issue precisely in order to provide this explanation. But they carry with them also the implication that the teller of the tale is no less inauthentic than "Averroes", caught as he is in an infinite circularity of cause and effect which seems to deprive him of any individual reality. Part of the ending of "La busca de Averroes", that is, is connected to its beginning and to the theme of Averroes enclosed within the boundaries of Islam and thus limited by his culture, as we all are. But another part is concerned with something quite different: not the defeat of the intellect, but the threat to the personality posed by the concept of the infinite, and applicable both to Averroes and the narrator. This is what accounts for the "double-take" effect. Let us look at other examples.

We noticed earlier the symmetry which links the ending of "El Aleph" to the beginning of the story so as to complete the frame in a satisfying way. What is distinctive about "El Aleph" in this respect is that the interaction between the frame and the core episode takes place essentially in the early part of the story. In the edition we have used, "El Aleph" occupies just over thirteen pages of text. The vision via the Aleph occurs between the tenth and the eleventh of these pages. It follows that the remainder of the story, less than a fifth of its total length, leaves Borges little room for manoeuvre. It is enough, however, for him to create one of his most baffling endings. To see why this is we need only contrast its technique with that of the ending of "La escritura del Dios", published four years later. In the latter the Aztec priest Tzinacán, having been granted what we can assume to be a vision of the cosmos fundamentally similar to that granted to the narrator of "El Aleph", is so crushed by it that life and activity lose all meaning and he elects to remain entombed in his prison. In "El Aleph", on the other hand, Borges attenuates the impact of total insight by reminding us of our fortunate ability to forget: the narrator is gradually able to shut out the horror of what he has seen and return to everyday life. The last adjective of "El Aleph", "tragic", is paradoxically ambiguous. For if "la trágica erosión de los años" (II, 125) (the tragic erosion of the years) blurs the narrator's memories of Beatriz, it saves him from the fate of Tzinacán or that of the narrator of "El Zahir".

But if this were all, the ending of "El Aleph" would be symmetrical with the beginning in all but length. The pattern would be: Beatriz > Daneri > The Aleph > Daneri > Beatriz. But in fact this is not the case. Instead Borges introduces a dubitative element which will not be present in the ending of either "El Zahir" or "La escritura del Dios": "... yo creo que el Aleph de la calle Garay era un falso Aleph" (II, 124) (I believe that the Aleph of the calle Garay was a false Aleph). There is nothing in the remaining two paragraphs of the story to substantiate such an opinion. The narrator merely records the apocryphal opinion of Burton that the only true Aleph exists inside a stone pillar in an Egyptian mosque, where its presence cannot be verified. He goes on to wonder whether he saw this "true" Aleph as part of the simultaneous vision of all things which he has so recently been granted, though it is not clear how this could possibly have been the case if the calle Garay Aleph were a false one. So far as I am aware, none of the critics who have discussed "El Aleph" has explained convincingly why Borges at the end makes his narrator change his stance about the authenticity of his discovery.

At the technical level what it constitutes is a sudden and completely unexpected anticlimax. The function of anticlimax in literature is to suggest contradiction. We are led, as readers, to form a certain expectation, and then that expectation is suddenly denied fulfilment or betrayed. Here our expectations relate to the meaningfulness of the Aleph-vision, that is to say, its correspondence to "reality". By breaking the symmetry of the ending of the story with this anticlimax, Borges is plainly sending the alert reader an intentional signal designed to subvert his provisional conclusions about the meaning of "El Aleph" as they have taken shape up to the end of the prepenultimate paragraph of the postscript. At this point the story unexpectedly dissolves into complete ambiguity. Either the Aleph was genuine and, as in "El Zahir" and "La escritura del Dios", the dominant theme is the horror of insight into the nature of reality, or the Aleph is merely a shared illusion and the dominant theme is revealed at the last moment to be the fallaciousness of any claim to possess a vision of reality. Perhaps the grotesquely inappropriate location of the Aleph and the undignified position which the narrator was obliged to adopt in order to receive the vision are related to this second possibility.

The use of sudden anticlimax at the end of "El Aleph" in order to question the meaningfulness of the core episode is a concluding stratagem which is typical of some Borges stories. For what it does is to alter the nature of the puzzle, to change the apparent thematic thrust of the tale and, at the eleventh hour, to destabilize the reader's reaction by producing a "double-take" ending. Few aspects of the stories are more indicative of the way in which the technique and *dispositio* in themselves function frequently as symbols of the way Borges views the world as devoid of fixed meanings. We already saw a prime example in our initial discussion of "La casa de Asterión". There, just as we seem to have come to terms with the questions of Asterion's identity and the significance of his labyrinth, Borges introduces, without warning, the concept of the "redeemer" to tease our intelligence yet again. The difference between the two cases under discussion is, of course, that while the ending of "El Aleph" seems to subvert the conclusion which the central episode of the story invited us to form, the ending of "La casa de Asterión" extends the tale's implications in a new direction. This is not an unimportant distinction. It reminds us that to identify some of Borges' main narrative devices, as we are attempting to do in this book, is only part of the task. We then have to see how he uses them, case by case. There are no short cuts. In the present instance the only generalization we can make is that certain concluding strategies, like certain pivotal episodes, tend to subvert the reader's "reception" of what he is reading and make him or her think again.

To the extent that ambiguity is preferable to horror, and

forgetfulness to tragic awareness, the ending of "El Aleph" is slightly reassuring. But subversion is not meant to be reassuring, as we see from the conclusion of "Tlön, Uqbar, Orbis Tertius". The "1947 postscript" is a classic example of a Borgesian end-game. The story, like "La muerte y la brújula", is an archetypal mystery story with a puzzle elaborated at the beginning, developed in the body of the tale and then apparently resolved at the end. Such tales suggest by implication that life's puzzles have a solution, that man is ultimately capable of understanding his circumstances and perceiving meaning in his experiences. This is one of the reasons why mystery stories, and their principal offshoot, detective stories, rarely obtain significant prestige as literature. For, however much we may wish to believe it, what they tell us is basically unconvincing. They are far more tidy than life and are hence recognizably unfaithful to our everyday awareness of its bizarre workings. For obvious reasons Borges is intensely drawn to the mystery story, but for equally obvious reasons he usually parodies it in order to break its interior metaphor. Such is the case in "Tlön, Uqbar, Orbis Tertius".

At first the "postscript" purports to be an explanation. Tlön turns out to be not a mysterious planet after all. It is simply an astoundingly complex cataloguization, in the form of a forty-volume encyclopaedia, of an imaginary world created by a group of dedicated individuals. The explanation is inherently satisfying. It resolves the mystery (up to a point, for we never learn, for instance, how the curious addendum appears in Bioy Casares' copy of the *Anglo-American Cyclopaedia*). In addition, it bears the implications that human fantasy is limitless and can compete with any presumed creator of the physical universe. To the degree that in Tlön the mind creates reality, while in the story of Tlön the minds of Buckley and his associates create the encyclopaedia, there is a happy parallelism. We grasp at the statement that "la carta elucidaba enteramente el misterio de Tlön" (I, 421) (the letter completely elucidated the mystery of Tlön) and begin to relax. But at once Borges turns the tables on us. Objects from Tlön begin to invade our reality. At the same time people all over the world become infatuated with the picture of Tlön presented by Buckley's encyclopaedia because it appears to fulfil their longing for an orderly universe.

 Not all critics have distinguished adequately between these two aspects of Borges' subversion of his own "explanation", nor have they always rightly explored the implications. This is admittedly difficult, because Tlön itself is not presented in a wholly consistent way. Borges is pursuing two not wholly compatible aims in his description of Tlön. On the one hand, he is asking one of his familiar "What if?" questions: what if the world were as philosophical idealism describes it, a purely mental creation, in this case with no God to guarantee that mental images reflect more or less accurately a reality external to themselves. On the other hand, as in "La Biblioteca de Babel", he is using the description of Tlön which thus emerges to satirize certain aspects of our culture related to philosophy, science, language and literature, as we comfortably envisage them. So that Tlön has to be at one and the same time both like our own world and radically unlike it, a fantasy and a caricature rolled into one. This raises two problems. The first is connected with the question of orderliness, predictability and the sequence of cause and effect. If the world of Tlön is a purely mental creation, then it is (as the text tells us) no more than "una serie heterogénea de actos independientes" (I, 414) (a heterogeneous series of independent acts). All objects are "convocados y disueltos en un momento" (I, 415) (convoked and dissolved in an instant). Time itself is discontinuous and exists only in the succession of present instants of mental awareness. There is no causality outside the mind. Nothing exists except discrete "mental processes". Or so it seems.

In these circumstances the world of Tlön can and must only be one of pure chaos: the random flickering on and off of mental events in the consciousness of separate individuals. Each of these events is unrelated to anything outside the head of the individual concerned and is restricted to the awareness of the individual who conceives it. But at the same time Borges insists that it is nonetheless "coherent": a "cosmos" with its own "intimate laws". How can this be? We have to remember that it is not a description of a world in the normal sense. What we have is not Tlön but an encyclopaedia of Tlön, which bears the same relationship to it as the *Encyclopaedia Britannica* does to our world. That is, it catalogues and systematizes it, imposing on its infinite variety (on its chaos, in fact) an orderly presentation based on an alphabetical, linguistic approach. We no more see Tlön as it "is" than a Martian reading the *Encyclopaedia Britannica* would see our world as it "is". The orderliness comes from the encyclopaedia, not from Tlön.

The second problem of consistency in the description of Tlön is concerned with objects. Despite the fact that, as we have just seen, they are supposed to exist only in the mind and to disappear the instant the mind ceases to imagine them, they actually subsist. They are "real" objects. The moon, for instance, is surprisingly described (surprisingly, that is, in a Tlönian sense) as "un objeto real" (I, 415) (a real object). And we hear not only of transparent tigers and towers of blood, but also of coins, pencils, amphoras, a wheel, an ancient sword, a gold mask and part of what seems to be a statue, all of which seem to have an existence outside the mind of some single inhabitant of Tlön. It seems that the minds of people in Tlön "create" reality, but after the moment of creation, that reality remains in existence.

Let us now return to the ending. The first part of the postscipt imposes what looks like a "closed" ending. We are promised, and appear to receive, a full and complete explanation. But solutions and closed endings are not what we associate with Borges' stock-in-trade. No sooner are we proferred them, in this case, than the solution is subverted and the closed ending pulled open again. We now see how the last part of the postscript interacts with the description of Tlön, and the reason for the inconsistent presentation of the planet in the body of the tale. The two elements in the postscript which follow the pseudo-explanation refer back to the "real" objects we have just mentioned. Characteristically, there is no indication that the story has, at the last moment, suddenly changed course. Just as he does in "La casa de Asterión" and "La lotería en Babilonia", Borges produces a shift unobtrusively, in the middle of a paragraph. With a completely straight face, and using the same technique of realistic detail in the background description that we saw in the beginning of the story (the date, the place, the circumstances), he introduces an object from Tlön rapidly followed by another. The symbolism of these objects seems clear: a compass indicates a reliable direction; a cone, like a church-spire, points upwards towards transcendence. But what is their function? It is to link Tlön in a new way (no longer parodic) with our world. Ceasing to be a merely imaginary creation, it suddenly invades our reality with its reality. Just as the participants in the Babylonian lottery prefer to believe in an illusory order imposed on events by the Company, rather than accepting a world of pure chance, so at the end of "Tlön, Uqbar, Orbis Tertius" the inhabitants of our world prefer the illusory order of Tlön to the disorder of the universe as we know it. At the same time the objects "from Tlön" with their reassuring symbolism appear to endorse the planet's "real" existence.

What does all this mean? It means surely that the ending of "Tlön, Uqbar, Orbis Tertius" is designed to alter the puzzle. It is no longer a question of what the world would be like if the philosophical idealists were right. It is a question now of how far people will go to create for themselves a comforting picture of existence. If Tlön is simply the mental creation of Buckley and his associates, it makes no difference whether it is coherent or not, so far as the production of objects in Tlön is concerned. They would still be mere words in an encyclopaedia. Where, then, do the compass and the cone come from? Plainly they are *hrönir* brought into being by our aspirations, and so probably was the interpolation in Bioy Casares' copy of the *Anglo-American Cyclopaedia* with which the tale began. Because people are so desperately anxious to find an orderly world to inhabit, humanity, "Encantada por su rigor" (I, 424) (Enchanted by its rigour), embraces hungrily the world of Tlön and creates the "proofs" of its existence. In the last resort these "proofs" extend to the creation of the Encyclopaedia of Tlön itself, created in rivalry to the Christian God-ordained world. Tlön, in fact, turns out to be an anti-Aleph. The Aleph offers a vision of reality in terms of repulsive chaos and horror; Tlön appears to offer a vision of a rigorously orderly world more acceptable than our own. Both visions may be illusory. But whereas the anticlimactic ending of "El Aleph" is designed to emphasize this last point, the trick ending of "Tlön, Uqbar, Orbis Tertius" stresses something quite different: man's overmastering desire for a reassuring conception of a world according to design. A tale which began as a "What if?" story turns into a bitter fable of human credulity. The last few lines contain a prophecy and an assertion of indifference. The prophecy is that the process already described in the postscript will continue inexorably, fuelled as it is by a universal aspiration. As the First Encyclopaedia of Tlön has come into being in response to human longing, so inevitably will the Second Encyclopaedia appear in order to confirm and extend the impact of the first. But the narrator is not interested in participating in the collective dream. Pointless activity for pointless activity, he prefers a more literary form of futility.

"Abenjacán el Bojarí, muerto en su laberinto" (II, 91-99) could be seen as a story whose technique illustrates the kind of framing device described in Chapter 4. One could take the opening paragraphs, up to and including the description of the brick-built labyrinth, as the first part of the frame. The story of Abenjacán, the tyrannical sheik, Zaid, his treacherous vizir, and the stolen treasure, recounted by Dunraven as he and his companion Unwin thread their way through the labyrinth to its circular central chamber, would correspond to the core element. The attempts of the two men to explain the story would then complete the frame. A puzzle is announced at the beginning, details are supplied in the middle, and the explanation is reached at the end. This is essentially how Balderston reads the tale, that is, applying the model of a mystery story and emphasizing the parallels with a fragment of Stevenson's *The Master of Ballantrae*. However, such a reading depends on the notion that Unwin's explanation of the puzzle is correct and Dunraven's wrong.[6] In fact, Balderston asserts: "Un cuentista inocente y romántico como Dunraven repite la versión errónea; sólo Unwin, debido al rigor lógico con que examina el problema puede percibir que la serie [de acontecimientos] fue establecida para condicionar una deducción errónea por parte de aquellos espectadores incapaces de analizar las premisas defectuosas en que se basó la deducción" (An innocent and romantic story-teller like Dunraven repeats the false version; only Unwin, because of the logical rigour with which he examines the problem, can see that the series of events was set up in order to produce a false deduction on the part of those spectators who are incapable of analysing the defective premisses on which the deduction was based).

Such a reading, though it has the merit, for our purposes, of fixing attention on the ending, seems implausible for several reasons. In the first place, it makes the solution far too neat and rational. Balderston himself praises it for that very reason, describing it as "elegante por su lógica y la economía de sus términos" (elegant because of its logic and the economy of its terms) and relating it to "las series algebraicas y la lógica formal" (algebraic series and formal logic). Such reassuring endings, implying confidence in man's ability to comprehend and resolve the enigmas by which he is confronted, are, as we have tried to show, just the kind of endings which Borges avoids, at all events in those of his stories which fall fully within the category of tales of mystery. In the second place, it overlooks an important aspect of the opening strategy of the story: the comic presentation of both Dunraven and Unwin. The former is a poet, the author of an epic poem of doubtful scansion, whose theme he has still to discover. The latter is a mathematician whose only publication seems to be a study of a non-existent theorem. On this evidence neither qualifies as a very reliable problem-solver. It hardly seems likely that Borges would have made fun of both of his characters impartially, in the way he does, if afterwards he intended simply to endorse the explanation advanced by one of them. In the third place, what Unwin passes off as a "wise reflection" of his mathematically-trained mind was, in fact, a dream, we are told by the omniscient narrator. There seems to be a hint of Borgesian irony present in this, which undermines our confidence in Unwin's explanation. In separate articles, Boldy and I have suggested quite different interpretations.[7] However, we agree on one point. In Boldy's words: "El relato ofrece dos versiones contradictorias de un mismo acontecimiento. Postulamos que Borges no cree en ninguna de las dos" (The story offers two contradictory versions of the same event. We postulate that Borges does not believe in either of them).[8]

Boldy makes the assumption that it is Zaid who constructs the labyrinth, but that he is finally killed by Abenjacán for the crime of having usurped his name and power. The approach employed is ingenious and produces important insights, especially in regard to certain parallels between the two Englishmen and the two Arabs. It also cleverly links this to other Borges stories with cognate elements. But it is flawed by the fact that it places too much strain on the evidence and hardly fits in with the final sentences of the story, which would lose a large part of their meaning if Boldy's assumption were correct.

The strategy of "Abenjacán el Bojarí ..." is not quite as Balderston and Boldy have perceived it to be. It is, in fact, a further illustration of Borges' tendency in his more fantastic stories to subvert the ending which we have been led to expect, rather than simply closing the frame. The last part of the tale interacts with the rest of the story in two ways. The first relates to the story as a puzzle-story and to its possible solution. Borges has referred to it as a parody of a detective story.[9] But in what sense? In a normal detective story we expect a solution, however unforseen. Balderston asserts that this is what we get: Unwin analyses and interprets the ambiguous evidence better than Dunraven and his version is what we are intended to accept. Boldy rejects both Unwin's and Dunraven's solutions in favour of one of his own, which he considers fits all the evidence (including

---

[7] Steven Boldy, "Eramos pocos y parió la abuela: más versiones borgianas", *Revista Canadiense de Estudios Hispánicos*, 6, no. 2 (1982), 257-61; Donald L. Shaw, "En torno a 'Abenjacán el Bojarí, muerto en su laberinto'", *Actas del séptimo Congreso de la Asociación Internacional de Hispanistas*, ed. Giuseppe Bellini (Rome: Bulzoni, 1982), pp. 763-70.

[8] Boldy, p. 257.

[9] Jorge Luis Borges, "An Autobiographical Essay", in *The Aleph and Other Stories*, ed. and trans. Norman Thomas di Giovanni (New York: Dutton, 1970), p. 274.

parallels with other Borges stories) better than either of theirs. My own view is that the parody of the detective story arises from the fact that neither of the explanations put forward by Unwin and Dunraven is convincing. Borges, following Chesterton, is manipulating the genre in a familiar way. Detective stories in general belong to "popular" literature, which usually operates by bringing originality and invention to bear on conventional situations and often stereotyped characters. "High" literature, by contrast, tends to challenge conventions both in regard to thematic content and the presentation of characters and events. It demands of the reader a certain willingness to tolerate, if not accept, ideas, attitudes and values which contradict received ones. In "Abenjacán el Bojarí ..." the parody of the detective story which Borges refers to is connected with this distinction. Detective stories, and in general puzzle-stories where the puzzle is resolved at the end, are implicitly reassuring. By avoiding this type of ending here, Borges is parodying the genre. But at the same time he is lifting it to another level of significance and, by thwarting expectations and removing the reassurance, he is wholly altering its impact on the reader.

The key is to be found near the opening, when Dunraven points out that mysteries may be simple, as Unwin proposes, but also that they may be as complicated as the mystery of the universe, that is to say, insoluble. In "La muerte y la brújula", we recall, the puzzle, like this one in "Abenjacán el Bojarí ...", is in itself brilliantly conceived and worked out. But it alludes to a deeper theme in the story: whether the strict rationalism on which Lönnrot prides himself is ultimately a help or a hindrance in understanding a reality which may not operate according to rational assumptions. The ending and the role of Treviranus suggest that Lönnrot would have been wiser to show more caution before jumping to his logically compelling, but fatal, conclusions. What we find at the end of "Abenjacán el Bojarí ..." is a variant of the same technique. The fact that the puzzle itself includes a circular labyrinth with death at its centre seems enough to indicate that here, too, there is a deeper theme behind the story of the ruler and his vizir. Borges does not construct puzzles for their own sake: the mystery here implies the mystery of reality.

Dunraven is a poet. He represents intuitive vision and creative imagination as guides to the understanding of this mystery. What he sees in the puzzle is a ghost story, the triumphant vengeance of the murdered vizir. Like all ghost stories, it is predicated on the notion of a hidden, inexplicable dimension behind everyday experience. Unwin, the mathematician, corresponds closely to Lönnrot. He represents analytic reasoning as the means of deciphering reality. Dunraven's version of events is a story; Unwin's is an argument. It is a dissection of the various elements contained in his friend's account of the events and is designed to refute the latter's conclusion and to present what seems at first sight to be a more logical solution. But is it really any more convincing? Except for the fact that it eliminates the supernatural, it is not. It does not explain why Zaid has the courage to kill a vengeful Abenjacán in the labyrinth when he did not dare to do so when the latter was peacefully asleep in the tomb. Nor does it indicate why Zaid should apparently spend all the wealth he had stolen on the construction of his labyrinth, thus gaining nothing from his crime. Taken together with the initial presentation of Unwin and Dunraven, it seems that the versions offered by both men are intended to suggest that neither poetic insight nor cold ratiocination, neither acceptance of the supernatural nor rational analysis, can solve the mysteries by which we are surrounded.

The problem with this ending is that in itself it contains an anticlimax. We may, like Balderston, be initially convinced by Unwin's explanation of events, but subsequent reflection suggests that although it is ingenious and, as Dunraven admits, fits the conventions of the mystery story by neatly reversing the obvious conclusion, it will not really stand up. So we are left with no satisfactory explanation, but with yet another illustration of Borgesian scepticism. Borges, as so often, shows himself not to be in the business of providing answers, but in that of asking questions, the more disturbing in their implications the better. If Unwin's solution had been a genuine solution, it would have contradicted one of the main thrusts of Borges' work. The defect of conventional mystery stories, from Borges' point of view, is precisely that at the end they usually destroy the mystery. In this case, if the present approach is correct, Borges has successfully avoided this defect. But it leaves him with a problem. If Unwin's explanation is not the answer, how is the story to be brought to an end? It was suggested earlier that the ending interacts with the rest of the story in two ways. The first was by providing contrasting solutions to the central mystery. We have tried to show that the result was inconclusive and, therefore, inadequate as an ending. To see that this is the case, we only have to read the story as if the fourth sentence from the end — "Lo esencial era que Abenjacán pereciera" (The essential thing was for Abenjacán to perish) — were the last line. Murillo has correctly noted that this will not do: "The ironical ending is complete, of course, only when we understand that once the king is dead, there can be no identity for the living Zaid. He is simply a nobody. His fate was ultimately bound, through envy, hatred and fear, to Abenjacán's."[10] Borges conceals the anticlimax and causes the ending to interact with the rest of the story in a new way by introducing in the last three sentences the question of individual identity. Boldy makes a certain amount of play with the parallel between Zaid's situation at the end and those of Otálora in "El muerto" and Villari in "La espera", who are also usurpers of a similar kind. But there is a much more obvious similarity. That is, between the ending of "Abenjacán el Bojarí ..." and those of "El fin" and "El inmortal". In the case of "El fin" we read: "... ahora era nadie. Mejor dicho, era el otro: no tenía destino sobre la tierra y había matado a un hombre" (I, 524) (now he was no-one. Or rather, he was the other: he had no destiny on the earth and he had killed a man). At the end of "Abenjacán el Bojarí ..." we read: "Simuló ser Abenjacán, mató a Abenjacán y finalmente *fue Abenjacán* [...] antes de ser nadie en la muerte" (He pretended to be Abenjacán, he killed Abenjacán, and finally he was Abenjacán [...] before being no-one in death). The last words of "El inmortal", before the postscript, are: "... en breve, seré Nadie, como Ulises; en breve, seré todos: estaré muerto" (II, 22) (before long I shall be No-one, like Ulysses; before long I shall be everyone: I shall be dead). The connection between the three endings is patent. Inevitably also we recall the ending of "Los teólogos", in which Juan de Panonia, after the death of his rival Aureliano, discovers that in the mind of God he and Aureliano are the same person. The clearest similarity is with "El fin". In both cases we have a story of vengeance in which two factors are involved. One is the idea that the character who seeks revenge has surrendered himself so totally to that desire that, when he achieves it, he finds himself without any remaining identity. The other factor, which is closer to "El inmortal" and "Los teólogos", involves the idea that individual identity is an illusion in any case, that one man is all men, and hence that rivalry and vengeance are absurd and futile.

Up to the last three sentences "Abenjacán el Bojarí ..." is a whodunnit. The puzzle is: who killed whom? In the last three sentences there is a sudden shift of emphasis from the answer to that

---

[10] Luis Andrew Murillo, "The Labyrinths of Jorge Luis Borges. An Introduction to the Stories of *El Aleph*", *Modern Language Quarterly*, 20 (1959), p.263.

question, whatever it is, to something quite different. The courage
and moral integrity shown by Dahlmann at the end of "El Sur", by
Cruz in "Biografía de Tadeo Isidoro Cruz" or by Rosendo in
"Historia de Rosendo Juárez" produce for them a moment of
illumination about their real selves. By contrast, Zaid's cowardly
murder of his master is presented by Dunraven (who has accepted
Unwin's explanation of the events as substantially correct) as
bringing with it only the awareness of his lack of true identity, which
will be confirmed by his own death, the final destroyer of all
individuality.

The suddenness with which this radical shift takes place is perhaps
a defect in the story's technique. But the new theme of the non-
existence of individual identity is not unrelated to the rest of the tale.
In the main part of the final dialogue between Unwin and Dunraven
Borges has been concerned to indicate to us how ill-equipped we are
to solve the puzzles with which life confronts us. In the last sentences
he rounds the tale off by adding the further disturbing implication
that perhaps we do not know who we are, since the concept of
identity may be illusory.

A more baffling Borges story ending is that of "El otro" (II, 457-
64). Like "El Congreso", this is a tale which shuffles together a
number of easily recognizable Borgesian themes and ploys, but the
essential element is the questioning of one of our most cherished
assumptions: that of the reality of our personality and its continuity
despite the passage of time. In the tale both the "Borges" of 1969 and
his younger self of 1918 wish to believe that they are real and not the
figments of a dream or the projections of each other's minds. After
some preliminary exchanges, the older Borges adduces two proofs
intended to establish conclusively that he is the more "real" of the
two. This is the crucial part of the tale, the general strategy of which is
rather complex, despite Borges' slightly disingenuous suggestion to
Sorrentino that his later stories might be regarded as more traditional:
"¿Por qué no suponer que, cansado de todo eso, yo haya querido
escribir cuentos un poco a la manera de todos?" (Why not suppose
that, weary of all this, I had wanted to write stories somewhat in the
way everyone else does?).[11] The first three paragraphs of "El otro"
prefigure the rest by placing "Borges", the narrator, beside a river
representing the disintegrating force (time) which operates on the
personality. Subsequently Borges encapsulates references to time as

[11] In Sorrentino, p. 16.

simultaneous (both 1918 and 1969 are "now") and cyclic (the battle for Berlin in World War II was a remake of the Battle of Waterloo) within a frame consisting of the discussion between "Borges" and his younger self about each other's reality.

The discussion is both Borgesian and Unamunesque. If we accept the postulate of two people each of whom (to different degrees) reluctantly harbours the suspicion that he may have no objective existence outside the other's mind, where does that leave us, the readers? Presumably, contaminated with unreality. The theme of "El otro", that is, seems not unrelated to the kind of ontological insecurity which had surfaced in Unamuno, notably in *Niebla*, in *La historia de don Sandalio, jugador de ajedrez* and in *Soledad*. The mere suspicion that our existence may be no more than a hallucination or an illusion justifies Borges' use of "atrocious", one of his favourite adjectives, at the beginning of the story and his mention of horror at the end. This is what makes the proofs of his greater reality advanced by the older "Borges" so crucial. The author's strategy with regard to them is a familiar one. He offers us what seems to be a conclusive argument, only to follow it with one which totally undermines its validity.

The first argument used by the older figure admits of little reply and, in fact, the young "Borges" rather surprisingly admits it, though without appearing to appreciate its consequences for him. In the earlier exchanges, what is at stake is simply that the older "Borges" knows certain facts, including intimate ones, about his younger self. First, his address and where the house is situated. When this evidence has no effect on his younger interlocutor, the older "Borges" is provoked to use the word "proof" specifically, after which he details information about the young man's books and about his (presumably sexual) behaviour in the calle Dufour. The shortcoming of these two proofs is that they are known to the younger figure. Hence they could credibly emerge in a dream which he might be having of meeting his older self.

Borges does not proceed directly from these two less adequate proofs to the second two. Instead, he places at the centre, the core, of the story the references to time as possibly simultaneous and/or cyclic which we mentioned above. As always, the core and the frame are designed to interact. For when we come to the conclusive proof, we see that the difference between it and those produced in the earlier part of the frame-dialogue is precisely that it involves time. The older Borges, that is, quotes a line by Victor Hugo which he had memorized only after 1918 and which his younger self, therefore, could not have known. At this point the conclusion is inescapable that, if one of the two is dreaming the other, it must be the older "Borges" dreaming the younger.

The story seems to be over, and if a similar story had been written by a nineteenth-century author, this is no doubt where it would have ended. That is, on a note of reassurance, for now everything seems to fit neatly into place. An old man on a park bench falls asleep and dreams of his younger self. The dream is disturbing but not ultimately a threat to the ontological security of the dreamer, who is able to assert his "reality" over that of the figure about whom he dreams. But Borges is not in the business of reassurance. The parallel between "El otro" and "Las ruinas circulares" is hard to overlook. In the latter both the wizard and his "son" are shown in the end to be equally unreal. It would be quite contrary to the entire thrust of Borges' thinking to offer the reader a story in which the younger "Borges" is a figment, while the older "Borges" is comfortably real. Borges' problem, therefore, at the end of the tale is to find a device to undermine the reality of the narrator, just as he had undermined the reality of his interlocutor. The test of the tale's success is whether this concluding device works. At first sight the last proof of the older "Borges" is almost as conclusive as the preceding one, and once more it includes a specific ingredient of time. He gives his younger self a United States banknote dated 1964 (in some editions 1974). At this point, in spite of the fact that, logically speaking, the latter could perfectly well dream of a 1964 banknote in 1918, he perceives the implication and angrily destroys this further evidence of his own unreality.

But now our troubles as readers begin. In the first place, the narrator (who now for the first time mentions his semi-blindness) is led to believe — wrongly — that American banknotes do not bear a date. What are we to make of this? It is, of course, possible that Borges himself made a genuine mistake about what was after all foreign currency to him. But this is extremely unlikely. Excluding that possibility, we are left with the paradox, at the conclusion of the tale, that the narrator produces a very good additional proof of his own reality and of the unreality of his interlocutor, but mistakenly disbelieves it. Why should Borges wish to place his character in such a tortuous situation? "El otro" ends with an "explanation" offered by the narrator. It contains three affirmations: i) the meeting actually happened; ii) his younger self was dreaming the meeting and dreamed of the "impossible" date on the banknote; iii) he, the narrator, was awake. Plainly, however, the second affirmation is flawed, since United States banknotes do, in fact, carry a date, though it is not clear how many readers would actually know this or would take the trouble to find out. But the flaw is objectively there and we must conclude that Borges intended us to deduce that the narrator's explanation was not to be taken on trust. The only alternative to it is that *both* figures in the tale were dreaming. In that case, the narrator's view that he was awake symbolizes afresh our inability to distinguish between reality and fantasy.

There is another twist to the ending. The text states: "Hizo pedazos el billete y guardó la moneda. Yo resolví tirarla al río" (II, 463) (He tore up the note and put away the coin. I decided to throw it in the river). There is no indication that the older "Borges" accepted the coin offered by his younger self, but even if we are to presume that he had done so, the text would have said: "Yo resolví tirar la mía al río" (I decided to throw mine in the river). The coin in question seems, therefore, to be the same one. But how can the narrator resolve to toss into the river a coin which his other self has just put back into his pocket? We must assume that Borges is additionally hinting to us that the difference between the two protagonists is purely illusory: during the whole course of the story they are one and the same. The difference of age is a mere illusion suffered in his dream by the narrator. Once more, Borges is aiming at a "double-take" ending, but it is open to question whether, in this case, it is not too over-elaborate to be fully successful.

One of the most memorable of Borges' later stories is "Ulrica" (II, 465-68), about a meeting between an elderly Spanish American professor and a Scandinavian girl in the ancient English city of York. Borges himself in the early 1980s described it as "mi cuento preferido" (my favourite story).[12] It is not immediately obvious why Borges should prefer it to other late stories, but we may conjecture that, apart from its theme, involving a rare, characteristically low-key presentation of love and sexuality, it reminded him of his earlier favourite, "El Sur". A feature of both these stories is that we have to work back from the endings to a recognition of the tales' fundamental ambiguity. The last words of "Ulrica" — "... poseí por primera y última vez la imagen de Ulrica" (I possessed for the first and last time the image of Ulrica) — create a slightly disconcerting effect. They

[12] In Roffé, p. 3.

constitute the climax of the story, but it is not, as in "El Sur", an unexpected climax suddenly shifting an uneventful narrative into a tense, life-threatening situation. On the contrary, it is the fully anticipated outcome of the third sentence: "Quiero narrar mi encuentro con Ulrica" (I want to tell of my encounter with Ulrica). And yet it betrays our anticipation. Why "poseí la imagen de Ulrica" (I possessed the image of Ulrica) and not simply "poseí a Ulrica" (I possessed Ulrica)? We feel a sense of anticlimax, without quite being able to identify the reason.

Reading the story again with the last words in mind, we slowly come to see that from the very beginning Borges has been leading up to its final statement. The epigraph is no great help to those of us who (remembering Borges' quip about his acquaintance with Sanskrit) only know the Old Norse that everybody knows. It means, in fact: "He takes the sword, Gram, and lays it naked between them." Did we but realize it, the emphasis is already on separation rather than on consummation. The opening sentence — "Mi relato será fiel a la realidad o, en todo caso, a mi recuerdo personal de la realidad, lo cual es lo mismo" (My story will be faithful to reality or, in any event, to my personal memory of reality, which is the same thing) — again acquires a new significance in the light of the ending. For it not only hints that the tale will have to do, more than usually, with "reality", but also that reality is created by the mind and that there is no reality of the past outside the individual memory. We eventually perceive that these are ideas which are crucial to a clear understanding of the tale. The next clue is Ulrica's curious remark, which for the first time fixes the narrator's interest on her: "Inglaterra fue nuestra y la perdimos, si alguien puede tener algo o algo puede perderse" (II, 466) (England was ours and we lost her, if anyone can have anything or anything can be lost). The sentence prefigures the tale's concluding words. Can one ever possess the reality of anything (England) or of anyone (Ulrica)? The remark is immediately followed by the first of a series of literary references which associate Ulrica with Blake, with De Quincey, with Ibsen and, above all, with Brynhild of the *Völsung Saga* and with William Morris, its translator. We recall that Morris' *Sigurd the Volsung* was one of the first books Borges remembers reading. These associations are not introduced casually. Together with the idea that the mind creates its own reality and the epigraph's implication that the destiny of the couple is separation, they hint to the alert reader that the final development of the tale is no more than a dream in Professor Otálora's mind, generated by a casual encounter and coloured by literary reminiscences.

If we adopt this hypothesis, many of the odd details in the body of the story fall into place. The key element in the presentation of Ulrica is her grey eyes. Grey in Borges is the colour of unreality: Cartaphilus in "El inmortal", for instance, also has grey eyes. The remaining details fit, her general air and smile conveying mystery and distance. Her remark that to be Norwegian is an act of faith reinforces her earlier comment on possession and loss: all attempts to comprehend and keep a grip on reality, including that of the self (nationality being an essential part of one's self-image) are mere acts of faith without objective supports. The difference between Ulrica and Otálora is that she appears to be aware from the outset that she is a phantom. Her remark apropos of the loss of England by Norway seems to contain a warning to Otálora that such is the case. She is moved more by the swords in York Minster than by the Viking long ships in Oslo because of what they symbolize: loss, in this case the loss of York by Norway. This is clearly related to the fact that both in the epigraph and in Otálora's final remark to her a sword is associated with loss of love's fulfilment and with separation. Real contact between the couple is impossible, since they are simply enacting, inside his mind, an episode suggested by the *Völsung Saga*.

Like "El Sur", the story has no pivotal episode. We move imperceptibly from what Otálora — by his initial use of the words "the facts" — implies is a real situation in a hotel in York to his dream of love and possession at the end. So imperceptibly do we move, indeed, that on first reading we are unaware of what has happened until the final sentence breaks the spell. But we can assume, on further reading of the tale, that the shift comes with the sentence "Al día siguiente bajé temprano al comedor" (II, 466) (Next day I went down early to the dining-room). From here on the atmosphere of the story is different: perhaps the snowfall, which alters the appearance of the moors, is symbolic of the change which now overtakes the tale. In addition, Otálora's Schopenhauerian joke, strategically situated at this point, already strongly hints at the unreality of his companion. At all events, as the couple "leave" the hotel (the fact that the one they arrive at in Thorgate has the same name casts doubt on their setting out) they pass into a different dimension of reality. Three elements underline the difference between this dimension and that of conventional experience. The first is the wolf-howl which, as we later realize, suggests that Otálora has transported himself, with part of his mind, to the historical period of the Norwegian domination of Yorkshire. The second is Ulrica's forecast of the birdsong, which marks her off from the limitations of ordinary human beings. The third is her enigmatic reference to her own imminent death. Partly, this sense of love (she has just promised herself to Otálora) leading to death stresses her identification with Brynhild. But also it seems to imply an awareness on her part that she "lives" only in Otálora's dream-fantasy and hence that as soon as he realizes that he possesses no more than her "image", a simulacrum, her imaginary life will come to an end. The couple's last spoken words are similarly indicative. The reference to the "tragic story" of Sigurd and Brynhild causes Ulrica to slacken her pace. Otálora reproaches her for this with the suggestion, referring back to the epigraph, that she wished the symbolic separation to take place. In reality, we must assume that the mention of the *Völsung Saga* characters reawakens Ulrica's awareness of her fantasmal situation, her consciousness (which is the essence of her fascination) of existing precariously inside Otálora's dream. By walking more slowly she wishes to prolong the dream, but the sudden arrival of the couple at the inn seems to bring on the opposite fear: that (perhaps because the inn-name is the same) Otálora may realize that he is cherishing a fantasy and bring it to an end before their final embrace. The William Morris wallpaper clues us in afresh to who was the original begetter of Otálora's dream of love before it reaches its ambiguous climax. A final interesting inlaid detail is the last paragraph's reference to *Corinthians*, 13. 12: "... la bruñida caoba me recordó el espejo de la Escritura" (the polished mahogany reminded me of the mirror in the Scriptures).[13] The notion of Otálora's seeing "as in a glass darkly" implies what the reference to "the image" of Ulrica confirms: that he is not "face to face" with reality but seeing only a reflection of it in the mirror of his literature-impregnated mind.

---

[13] Leon Bloy's obsession with this verse is the subject of the essay "El espejo de los enigmas", the thrust of which is once more to emphasize our inability to understand either the enigmatic laws which may govern reality or "el Abismo verdadero, que es el alma del hombre" (II, 239) (the real Abyss, which is the soul of man).

CHAPTER 9

CONCLUSION

At the end of his interesting *La filosofía de Borges*, Juan Nuño recognizes the perversity of his preceding commentary on Borges' philosophical ideas: "Es innegable que Borges encierra temas de valor metafísico, pero justamente eso: el encierro vale más que los temas. Y el temor del comentarista es siempre el de maltratar o echar a perder o preterir la maravillosa envoltura" (Borges undeniably incorporates themes which have metaphysical value, but that is just it: the way he incorporates them matters more than the themes. And the commentator is always afraid of harming or spoiling or subordinating the marvellous wrapping).[1] This is an understandable fear, though unjustified in Nuño's case. However, the aim of the foregoing pages has been rather to try to show that the fictional "wrapping" of Borges' themes is really inseparable from the themes themselves and has to be examined in relation to them. The view popularized by the Russian Formalists that new forms (new wrappings) come about, not in order to express new contents, but in order to replace old, worn-out forms, runs counter to this approach. But it is a view which is objectively difficult to sustain. Hume, for instance, indicates rather convincingly that the evolution of fantasy literature has closely followed changing attitudes to reality: "Techniques for attacking the beliefs of the audience have little in common," she concludes; what is consistent is "the author's attack on the reader's assurance".[2]

---

[1] Juan Nuño, *La filosofía de Borges* (Mexico City: Fondo de Cultura Económica, 1986), p. 138.

[2] Hume, p. 125.

Borges' art is not independent of the outside world, a closed realm unconnected with anything but itself. We may, like Alazraki, Wheelock, Sturrock or Zlotchew, read Borges this way if we choose, with or without ritual obeisances to Ricardou, Morisette and other post-formalist critics.[3] But it is not the only way to read him, and to write as though it were is to falsify the issues. The fact that Borges has frequently asserted that reality is unknowable, and in any case not expressible in verbal terms, does not mean that his fictional work is only mimetic of the activity of the artist himself, as Sturrock contends.[4] Wheelock, likewise, dogmatically overstates the case:

> ... the work does not finally impart or signify anything except that it comprises art, which is artifice having an aesthetic effect; the only reality offered is the literature itself, self-enclosed and distinct from anything else: ars, ars est. Borges' fiction is by no means devoid of familiar truth, but it is only there as building material[5]

Because they cannot know the ultimate nature of reality or "penetrate the divine scheme of the universe", writers are not necessarily precluded from writing about reality *as if* it were partially comprehensible. Nor does it follow that, because the relation between the signifier and the signified is arbitrary, writers cannot assume a certain consensus among speakers and readers of a given tongue which allows some sort of meaningful communication about the outside world. It is possible to make sense of Borges' stories as self-referential sign-systems whose encoded meanings are not to be thought of as relating in any way to human experiences beyond the act of reading, but to do so is surely to impoverish our response to them.

This is not to deny that our response, as twentieth-century readers, especially to contemporary texts, has undergone a significant modification in recent years. Not only has the presentation of "reality" by writers altered, but our expectations of the text have also changed. We read not only for entertainment and then significance,

---

[3] Jaime Alazraki, "Borges' Modernism and the New Critical Idiom", in his *Borges and the Kabbalah* (Cambridge: Cambridge Univ. Press, 1988), chapter 13; Carter Wheelock, "Borges and the Death of the Text", *Hispanic Review*, 53 (1985), 151-61, and "Borges, Cortázar and the Aesthetic of the Vacant Mind", *International Fiction Review*, 12, no. 1 (1985), 3-10; John Sturrock, *Paper Tigers. The Ideal Fictions of Jorge Luis Borges* (Oxford: Clarendon Press, 1973); Clark Zlotchew, "Fiction Wrapped in Fiction: Casuality in Borges and the *Nouveau Roman*", *INTI*, 15 (1982), 25-32.

[4] Sturrock, p. 33.

[5] Wheelock, "Borges, Cortázar ...", p. 9.

but also for the pleasure of recognizing literary patterning, of
colluding with the author and of detecting the devices and mechanisms which are part of the literary artefact and which are nowadays
quite often deliberately foregrounded. When Borges writes in "El
duelo": "Dictar este relato es para mí una modesta y lateral
aventura" (II, 406) (To dictate this story is for me a modest and
lateral adventure), or in "La señora mayor": "En la fecha de mi
relato ..." (II, 402) (On the date of my story ...), he is deliberately
removing any illusion that what we are reading is other than a fiction.
But, again, it does not follow that this constitutes an invitation to
resist any temptation to relate the fiction to life. It is, of course,
unfashionable (and, to be sure, sometimes unwise) to pay attention
to what writers say about their own work. But perhaps we ought not
to overlook the fact that of "La Biblioteca de Babel", for example,
Borges said to Charbonnier that the tale contained "l'idée d'être
perdu dans l'univers, de ne pas le comprendre, l'envie de trouver une
solution précise [...] le sentiment de la solitude, de l'angoisse, de
l'inutilité, du caractère mistérieux de l'univers, du temps, ce qui est
plus important: de nous mêmes" (the idea of being lost in the
universe, of not understanding it, the wish to find a precise solution
[...] the feeling of loneliness, of anguish, of uselessness, of the
mysterious character of the universe, of time, what is even more
important: of ourselves).[6] These are all familiar preoccupations of
Borges in his essays, and universal human preoccupations to boot. Is
it really plausible to suggest that we should ignore them entirely in
interpreting the story in question, or others like it?

What has been contended here, in other words, is that we can and
should be consciously aware of the strategies which Borges uses in his
fiction. As with other contemporary writers, we should expect to
have to work at them as part of the task of understanding the tales as
fully as we can. But not with the accompanying belief that we are in
the presence of "The Death of the Text". The possible paradox
subsists: a work of fiction is necessarily an organized, structured
attempt to represent a reality which is random, elusive, even possibly
unknowable. But the fact that we have a text in front of us which, in
the opinion of reputable readers, clearly tries to comment on
something other than itself, indicates that there are at least two views
of the problem. Borges himself sets us an example. Although he
himself was perfectly aware, as his repeated affirmations attest, that

[6] Charbonnier, p. 20.

reality is not verbal, he continued to write and (it is argued here) to write about reality and not just about writing. Although he seems to have regarded our awareness of reality as awareness of chaotic flux, he continued to structure his tales meticulously. We, too, can be aware of the paradox, without allowing it to distort our critical response. With all the appropriate ifs and buts, we can assume a relationship of some sort between art and life. If this is an illusion, it is a necessary illusion in dealing with Borges.

That being said, we are left with the traditional view that in literature there is frequently an interrelation between form and meaning, whether in the sense that form can at times become a symbol of meaning or in the sense that form is simply the external expression of an inner meaning. To the extent that many Borges stories pose problems of interpretation to the reader and on inspection reveal more than one level of meaning, their form is in a broad sense often symbolic of the mysterious nature of the reality to which they seem to refer. Certain specific formal elements, such as the use of hidden elements, *mise en abîme*, internal reduplication, circularity and the like, may be more readily interpreted symbolically than others, such as foreshadowing, anticlimax, framing or inlaid details, which are more immediately functional. The aim here has been to try to identify some of the more important and frequently employed techniques and the way Borges uses them to solve the problems presented by the telling of individual tales. It is not really possible to produce a "grammar" of Borges' narratology. In the last resort we cannot get beyond Borges' own comment: "... creo que cada cuento impone su técnica" (I think every tale imposes its own tecnique).[7] What we can do is notice that Borges has a certain repertoire of devices which occasionally recur and which we can recognize and examine. No claim is made here to have identified all the devices or to have examined examples from every story. Nor is it even possible to argue that a study of Borges' narrative strategies will in itself answer the question of why and how Borges' later stories differ in many cases from those of *Ficciones* and *El Aleph*. However, it seems plausible to suggest that as time went on Borges became gradually less able to invent the impressive ploys he had so brilliantly conceived earlier.

If the examination we have attempted to carry out leads to any overall conclusion, that conclusion must emphasize the variety of the

[7] Roffé, p. 9.

strategies which Borges invents and deploys. If there is a bane of Borges studies, so far as his fiction is concerned, apart from the unrelenting search for meaning combined with inadequate attention to technique, it is the tendency to try to reduce the formal elements in his stories to one basic model and make them into variants of some sort of Borgesian ur-text. Alazraki's *Versiones, inversiones, reversiones*, which we have criticized for this tendency, has been followed *inter alia* by Cédola's *Borges o la coincidencia de los opuestos*, which promises to reveal the "structuring" of the thirteen stories of *El Aleph* only to disappoint us by positing a similar binary structure in every case.[8] It must be pointed out that such approaches, however valid the insights they occasionally yield, are apt to be unhelpful because they tend to proceed by elimination rather than by accretion. It seems more profitable to examine the variety of Borges' techniques, tailored as they are to the exigencies of each individual story. Such an examination cannot be exhaustive. Just as his themes have been and will be interpreted in very different ways, so his narrative strategies are likely to go on being unravelled in different ways and fresh ones to go on being identified. The aim here has been to examine Borges chiefly as a practitioner of the craft of writing, as an inventor of functionally effective ways of telling tales. To see his stories as artefacts, as well as reflecting on them as statements, is to make a small contribution, or so it is hoped, to enriching the dialogue between Borges and his readers.

[8] Estela Cédola, *Borges o la coincidencia de los opuestos* (Buenos Aires: Eudeba, 1987).

BIBLIOGRAPHY

The following bibliography is deliberately selective. It contains references to works cited in the text and to material primarily relevant to Borges' fictional technique.

1. WORKS BY BORGES

Prosa completa, 2 vols. (Barcelona: Bruguera, 1980)

Veinticinco agosto 1983 y otros cuentos (Madrid: Siruela, 1983)

Obra poética, 1923-1977, 3rd ed. (Madrid: Alianza, 1983)

"An Autobiographical Essay", in *The Aleph and Other Stories*, ed. and trans. Norman Thomas di Giovanni (New York: Dutton, 1970)

A Universal History of Infamy, trans. Norman Thomas di Giovanni (Harmondsworth: Penguin, 1985)

Fictions, trans. Anthony Kerrigan (London: Calder, 1985)

The Aleph and Other Stories, trans. Norman Thomas di Giovanni (London: Cape, 1971)

Dr. Brodie's Report, trans. Norman Thomas di Giovanni (Harmondsworth: Penguin, 1985)

The Book of Sand, trans. Norman Thomas di Giovanni (Harmondsworth: Penguin, 1986)

2. CRITICAL WORKS

Agheana, Ion, *The Meaning of Experience in the Prose of Jorge Luis Borges* (New York: Peter Lang, 1988)

Alazraki, Jaime, *La prosa narrativa de Jorge Luis Borges* (Madrid: Gredos, 1968)

—, "Estructura y función de los sueños en un cuento de Borges", *Ibero-romania*, New Series, 3 (1975), 9-38

—, *Jorge Luis Borges, el escritor y la crítica* (Madrid: Taurus, 1976)

—, *Versiones, inversiones, reversiones: el espejo como modelo estructural en los cuentos de Borges* (Madrid: Gredos, 1977)

—, *Borges and the Kabbalah* (Cambridge: Cambridge Univ. Press, 1988)

Alonso, Amado, "Borges narrador", in his *Materia y forma en poesía*, 2nd ed. (Madrid: Gredos, 1960), pp. 341-54

Anderson Imbert, Enrique, "El punto de vista en Borges", *Hispanic Review*, 44 (1976), 213-21

Balderston, Daniel, *El precursor velado: R.L. Stevenson en la obra de Borges* (Buenos Aires: Sudamericana, 1985)

Barrenechea, Ana María, *Borges the Labyrinth Maker* (New York: New York Univ. Press, 1965)

—, "Borges y los símbolos", *Revista Iberoamericana*, 100/101 (1977), 601-08

—, "Borges y la narración que se autoanaliza", in her *Textos hispanoamericanos* (Caracas: Monte Avila, 1978), pp. 127-44

Barrientos, Juan José, *Borges y la imaginación* (Mexico City: Bellas Artes-Katún, 1986)

Bell-Villada, Gene, *Borges and his Fiction* (Chapel Hill: North Carolina Univ. Press, 1981)

Bickel, Gisèle, "La alegoría del pensamiento", *Modern Language Notes*, 88 (1973), 295-316

Borello, Rodolfo, "El evangelio según Borges", *Revista Iberoamericana*, 100/101 (1977), 503-16

Boldy, Steven, "Eramos pocos y parió la abuela: más versiones borgianas", *Revista Canadiense de Estudios Hispánicos*, 6, no. 2 (1982), 257-61

Burgin, Richard, *Conversations with Jorge Luis Borges* (New York: Avon, 1968)

Campra, Rosalba, "Fantástico y sintaxis narrativa", *Río de la Plata*, 1 (1985), 95-111

Carlos, Alberto J., "Dante y el Aleph de Borges", *Duquesne Hispanic Review*, 5, no. 1 (1966), 35-50

Cédola, Estela, *Borges o la coincidencia de los opuestos* (Buenos Aires: Eudeba, 1987)

Charbonnier, Georges, *Entretiens avec Jorge Luis Borges* (Paris: Gallimard, 1967)

Christ, Ronald, *The Narrow Act. Borges' Art of Allusion* (New York: New York Univ. Press, 1969)

—, "Forking Narratives", *Latin American Literary Review*, 7, no. 14 (1979), 52-61

Cortázar, Julio, "Algunos aspectos del cuento", *Casa de las Américas*, 2, nos. 15/16 (1962-63), 3-14

Cortínez, Carlos, "Hacia el éxtasis: 'El Congreso' de Borges", *Hispanic Review*, 54 (1986), 313-22

Costa, René de, "A Note on Narrative Voice in Borges's Early Fiction", *Modern Philology*, 76 (1978-79), 193-96

Dauster, Frank, "Notes on Borges' Labyrinths", *Hispanic Review*, 30 (1962), 142-48

Del Río, Carmen, *Jorge Luis Borges y su ficción: el conocimiento como invención* (Miami: Universal, 1983)

Devoto, Daniel, "Aleph et Alexis", in *Jorge Luis Borges*, ed. Dominique de Roux and Jean de Milleret (Paris: L'Herne, 1964), pp. 280-92

Di Giovanni, Norman Thomas, Daniel Halpern, and Frank MacShane, eds., *Borges on Writing* (New York: Dutton, 1973)

D'Lugo, Marvin, "Binary Vision in Borgean Narrative", *Romance Notes*, 13 (1971-72), 425-31

Efron, Arthur, "Perspectivism and the Nature of Fiction: Don Quixote and Borges", *Thought*, 50, no. 197 (1975), 148-75

Foster, David William, "Borges and Structuralism: Toward an Implied Poetics", *Modern Fiction Studies*, 19, no. 3 (1973), 341-51

—, "Para una caracterización de la *escritura* en los relatos de Borges", *Revista Iberoamericana*, 100/101 (1977), 337-55

—, *Jorge Luis Borges. An Annotated Primary and Secondary Bibliography* (New York: Garland, 1984)

Frank, Roslyn M., and Vosburg, Nancy, "Textos y contratextos en 'El jardín de senderos que se bifurcan'", *Revista Iberoamericana*, 100/101 (1977), 517-34

Friedman, Mary Lusky, *The Emperor's Kites* (Durham: Duke Univ. Press, 1987)

García Montero, Antonio, "Subtexto en 'El Inmortal' y 'Deutsches Requiem'", *Hispamérica*, 21 (1978), 3-10

Gertel, Zunilda, " 'El Sur' de Borges: búsqueda de la identidad en el laberinto", *Nueva Narrativa Hispanoamericana*, 1, no. 2 (1971), 35-55

Hall, J.B., "Deception or Self-deception? The Essential Ambiguity of Borges' 'Emma Zunz'", *Forum for Modern Language Studies*, 18 (1982), 258-65

Haberly, David T., "The Argentine Gospels of Borges", *Bulletin of Hispanic Studies*, 66 (1989), 47-54

Hirsch, Eric D., *Validity in Interpretation* (New Haven: Yale Univ. Press, 1967)

—, *The Aims of Interpretation* (Chicago: Chicago Univ. Press, 1976)

Hume, Kathryn, *Fantasy and Mimesis* (London: Methuen, 1984)

Irby, James E., "Sobre la estructura de 'Hombre de la esquina rosada'", *Anuario de Filología* (Venezuela), 1, no. 1 (1962), 157-72

—, *Encuentro con Borges* (Buenos Aires: Galerna, 1968)

Klein, Lucy B., "Los falsos indicios en la narrativa de Jorge Luis Borges", *Symposium*, 28, no. 2 (1974), 146-53

Lyon, Thomas E., "Borges and the (Somewhat) Personal Narrator", *Modern Fiction Studies*, 19, no. 3 (1973), 363-72

McGrady, Donald, "El Redentor del Asterión de Borges", *Revista Iberoamericana*, 135/136 (1986), 531-35

—, "Prefiguration, Narrative Transgression and Eternal Return in Borges'

'La forma de la espada'", *Revista Canadiense de Estudios Hispánicos*, 12, no. 1 (1987), 141-49

McMurray, George R., *Jorge Luis Borges* (New York: Ungar, 1980)

Madrid, Lelia, *Cervantes y Borges: la inversión de los signos* (Madrid: Pliegos, 1987)

Magliola, Robert, "Jorge Luis Borges and the Loss of Being", *Studies in Short Fiction*, 15, no. 1 (1978), 25-31

Merivale, Patricia, "The Flaunting of Artifice in Vladimir Nabokov and Jorge Luis Borges", *Wisconsin Studies in Contemporary Literature*, 8 (1967), 294-309

Molloy, Silvia, "Borges y la distancia literaria", *Sur*, 318 (1969), 26-37

—, "La composición del personaje en la ficción de Borges", *Nueva Revista de Filología Española*, 26 (1977), 130-40

—, *Las letras de Borges* (Buenos Aires: Sudamericana, 1979)

Murillo, Luis Andrew, "The Labyrinths of Jorge Luis Borges. An Introduction to the Stories of *El Aleph*", *Modern Languages Quarterly*, 20 (1959), 259-66

—, *The Cyclical Night. Irony in James Joyce and Jorge Luis Borges* (Cambridge, Mass.: Harvard Univ. Press, 1968)

Natella, Arthur A., "Symbolic Colors in the Stories of Jorge Luis Borges", *Journal of Spanish Studies*, 2 (1974), 39-48

Newman, Charles, and Kinzie, Mary, eds., *Prose for Borges* (Evanston: Northwestern Univ. Press, 1972)

Nuño, Juan, *La filosofía de Borges* (Mexico City: Fondo de Cultura Económica, 1986)

Orgambide, Pedro G., *Horacio Quiroga, el hombre y su obra* (Buenos Aires: Stilcograf, 1954)

Oviedo, José Miguel, "Borges sobre los pasos de Borges: *El libro de arena*", *Revista Iberoamericana*, 100/101 (1977), 713-19

Paoli, Roberto, *Borges, percorsi di significato* (Messina-Firenze: D'Anna, 1977)

Pérez, Alberto C., *Realidad y suprarrealidad en los cuentos fantásticos de Jorge Luis Borges* (Miami: Universal, 1971)

Prieto, René, "Mimetic Strategies: The Unreliable Narrator in Latin American Literature", *Revista de Estudios Hispánicos*, 19, no. 3 (1985), 61-73

Pupo-Walker, Enrique, ed., *El cuento hispanoamericano ante la crítica* (Madrid: Castalia, 1973)

Quiroga, Horacio, *Sobre literatura* (Montevideo: Arca, 1970)

Rest, Jaime, *El laberinto del universo: Borges y el pensamiento nominalista* (Buenos Aires: Fausto, 1976)

Rivero Potter, Alicia, *Autor, lector* (Detroit: Wayne State Univ. Press, 1989)

Rodriguez Monegal, Emir, "Borges y la *Nouvelle Critique*", *Revista Iberoamericana*, 80 (1972), 367-90

—, *Jorge Luis Borges. A Literary Biography* (New York: Dutton, 1978)

Roffé, Reina, ed., *Espejo de escritores* (Hanover, N.H.: Ediciones del Norte, 1985)

Rosa, Nicolás, "Borges o la ficción laberíntica", in *Nueva novela latinoamericana*, ed. José Laforgue (Buenos Aires: Paidos, 1972), II, pp. 140-73

Santander, Carlos, "Estructura narrativa en 'Hombre de la esquina rosada'", *Revista Chilena de Literatura*, 1 (1970), 23-30

Santí, Enrico-Mario, "Escritura y tradición: Martín Fierro en dos cuentos de Borges", *Revista Iberoamericana*, 87/88 (1974), 303-19

Shaw, Donald L., *Borges: Ficciones* (London: Grant and Cutler, 1976)

—, "Acerca de la crítica de los cuentos de Borges", *Cuadernos Hispanoamericanos*, 346 (1979), 130-43

—, "En torno a 'Abenjacán el Bojarí, muerto en su laberinto'", *Actas del séptimo Congreso de la Asociación Internacional de Hispanistas*, ed. Giuseppe Bellini (Rome: Bulzoni, 1982), pp. 763-70

Sorrentino, Fernando, *Siete conversaciones con Jorge Luis Borges* (Buenos Aires: Pardo, 1974)

Sosnowski, Saul, "The God's Script: A Kabbalistic Quest", *Modern Fiction Studies*, 19 (1973), 381-94

Sturrock, John, *Paper Tigers. The Ideal Fictions of Jorge Luis Borges* (Oxford: Clarendon Press, 1973)

Volek, Emil, "Aquiles y la tortuga: arte, imaginación y la realidad según Borges", in his *Cuatro claves para la modernidad* (Madrid: Gredos, 1984)

Wheelock, Carter, *The Mythmaker. A Study of Motif and Symbol in the Short Stories of Jorge Luis Borges* (Austin: Univ. of Texas Press, 1969)

—, "Borges, Cortázar and the Aesthetic of the Vacant Mind", *International Fiction Review*, 12, no. 1 (1985), 3-10

—, "Borges and the Death of the Text", *Hispanic Review*, 53 (1985), 151-61

Zlotchew, Clark, "Fiction Wrapped in Fiction: Casuality in Borges and the *Nouveau Roman*", *INTI*, 15 (1982), 25-32

INDEX OF STORIES

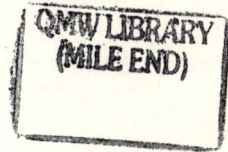

QMW LIBRARY
(MILE END)

LIVERPOOL MONOGRAPHS IN HISPANIC STUDIES
ISSN 0261-1538
General Editors: Peter A. Bly, James Higgins
Assistant Editor: Roger Wright

The Poet in Peru
Alienation and the Quest for a Super-Reality
JAMES HIGGINS
0 905205 10 3. LMHS 1. x+166pp. 1982.

Readings of the work of six modern Peruvian poets—Eguren, Vallejo, Belli, Cisneros, Moro, Adán—reveal, in spite of wide differences between the poets, a common dilemma (how to reconcile the dichotomies of their society) and a common artistic stance (that of the outcast who perceives a higher reality in a visionary, surreal world).

"Higgins has set himself a difficult task in this intriguing volume, and to say that it perhaps raises more questions than it answers is in no way anything but an appreciation of the way in which he has carried out a complex and difficult undertaking" (*Hispanic Review* 1984).

Galdós's Novel of the Historical Imagination
A Study of the Contemporary Novels
PETER A. BLY
0 905205 14 6. LMHS 2. xii+195pp. 1983.

Professor Bly argues that in the *serie contemporánea* Benito Pérez Galdós (1843-1920) created a special type of historical novel which, by drawing subtle parallels between fictional action and political events, allegorises the political history of the recent Spanish past.

"*Galdós's Novel of the Historical Imagination* is one of the most fruitful studies of Galdós to appear in recent years; it deserves a place in the library of every *galdosista*" (*Critica Hispánica* 1983).

The Deceptive Realism of Machado de Assis
A Dissenting Interpretation of Dom Casmurro
JOHN GLEDSON
0 905205 19 7. LMHS 3. viii+215pp. 1984.

This reading of *Dom Casmurro* (1899) lays the basis for understanding in more 'realistic' terms the work of the major Brazilian novelist, Machado de Assis. Dr Gledson first disentangles the 'plot' of the novel from the biased and twisted version of events presented by the narrator and central character, Bento. This leads to a new perception of Machado's veiled commentary on the contemporary political and social situation—issues such as slavery, the growth of capitalism and the influence of organised religion within the state form a vital (though covert) part of Machado's narrative structure.

"There is no gainsaying that this is a remarkable, thought-provoking addition to the critical literature on Machado de Assis. In subtlety of analysis as well as conversancy with Machado's oeuvre in prose it bears comparison with the best work to date on *Dom Casmurro*" (*Times Literary Supplement* 1985).

The Structured World of Jorge Guillén
A Study of Cántico and Clamor
ELIZABETH MATTHEWS
0 905205 23 5. LMHS 4. x+326pp. 1985.

In this study of the work of Jorge Guillén (1893-1984), one of the greatest poets of twentieth-century Spain, Dr Matthews argues that his vision of the world as an ordered harmonious unity is echoed in the structural symmetry of his work. Close analysis of twelve long poems, forming ideological and structural pillars of the *Cántico* and *Clamor* volumes, reveals the intricacies of Guillén's mimesis of cosmic harmony. The first English translations of the twelve poems appear in an appendix.

"Matthews offers a precise study of the poet's main themes which, without modifying in a major way earlier overviews, contributes many new insights and deepens our general vision of his work" (*Hispanic Review* 1986).

Reading Onetti
Language, Narrative and the Subject
MARK MILLINGTON
0 905205 26 X. LMHS 5. vi+345pp. 1985.

The Uruguayan Juan Carlos Onetti (born 1909) is one of the leading exponents of the new Spanish American novel. This study offers a close reading of the novels published between 1939 and 1964, and of *Dejemos hablar al viento* (1979). Dr Millington traces the various stages of Onetti's existential and artistic evolution and utilises recent developments in narrative theory to illuminate Onetti's complex fictional world. The analyses in this book rarely offer a straightforward exposition of Onetti's ideas or seek simply to celebrate Onetti; rather there is an implicit respect for the novels' capacity to stand up to and reward rigorous analysis.

"*Reading Onetti* is an intelligent and stimulating book, highly serious in conception and execution, lucid and rigorous in its methodology: an essential contribution to the understanding of the mysterious Uruguayan." (*Modern Language Review* 83)

Vision and the Visual Arts in Galdós
A Study of the Novels and Newspaper Articles
PETER A. BLY
0 905205 30 8. LMHS 6. x+242pp. 1986.

The keen interest which Galdós took throughout his life in the visual arts is documented in Parts I and II of this book, which discuss his art journalism and his artistic contributions to the illustrated edition of his historical novels. But the main focus (Part III) is on Galdós' frequent use of the visual arts and pictorial landscapes in his fictional work, particularly the *seria contemporánea*. Professor Bly's study contributes greatly to the understanding of aesthetic and moral perception in Galdós's novels, and suggests wider implications for the literary and aesthetic theories of the nineteenth century.

"This is a stimulating book, original in its conception, well-documented and thought-provoking. Whilst one may sometimes feel that the way in which the author has chosen to organise such a wealth of material has led to over-rigid demarcations between novels, one is glad for the challenges to different formulations that the author's comments present." (*Revista Canadiense de Estudios Hispánicos* 1989)

A History of Peruvian Literature
JAMES HIGGINS
0 905205 35 9. LMHS 7. xiv+379pp. 1987.

Professor Higgins sets in context and appraises, with ample quotation and analysis, all of the more significant Peruvian writings from the Renaissance onwards. Individual bibliographies for each of the authors discussed are provided in addition to a general bibliography.

"This book is a major critical achievement. Those readers requiring an introduction to internationally famous authors like Vallejo and Vargas Llosa will be more than satisfied. Those looking for a more general survey will not be disappointed. There is no attempt to be comprehensive, but this creates the advantage that the main authors and works are dealt with at sufficient length to arouse our interest ... a genuinely new contribution to the field by an acknowledged authority." (*Bulletin of Hispanic Studies* 1989)

The Early Pardo Bazán
Theme and Narrative Technique in the Novels of 1879-89
DAVID HENN
0 905205 63 4. LMHS 8. viii+231pp. 1988.

Emilia Pardo Bazán, born in the north-west Spanish region of Galicia in 1851, remained active as a prolific novelist, short-story writer and literary critic almost up to her death in 1921. David Henn examines Bazán's main thematic concerns in her first decade as a novelist: social tensions; environment and heredity as influences on character; the feminist question and the narrative portrayal of the female; political controversies. She is revealed as an acute, if tendentious, commentator on the affairs of her day. She was also vigorously engaged with current French and Spanish literary polemic; and her contributions to this area of vital literary debate are collated in this study, which makes the first full and systematic test of her early fictional practice in relation to her theoretical stance.

"Dr Henn's cool and well-judged appraisal of Pardo Bazán's early work will open up a critical debate in his readers' minds, whenever they next come to a reading, or return to a rereading, of the novels that he discusses in these pages." (*Modern Language Review* 85)

José Donoso: The "Boom" and Beyond
PHILIP SWANSON
0 905205 63 2. LMHS 9. viii+181pp. 1988.

The work of José Donoso, Chile's most renowned writer of fiction, is surveyed in this volume, which concentrates on his novelistic production up to 1981. Philip Swanson analyses each novel in detail and plots the twin development of narrative technique and existential outlook.

"Philip Swanson's lucid textual study of Donoso's fiction between 1957 and 1981 sets his work in the context of the "boom", as is unavoidable, and seeks to show 'a consistent pattern of development which allows us to perceive an overall unity in the process of evolution'. ... This general picture, based on close and essentially thematic readings of the novels ... is patiently elaborated and convincing. Swanson's work is undoubtedly a useful addition to the literature in English on Chile's most important novelist of the past thirty years, and it will be especially helpful for undergraduate teaching." (*Bulletin of Latin American Research* 1989)

Lorca's Late Poetry
ANDREW A. ANDERSON
0 905205 78 2. LMHS 10. xiv+462pp. 1990.

This is the first large-scale book to focus on Lorca's poetic output in the last years of his life, from 1931 to 1936. It offers extensive analyses of the poems of the four collections of these years: *Diván del Tamarit* with its Arab-Andalusian flavour and stylization; *Llanto por Ignacio Sánchez Mejías*, a sustained lament on the death of a famous bullfighter; *Seis poemas galegos*; and *Sonetos*, love poetry in the tradition of Petrarch, Shakespeare and Góngora. An Appendix gives English translations of all the poems in the four collections (other quotations from Spanish are translated where they occur in the text). Professor Anderson rejects categorizations of this body of poetry into any of the 'isms' prevalent today or in the '20s and '30s, and gives a new appraisal of Lorca's creative development.

"This is a meticulously researched, carefully wrought assessment of Lorca's later poetry elaborated upon the background of the literary and cultural activities which concerned Lorca during these years." (*Hispania* 1991)

Borges' Narrative Strategy
DONALD L. SHAW
0 905205 84 7. LMHS 11. viii+191pp. 1992.

César Vallejo: a Selection of his Poetry
with Translations, Introduction and Notes
JAMES HIGGINS
0 905205 36 7 (Cloth) 0 905205 67 7 (Paper). xxviii+126pp. 1987

The Peruvian César Vallejo (1892-1938) is not only Spanish America's foremost poet but, arguably, the most important poet of the Spanish-speaking world in modern times. In this new anthology of his work the poems are accompanied by English verse translations; and, because of the density and difficulty of Vallejo's work, the introduction offers guidance by commenting on each of the poems included in addition to outlining his career and poetics. There is a select bibliography.

"The introduction is excellent, concise but also very concentrated, with comments on each poem selected. Both student and general reader are provided with all the basic information necessary for an approach to these demanding poems. This edition will surely establish itself as the text for undergraduate students." (*Modern Language Review* 85)

CAREERS ABC
2005
004 YAR
SHORT
LOAN

THE ✤ TIMES

careers & jobs
in IT

☷ BCS®

THE BRITISH COMPUTER SOCIETY

david yardley

JOSEPH PRIESTLEY COLLEGE

18520

For Jack

Publisher's note
Every possible effort has been made to ensure that the information contained in this book is accurate at the time of going to press, and the publishers and authors cannot accept responsibility for any errors or omissions, however caused. No responsibility for loss or damage occasioned to any person acting, or refraining from action, as a result of the material in this publication can be accepted by the editor, the publisher or any of the authors.

First published in Great Britain in 2004

Apart from any fair dealing for the purposes of research or private study, or criticism or review, as permitted under the Copyright, Designs and Patents Act 1988, this publication may only be reproduced, stored or transmitted, in any form or by any means, with the prior permission in writing of the publishers, or in the case of reprographic reproduction in accordance with the terms and licences issued by the CLA. Enquiries concerning reproduction outside these terms should be sent to the publishers at the undermentioned address:

Kogan Page Limited
120 Pentonville Road
London N1 9JN
United Kingdom
www.kogan-page.co.uk

© David Yardley, 2004

The right of David Yardley to be identified as the author of this work has been asserted by him in accordance with the Copyright, Designs and Patents Act 1988.

The views expressed in this book are those of the author, and are not necessarily the same as those of Times Newspapers Ltd.

British Library Cataloguing in Publication Data

A CIP record for this book is available from the British Library.

ISBN 0 7494 4245 X

Typeset by Saxon Graphics Ltd, Derby
Printed and bound in Great Britain by Clays Ltd, St Ives plc